Praise for *Relief Chief: A Manifesto for Saving Lives in Dire Times*

"A detailed, practical, and humane agenda for saving lives and reducing suffering. Mark Lowcock's valuable new book based on his outstanding service as head of humanitarian relief at the United Nations is timely and topical in the face of ever-growing crises from Afghanistan to Yemen and the deepening impact of the COVID-19 pandemic in the most vulnerable countries."
—*Gordon Brown*

"An insider's view on the major humanitarian crises of our time. Full of insight, compassion, and ideas for how we could build a better system to support the most vulnerable people in the world."
—*Minouche Shafik*

"This is an important book. It gives a clear account of recent humanitarian crises, what was achieved, and what could have been done better. It argues that a preventative approach could always achieve more. The world has achieved great progress in development in recent years and is now going backwards. This book could help us to reverse this."
—*Clare Short*

"This guide to humanitarian failures and challenges is indispensable reading for those who care about our fellow men and women caught up in great jeopardy. Drawing on a lifetime of experience, Mark Lowcock tells it like it is."
—*Andrew Mitchell*

"Mark Lowcock's arresting first-hand account of how the UN and other agencies mobilize aid for those who need it the most is both jarring and hopeful. Essential reading for anyone who wants to understand one of the world's biggest current challenges."
—*Toni G. Verstandig*

RELIEF CHIEF

Relief Chief

A MANIFESTO

FOR SAVING LIVES

IN DIRE TIMES

Mark Lowcock

For the victims and survivors.

CONTENTS

CONTENTS

PREFACE

WHEN THE CALL CAME THROUGH, I was in the United Kingdom (UK) office at the World Bank in Washington, D.C., chatting to colleagues and drinking sour, lukewarm coffee in a vain attempt to fight off jet lag. I moved out into the corridor, and found myself looking down into the atrium in which Jim Kim, the president of the World Bank, had established an open-plan working area in a short-lived fit of modern management. The desks and chairs were now all empty.

"Hello?"

"Mr. Lowcock?"

"Yes, it's Mark speaking."

"Please hold for the Secretary-General of the United Nations."

He came on the line.

"Hello? I think you know why I am calling."

I laughed. "Yes."

"I am pleased I can now offer you the job."

"I am very happy to accept."

It transpired that we were both attending the same lunch meeting the following day, so we agreed to talk further then.

This conversation, on 20 April 2017, was the culmination of a saga that had been running for five months and led eventually to my appointment as the person responsible for humanitarian issues at the

UN—the Under-Secretary-General for Humanitarian Affairs and Emergency Relief Coordinator, or ERC.[1]

António Guterres was elected UN secretary-general in November 2016. Like his predecessors, he wanted a new management team to support him. There was a long-standing practice of each of the P5—the five permanent members of the United Nations (UN) Security Council, namely China, France, Russia, the United Kingdom, and the United States—having one of their nationals in an under-secretary role in the UN Secretariat in New York. Whether that is a good idea is much debated, but it remains an established arrangement. Some of the senior staff Guterres had inherited wanted to stay on, and transitioning them out took a little time. But Guterres was clear from the outset that he was going to pick his own team, including having a new person as the ERC. That was the under-secretary role that a series of British nationals had filled for the previous decade. The current incumbent, Stephen O'Brien, was a former member of Parliament and junior minister in the Department for International Development (DFID).

The powers that be in the United Kingdom, battered by the 2016 Brexit referendum and anxious to demonstrate Britain's continuing relevance and status in the world, wanted to retain the job, which was the most senior UN post held by a British national. Fi Hill, one of the chiefs of staff to Prime Minister Theresa May, asked the civil service to provide a list of potential candidates. She did not like the look of any of the initial names, so she concocted an eyebrow-raising list of her own—mostly friends and contacts, none of whom had much relevant background in international humanitarian issues. Matthew Rycroft, Britain's hard-working, honest, and respected ambassador in New York, was instructed to pass the names to Guterres' team. I heard later that they thought the list was so bizarre that it must be part of a cunning British plot to consolidate the case for retaining Ste-

---

1. The different shortened forms of this position include the USG, the Relief Chief, and the head of OCHA (Office for the Coordination of Humanitarian Affairs). Here, for simplicity, I will stick to ERC.

phen O'Brien. Guterres stalled for weeks, asking whether the British would instead like to nominate candidates for some other role—like the top job reforming the management of the UN, or the post of administrator of the UN Development Programme. Anxiety in London grew.

I knew Guterres slightly, admired what he had done as the head of the UN refugee agency, and liked his vision for his tenure as secretary-general. I had then been permanent secretary, the most senior civil servant, at DFID for approaching six years, on the back of a 30-year career dealing with international development and humanitarian issues. I felt we had achieved a lot: the United Kingdom had finally met the UN commitment to provide 0.7 percent of national income as official development assistance, a previously unfulfilled promise going back more than 30 years. Consequently, I oversaw big increases in the DFID budget. The department was widely respected across the globe. But I was starting to think it might be time to move on. I was approached by people I respected enquiring whether I would be interested in the ERC job. After discussing it with my wife Julia and weighing up the family issues, I decided in mid-December to let it be known informally that I might be persuadable to let my name go to Guterres. Between Christmas and New Year, this got back to my civil service boss, Jeremy Heywood, the brilliant, omniscient cabinet secretary and Britain's most senior civil servant. He rang me and asked if I would be willing to be nominated. Yes, I said, provided the prime minister would back my candidacy and I was the sole nominee she was supporting, not simply another name added to the list.

On 31 December 2016, I found myself on the front pages of several of the British tabloid newspapers when it was announced that I was being awarded a knighthood. Earlier in the year, DFID had attracted a lot of negative publicity over the construction of a £250 million airport on St. Helena, a small island in the Atlantic which had been a British territory for hundreds of years and which was hitherto accessible only by sea. The airport construction was completed on time and to budget, but it then transpired that air turbulence around the island meant that the original intention to fly in Boeing 737s was not viable. It looked to some people as though the government had wasted money on a white elephant. In June 2016, I had been summoned to Parliament to be harangued, and on 16 December the Parliamentary Public Accounts Committee published a damning report describing the project as a fiasco. The award of my knighthood therefore unsurprisingly attracted more criticism. In fact, this was all a storm in a tea cup. In 2017, other aircraft were found that could use the airport successfully, and a weekly air service was established. We launched a legal case against the consultants who had recommended the Boeing 737. It was settled out of court, with the consultants both denying any wrongdoing and making a seven-figure payment to DFID. However, when the tabloids were published on New Year's Eve 2016, the end of the story remained unclear, and I wondered if I would be regarded as damaged goods and if it would affect the UN job.

But in early January, I was summoned for an interview with Fi Hill in Downing Street. A few days after that, while on a visit to Sudan, I was told that the prime minister wanted to talk to Guterres personally to make the case to him for appointing me as ERC. She would be seeing him soon at the annual meeting of the World Economic Forum in Davos, Switzerland, and planned to raise the issue then. Send us a CV and material on why I was the person for the job, Downing Street told me.

Theresa May duly met Guterres. When, subsequently, I saw the record of the meeting, it was clear that this was her main topic. She spoke to my qualifications to be the ERC, and repeatedly pressed him to appoint me. He was noncommittal, saying nothing but nodding in response to her description of why I was the right person, given my background and experience.

At that point, Downing Street decided that we had better put Priti Patel—who as secretary of state for international development was my political boss at DFID—in the picture. Earlier in the month, Jeremy Heywood had told her that I would want to move on before long. He floated the possibility that the UN might want me. I was asked now to tell Patel that the prime minister had decided to nominate me to be the ERC and had raised it with Guterres. In the meantime, Number 10 were also explaining the position to Stephen O'Brien, who had wondered whether he would be kept on. That consultation created its own dynamics. (In his diaries, which were published in 2021, Alan Duncan, then minister in the British Foreign Office, wrote on 10 January 2017, "[O'Brien] is for the chop, but doesn't know it yet. . . . Guterres wants someone better, but we have to be discreet as we have to push an alternative candidate before O'Brien knows he is on the way out.")

In January, I held a routine series of catch-up meetings with the DFID teams covering each of the main humanitarian crises: Syria, South Sudan, Somalia, Yemen, the Lake Chad Basin, the Democratic Republic of Congo, the various conflicts in Myanmar (Burma), and a variety of others. The overall picture was alarming. The Syria crisis was absorbing most of the political bandwidth available in the international humanitarian system. But there was also a credible threat of four famines in 2017, affecting Somalia, South Sudan, northeast Nigeria, and Yemen. In the most recent famine, which hit Somalia in 2011, a quarter of a million people lost their lives. I remembered it well. It had come early in my tenure as DFID permanent secretary. Like others, we were distracted by the Arab Spring and the Libyan crisis early that year. The Somali famine threat was difficult to deal with especially because of the behaviour of al-Shabaab extremists who exercised control over much of the affected area, and we missed the opportunity to take action in time. I had been in Somalia during the 1992 famine, and so I was familiar with the problem. I thought after 2011 that had I myself done some things differently that year, a better response might have been organised and lives might have been saved. I did not want to make the same mistake again.

I wrote a memo on 26 January 2017 to Mark Lyall Grant, the UK's national security adviser, and all my counterparts across Whitehall, describing the unfolding crises and the inadequacy of the response. It was an attempt to sound the alarm about the humanitarian prospects for the year. I made a series of recommendations: more UK relief aid, but also that Britain attempt to mobilise a wider and larger international response, collaborating with the UN, the World Bank, the leading nongovernmental organisations (NGOs), and the main international financiers of humanitarian response, especially the United States, the European Union (EU), and Germany. That week I also met most of the heads of the leading British development NGOs to seek their support.

A few days later I spoke to the DFID team in Mogadishu. They described a rapidly deteriorating situation, with a trajectory towards famine by the middle of the year. The international response was somewhere between tepid and lacklustre. I decided to visit Mogadishu myself and flew there on 3 February, meeting the DFID team and the UN, the NGOs, the Red Cross, and the Somali government. I wrote another memo to send round Whitehall on the way back to London. I recalled my previous experience with famine in Somalia, and said that without a big immediate scale-up in the international response, there would be another one by the middle of 2017. The death toll would run into hundreds of thousands or millions. This was still preventable. The United Kingdom should announce an immediate increase of £110 million in DFID support, and write to the UN secretary-general on the back of that offering to help him mobilise the international community. The UN were already thinking along similar lines. Guterres held a press conference on 22 February seeking support for efforts to stave off the four famines.

Everything was quiet for a while on the OCHA job. Guterres' appointment on 14 February of French diplomat Jean-Pierre Lacroix as under-secretary-general for peacekeeping set the Downing Street nerves jangling again. Why was there no news for us? Was Britain being deliberately snubbed? Foreign Secretary Boris Johnson was asked to raise the matter with Guterres when they met in the margins of the Munich Security Conference on 18 February. They had what I was told was a direct one-to-one exchange, with Johnson pushing the case aggressively and Guterres stonewalling. The emollient Alan Duncan then had a follow-up conversation with Guterres who, according to Alan when I spoke to him on 20 February, basically said people should calm down and it would be fine, but conveyed nothing more specific than that. This game of cat-and-mouse progressed in incremental steps over the next two months, with Matthew Rycroft periodically being instructed by Downing Street to go in again and push for a decision and announcement, and Guterres, who was trying to juggle lots of other senior appointments, giving ever-stronger hints that people should stop worrying but that he did not want to make Stephen O'Brien a lame duck too far before his contract ended at the end of May.

In early April, Guterres told Matthew Rycroft he would be appointing me and telling Stephen shortly. There was then a delay while Stephen was travelling. Meanwhile, Theresa May announced on 18 April that she was calling an election, and London were keen for my appointment to be announced before the election period formally began. Matthew raised that point with Guterres while they were sitting next to each other in the Security Council later that day. Guterres scribbled a note back, "I will try."

Then, on 20 April, Guterres called me. By then lots of people seemed to know I was being appointed. Several people I saw in Washington that day mentioned it to me, including UN Deputy-Secretary-General Amina Mohammed and World Bank Managing Director Kristalina Georgieva, as well as the deputy head of OCHA and a number of other World Bank staff.

By the end of April, the government in London wanted to begin recruiting my successor at DFID. But they could not do that until my departure was announced. On 4 May, I spoke to Guterres again asking when the announcement could be made. He was due in London the following week for a conference on Somalia. We agreed the announcement would happen then. And so it played out. Press stories started to appear on 11 May. The formal announcement was made by the UN at 5 p.m. London time on 12 May.

From mid-May, most of my attention was focused on my new job. I left DFID in June, and went to New York in July for a series of introductory meetings and to find an apartment, organise furniture, and sort out other practical matters.

I recount all this because it was illustrative of a lot of things I encountered in the UN and its dealings with member states over the following four years. The saga is symptomatic of what often goes on behind the scenes in international affairs. All sorts of considerations get mixed together: the personal, the political, the bureaucratic, the self-serving, the principled, the generous, the risible, the serious, and the mind-boggling. All these things are part of the meat and drink of the UN and everything around it. Humanitarian crises and how they are responded to are deeply serious. Most of the time, the important considerations are what determines decisions. This book is an account of my experience as the ERC, focusing mostly on the important things. But it is worth noting that there were often complicated underlying agendas, personalities, and interests just like those surrounding my appointment. Those things all needed to be managed and dealt with as well, and they often absorbed a lot of time and generated unnecessary frustrations.

As ERC I travelled on hundreds of aircraft around more than 50 countries—some of them many times. I sent and received tens of thousands of e-mails, tweets, and other messages. I sat in countless meetings, including more than a hundred meetings of the UN Security Council. I gave innumerable press interviews. I met and spoke to many politicians, warlords, and government officials as well as thousands of aid workers in far-flung places. Between 2017 and 2019, I privately recorded a dozen lengthy interviews about my ongoing experience in the role, the transcripts of which run to many more pages than this book. I gave speeches and lectures at universities and think tanks round the world, including at the Blavatnik School of Government at Oxford University, the London School of Economics, the Herthie School of Government in Berlin, Sciences Po in Paris, the Graduate Institute in Geneva, the Center for Global Development and the Center for Strategic and International Studies in Washington, D.C., and many similar places. I have drawn on all this material in what follows. In the acknowledgements section at the end of the book, I have tried to identify those—and they are many—who have particularly helped.

What has stayed with me most of all, however, is the stories I heard from people I met, especially women and children, in dozens of countries across four continents who found themselves caught up in crises, through no fault of their own, and needed help and protection just to survive. They are often frightened, typically powerless, always vulnerable, and rarely listened to. I have tried to bring their words and their experiences into these pages, and the book is dedicated to them.

Introduction

ON 24 JUNE 1859, A LARGE FRENCH ARMY led by Emperor Napoleon III faced an Austrian force near the historic and picturesque town of Solferino in what today is the Lombardy region of northern Italy. By the end of the day, 23,000 men lay wounded, dead, or dying across the battlefield, and no one seemed much bothered about them. One witness to their suffering was Henri Dunant, the son of a Swiss businessman, who had just written a flattering portrait of the emperor and brought it to Solferino in the hope of presenting it to him. Horrified by the sight of so many untended casualties, Dunant took it upon himself to organise help for those who could still be saved. He became instrumental in the founding in 1863 of the world's first major humanitarian organisation, the International Committee of the Red Cross. The following year saw the signing of the first Geneva Convention, which established international legal protections for both soldiers and civilians in armed conflicts.

The early 20th century saw the birth of some of the other international humanitarian agencies we have today. The International Health Office, set up in 1908, later formed the basis for the World Health Organisation (WHO). Save the Children, founded in 1919 in the wake of World War I, was one of the earliest nongovernmental organisations (NGOs). In the early 1930s, Albert Einstein helped establish the International Rescue Committee, among the largest operational international NGOs today. But it was only after World War II that today's humanitarian system began fully to take shape. The creation of the United Nations (UN) in 1945 was followed in 1946 by the creation of its children's agency, the United Nations International Children's Emergency Fund (now known as UNICEF). The Geneva Conventions, the bedrock of international humanitarian law, were consolidated into their modern form in 1949 (with subsequent additional Protocols covering new aspects of warfare). In 1951, the UN General Assembly established the United Nations High Commissioner for Refugees as the UN refugee agency, and the Refugees Convention agreed that year defined refugees and their rights, including the right not to be sent back to their country of origin against their will. The World Food Programme, today the largest of the humanitarian agencies, was set up in 1961.

Between the 1950s and the 1980s, much of the UN's humanitarian role played out in response to wars and the displacement they caused in East Asian countries like Korea, Vietnam, and Cambodia. Thereafter, the focus shifted further west. The major event of the mid-1980s was the famine in Ethiopia; in my first job after I left university, I was part of the response there. The tumultuous years after 1989 saw the end of the Cold War; the dismantling of the apartheid regime in South Africa; the 1990–91 Persian Gulf War; and conflicts in Somalia, Rwanda, and the Balkans. This era also saw the spread of democracy and an extension of market-based economic systems across many countries. One important effect was to drive up incomes across Asia and much of the rest of the developing world. A dramatic expansion of health and educational provision also was well underway. As time passed, these improvements reduced early death and increased life expectancy in poorer countries to levels achieved in the industrialised world in the first half of the 20th century.

In 1991, the UN General Assembly adopted Resolution 46/182, which created the post of the Under-Secretary-General for Humanitarian Affairs and Emergency Relief Coordinator (the ERC). The resolution asked the holder of this position to chair a committee, the Inter-Agency Standing Committee, to bring together all the UN agencies, Red Cross bodies, and major NGOs involved in international emergency relief.

Many emergencies were related to conflict, and effective support for potential victims required collaboration among the different specialised agencies (which focused on food, health, refugees, and the like). UN member states wanted the ERC to consolidate efforts to provide more comprehensive assistance. I frequently refer in what follows to the *humanitarian system*. By that I mean this large group of collaborating but independent international organisations. Most humanitarian action around the world is highly local, involving people helping their friends and neighbours, often through faith-based organisations. These local efforts are always the first and fastest to respond to tragedy, and frequently are the most generous. Nevertheless, international collaboration through the humanitarian system plays a crucial role, as I shall describe.

The ERC was put in charge of a new grouping in the UN Secretariat in New York, the Department of Humanitarian Affairs. Its first head was the highly regarded Swedish diplomat Jan Eliasson, who in 2012 would become deputy to Secretary-General Ban Ki-moon. Over the next 26 years, 11 more people served as ERC: several from Nordic countries, two Japanese, a Canadian (Carolyn McAskie, the first woman), and three before me from the United Kingdom. Arguably the most distinguished, and certainly the most charismatic, was Sérgio Vieira de Mello, a career UN staffer from Brazil who held the role from 1998 to 1999. The Pulitzer Prize–winning author Samantha Power, who went on to become head of the US Agency for International Development, wrote a memorable biography of him which was later turned into a Netflix movie. The ERC position was one in which people tended not to stay long: only Valerie Amos, my predecessor but one, reached the four-year mark. I was to be the thirteenth incumbent. I managed to speak privately to almost all of my predecessors about their experience in the role, and I learned a lot from what they said. (I was sorry not to have been able to talk to Sérgio Vieira de Mello, who had been killed in the suicide truck bombing of the UN headquarters in Iraq in August 2003.)

The structure that was put in place through Resolution 46/182 survives to this day, with only minor adjustments. In 1997, Kofi Annan took some of the operational responsibilities out of the Department of Humanitarian Affairs—such as the UN's work on land mines—beefed up its coordination role, and renamed it the Office for the Coordination of Humanitarian Affairs, or OCHA. OCHA's role was enhanced in 1999 when an initiative by Sérgio Vieira de Mello led to the Security Council passing Resolution 1265, which created more formal responsibilities to protect civilians in conflict situations. Although the impact of this resolution eroded over time, the precedent of initiating the ERC's engagement with the Security Council brought humanitarian issues more fully and consistently onto the UN agenda in New York, and elevated the role of humanitarian work to become one of the UN's key activities.

At the beginning of his second term as Secretary-General, Annan flirted with a more significant restructuring, which would have merged parts of the World Food Programme and the refugee agency with other entities to create a single agency responsible for emergency relief. That arrangement would probably have enabled the UN to improve its responses to crises. In the current structure, there are almost no problems to which one agency acting alone can respond effectively. In the case of famine, for example, any relief effort needs to go beyond just giving the hungry food or cash to buy it with. Most people who die in famines succumb to disease, often something like the measles or a common cold, which a healthy person can fight off but a starving one cannot. Famine response therefore needs to include health services, clean water, shelter, and protection, as well as efforts to deal with the hunger problem. Annan thought it would make sense to have all that work managed by one UN agency, coordinating with NGOs and the Red Cross.

His ideas, however, were resisted successfully by most UN agencies. They all feared losing their individual power and influence, and so the current structure was maintained. One important consequence is that a coordinator is essential. But the truth is that OCHA has limited power or leverage in fulfilling the role, because the operational agencies are much bigger and have their own large budgets, governance structures (in some cases independent even of the secretary-general), and support base. The trick, for the ERC and OCHA, is to be sufficiently useful to and valued by the agencies in the Inter-Agency Standing Committee in order to acquire the soft power necessary to exert influence to get the best possible overall response in each crisis.

The years around the turn of the millennium saw notable humanitarian tragedies, like the Rwanda genocide and the conflict in the Democratic Republic of Congo, which took millions of lives in the mid-1990s. The same period also witnessed the US-led invasion of Afghanistan in 2001, the 2003 Iraq War, and food crises in the Sahel. But across the world as a whole, there was continued progress in reducing poverty—one of humanity's greatest achievements—and reducing conflict, both of which had fuelled a lot of humanitarian need. There also were fewer new refugee and displacement problems. At the end of the 1990s, there were 35 million refugees and people displaced inside their own countries. The UN's annual humanitarian appeals at that time totalled around $2 billion, and aimed to provide support for an average of 34 million people. But overall, global progress in reducing extreme poverty was translating into lower humanitarian need. As António Guterres has recalled, in the early period of his tenure as the UN High Commissioner for Refugees—a post he took up in 2005—there was a serious conversation inside the agency as to whether they would be needed in future.

In the wake of the end of the Cold War, unconditional respect for sovereignty began more seriously to be questioned. In 1999, the then British Prime Minister Tony Blair argued in a speech in Chicago that "the principle of sovereignty must be qualified in important respects. Acts of genocide can never be a purely internal matter." The next five years saw international intervention in internal crises in Kosovo, Timor-Leste, and Sierra Leone.

The humanitarian sector also went through an important phase of professionalisation. Previously, a willingness to do good was often thought to be enough; now, a requirement to operate according to professional standards came to the fore. This process was reinforced as part of the backlash against one of the most serious reputational crises the UN has faced: the corruption and mismanagement of the UN Oil-for-Food Programme, which permitted Iraq to sell oil in exchange for food and other essential supplies for the Iraqi people.

The humanitarian aid sector also was permanently changed when jihadist groups bombed the UN headquarters in Baghdad in August 2003. The blue flag was no longer a protection: as well as Sérgio Vieira de Mello, 21 others were killed and many more injured. Attacks on aid workers, previously rare, have become routine over the past 20 years and have been increasing, with the highest number recorded in 2019. The sector has struggled to find an adequate response. Further complicating matters, antiterrorism laws introduced by many countries have had the (mostly unintended) effect of putting humanitarian agencies at risk of prosecution if they provide assistance to civilians living in areas with a terrorist presence.

In a marked change of trajectory, from early in the 21st century humanitarian needs and responses expanded. By 2005, UN appeals for humanitarian responses had trebled to $6 billion. A total of $4 billion of that was forthcoming in voluntary contributions to UN agencies (and through them to NGOs), primarily from the governments of Western countries. By 2010, with displacement caused by conflict increasing, the appeals totalled $7 billion, aiming to reach nearly twice as many people as a decade earlier.

Then things got substantially worse. At the end of 2016, some 130 million people required humanitarian assistance—a figure almost three times that of a decade earlier. Between 2007 and 2009, 72 percent of humanitarian needs were funded. Between 2013 and 2016, this figure fell to 61 percent. By 2017, as I was taking up my new job, the appeals had grown to $24 billion.

What had happened? The increase in need arose partly because the global population had increased by 1 billion between 2005 and 2017, with much of the growth concentrated in places with severe humanitarian problems. In addition, standards in meeting humanitarian need improved. Decades previously, responses tended to focus on the bare minimum life-saving requirements, typically revolving around food, shelter, and water. Now—and this is a good thing—the aims had expanded to cover health, education, protection (especially for women and girls), livelihoods, and early recovery. Humanitarian work contributed to increasing life expectancy. The work of UNICEF, the WHO, and others helped reduce child and maternal deaths. Fewer people were dying in humanitarian crises because both the quality and the coverage of the response was higher than it used to be. More comprehensive responses inevitably were more expensive.

But there was another major factor. The toppling of Saddam Hussein in Iraq in 2003 and the series of revolts and uprisings that constituted the Arab Spring from 2011 unleashed a wave of conflict and burgeoning humanitarian needs, including in refugee and displacement emergencies. A decline (by the beginning of the second decade of the current century) in the ability and willingness of the most powerful countries to prevent or resolve conflicts, together with a spate of insurgencies linked to terrorism and extremism, brought new, more complex, and more protracted problems. They were concentrated mostly across Africa and the Middle East, notably in places like the Lake Chad Basin, the Horn of Africa, Syria, Yemen, and Iraq. Conflicts themselves have causes, of course, and one increasingly visible common thread was the effect of climate change: more erratic rainfall patterns, droughts, floods, and storms added to demographic pressures and environmental stresses to increase competition over resources and fuel grievances. Those grievances were manifested in ever-more-violent ways.

Humanitarian agencies were largely successful in containing the loss of life, even as crises mushroomed. The spectre of the four famines in 2017—South Sudan, Somalia, Yemen, and northeast Nigeria—was averted. Agencies supported by the UN provided life-saving assistance to 13 million people in those four countries, despite dangerous conditions, funding gaps, and attempts to prevent help reaching those in need. Yet the underlying problems were not solved.

There is a paradox. On the one hand, over the past 50 years, a hundred previously poor countries have enjoyed dramatic economic and human development. There has been amazing progress in increasing life expectancy, ending acute hunger, reducing child and maternal deaths, expanding education, and making electricity, water, and the internet available to almost everyone. That trend continued through the second decade of the current century, with life improving in material terms year on year for most people in most countries. But on the other hand, those growing numbers at the bottom, the roughly 2 percent of the global population caught up in humanitarian emergencies, were left behind. This growing divergence is unfair, but it is also ultimately dangerous for everyone.

When I was appointed as ERC in 2017, having watched many poorer countries grow and develop their economies and provide better lives for their citizens in recent decades, I hoped it would be possible to get those at the bottom onto a more positive trajectory. I hoped to see less humanitarian need in the years ahead. On my first day in the job, gathering OCHA staff from around the world in a video town hall meeting, I said I wanted to contribute to three particular objectives.

First, I said, we needed to find ways to address the behaviour of combatants in conflict. Routinely, the international laws of war were being violated. People typically commit these heinous crimes when they think they won't be seen, won't be caught, or won't be punished.

Second, I hoped to see a reduction in the number of crises that escalated into food security catastrophes, sometimes verging on famine. Famine used to be ubiquitous across the world, but in the past 20 years (up to 2017) there had been just the one in Somalia in 2011. The horror of famine was becoming rarer and less lethal. That was partly because more countries had developed their economies and built better social protection systems for the poor. It was partly because in the modern world, politics in many countries now forces the authorities to deal with the problem before it gets out of control. And it was partly because when famine does threaten, the response is better—with modern therapeutic feeding programmes and immunisation dramatically reducing death rates. I said I saw no reason why famines could not be finally eliminated from the human condition during my lifetime. Staving off the four famines that threatened in early 2017 was evidence of that.

The third issue I had in mind was finding better solutions for the world's growing number of long-term refugees and displaced people. Above all, I wanted to ensure that people would have a chance to rebuild their lives sooner, either back at home where that is possible, or somewhere new where it is not.

I did not think achieving these things would be easy. But I did think it was possible.

Five years later, it is clear that things have not turned out as I hoped. Much of this book is about why: essentially, the causes of humanitarian crises mounted but only their symptoms were seriously addressed.

Part One deals with the largest crises in different parts of the world, those which were to absorb most of my time. Throughout, I have tried to keep a focus on people I met whose lives have been affected, what they said to me, and what they want. Many of them appear in these pages. From the beginning of September 2017, I was dealing with the tragedy of the Rohingya, forced out of their home country of Myanmar by a genocidal atrocity perpetrated by the military, backed by nationalist political sentiment. Chapter 1 deals with how the UN and others supported Bangladesh in providing the Rohingya with refuge. It is a story of how lives were saved but solutions proved elusive, and the current situation remains dangerous and unstable. The reputation of Burmese politician Aung San Suu Kyi, a Nobel Peace Prize laureate and an icon beloved of many, was destroyed.

Chapter 2 covers Yemen, which for years was the world's worst humanitarian crisis and could still deteriorate into a devastating famine involving a loss of life of historic proportions. The rotten thread weaving together the story of Yemen is how little any of the main protagonists—those men, and they are all men, who control the guns, missiles, and warplanes—weigh the lives and wishes of ordinary Yemenis in determining their actions. It was clear to me time and again that the powerful could not care less about the fate of so many ordinary people. That carelessness was the source of most of the problems plaguing humanitarian agencies in Yemen between 2017 and 2021.

I next move on to the decade of war in Syria. From the outset, it was inflamed by its geopolitical overlay, drawing in the armed forces of more than 30 nations and fighters from a hundred countries, but the huge multitude of its victims are Syrians themselves. This has been a disaster characterised by heinous atrocities and breaches of norms of behaviour in warfare of a sort and at a scale not seen since World War II. There is much to learn from what humanitarian agencies—many started and staffed by Syrians themselves—have confronted and how they have coped with it, and that is the focus of Chapter 3.

Chapter 4 deals with the Sahel, the region which when I think about the longer term worries me most of all. The problems are well understood, but much of what is happening addresses their symptoms, not their causes. That is not a recipe for improvement. Some of what needs to happen is clear, and I have tried to set it out. It is harder to get the necessary players to act on it.

I have spent a lot of time in and around the Horn of Africa over the past 35 years. That period has seen significant achievements, the remarkable economic development of Ethiopia (up to 2020) prominent among them. In recent years, progress in Somalia—which re-established normal relations with the international economic community and got its debt relieved—and the sweeping-away of the Bashir dictatorship in Sudan have opened up new opportunities. But conflict, poverty, drought, and climate change mean that chronic humanitarian problems remain, and at the end of my tenure as ERC the warning klaxon was again screeching loudly. As Chapter 5 describes, the past few years for humanitarian agencies have been a juggling act between staving off the worst while trying also to support progress for the future.

There is a danger in this job, where your daily diet is one disaster and example of human brutality after another, of succumbing to the sense that everything is getting worse everywhere all the time. That is of course not the case. The story of natural disaster response around the world over the previous generation is one of clear improvement. Hurricanes, cyclones, earthquakes, and volcanoes are a constant feature, and climate change is making some of them more ferocious. But the loss of life they cause is much lower than it used to be. I was closely involved in dealing with the Mexican earthquake in September 2017, Caribbean storms in 2017 and 2019, the Sulawesi earthquake and tsunami in 2018, and a host of similar events, and they are covered in Chapter 6.

Part Two, drawing on the regional analysis of the crises covered in Part One—and in many other places I visited or dealt with from afar—identifies key themes in humanitarian work in recent years, and describes the approach we took in the UN to reducing humanitarian needs and improving the work of the responding agencies. Chapter 7 deals with the organisational and management issues I faced in OCHA. When in February 2021 I announced I would be moving on, the *New Humanitarian*—one of the leading news websites for people working in the sector—noted, in assessing my tenure, that I had inherited a string of internal budget, administrative, and management challenges. That is an understatement. One of the reasons I was hired was to sort them out, and I have explained here how I approached both that and the task of getting the best out of the humanitarian system as a whole by making the Inter-Agency Standing Committee work as effectively as possible. I took the job in part because I was interested in contributing to broader UN reform beyond the humanitarian sector. António Guterres had set out a vision for a better UN as part of his manifesto as secretary-general. Some progress has been made, but much remains to be done.

The international humanitarian system is now a $25 billion a year enterprise, and the UN-coordinated element accounts for around 70 percent of it. Humanitarian agencies are effective in assisting and protecting people. But they operate primarily in a reactive mode, even though quite a lot of emergencies are predictable. It would be much cheaper, and save a lot of suffering, if action could be taken in anticipation of foreseeable problems occurring. Chapter 8 describes my work to promote a more rational, effective system for financing humanitarian action.

Chapter 9 grapples with the most intractable problem of all: that humanitarian suffering arises primarily from conflict and the behaviour of belligerents. Conflicts have been on the rise in recent years. This is partly a result of the state of geopolitics: the leading countries, not least in the Security Council, have proven less willing and able to resolve and prevent conflict in the past 10 years than in the 20 years before that. Another factor is the emergence of increasingly interconnected extremist groups that do not subscribe to the norms established in the Geneva Conventions and similar frameworks. These issues are difficult to address, and I have tried to describe why that is and what nevertheless can be done.

Most of the people affected by humanitarian emergencies are women and girls. This has always been true, but until quite recently the implications, in particular how this fact should affect what relief agencies do, were mostly ignored. The most harrowing conversations I had during my visits to crisis zones were with women. The humanitarian aid sector itself was shaken by sexual harassment and abuse scandals during my tenure—notably a prominent case affecting Oxfam in 2018—and we tried to use this as an opportunity for reform. What we did to improve protection and assistance for women and girls, and what more remains to be done, is the subject of Chapter 10.

In my final year in the position, everything changed. It is increasingly evident that the new coronavirus and the COVID-19 pandemic has inflicted its deepest, longest-lasting damage in the world's poorest, most fragile, and most vulnerable countries. Many of them were already mired in humanitarian disaster before the virus and its economic consequences wreaked further havoc. I spent most of 2020 and the first half of 2021 trying with too little success to mobilise more help for them, and Chapter 11 is devoted to those efforts.

Chapter 12 looks forward to what I think humanitarian agencies will face in the coming years and how the system can be improved to better meet the needs of people affected by crises. The causes of humanitarian problems in the most vulnerable countries are not being addressed with any degree of seriousness. It is therefore unrealistic to expect needs to decline. Humanitarian agencies do a good job, within the limits of their abilities, in saving lives and protecting the innocent. But they are far from perfect. There is a great deal of scope for the agencies to do better, especially in listening to what people say they want and giving it to them—and doing so faster.

PART ONE

ONE

The Tragedy of the Rohingya

I WAS HOT, TIRED, THIRSTY, HUNGRY, and wanted to get somewhere air-conditioned for a break. But the look on the woman's face and her one-word reply to my question stopped me short. She sat, hunched under a plastic sheet, her sister close on one side and a friend on the other, both of them cradling naked young children. They all looked shocked and traumatized. The woman who was speaking wore a long, pale-orange headscarf. There were bags under her eyes from tiredness or trauma, or both, but she spoke strongly and clearly. "Justice," she said, looking me full square in the eye and then waiting to see what I said next.

It was 4 October 2017. I was in the district of Cox's Bazar in eastern Bangladesh with Tony Lake, the executive director of UNICEF. Hundreds of thousands of refugees had flooded across the border from Myanmar (Burma) in the past six weeks, forced out in a brutal campaign of murder, rape, and ethnic cleansing by the Myanmar military. The conditions in the camp were abject. The terrain is hilly, was then covered in bushes and trees, and the refugees were squeezed into a very small area. It was hot and humid. The Bangladesh authorities, with a prominent role for their capable military engineers, were trying to establish basic road and water infrastructure, but it was taking time, partly because the space was overcrowded and there was little room to work. All the major aid agencies—the UN, leading NGOs, the Red Cross—had started operations. But they remained outfaced by the scale of the refugees' needs and limited by access restrictions imposed by the Bangladeshis, who were concerned about law-and-order problems and about the Myanmar military patrolling the border areas visible from the camps. Climbing to the crest of a hill to get a better sense of the situation, we saw we were surrounded by a sea of refugees, mostly women and young children, and the patchwork of plastic sheets that provided their only shelter.

I visited a counselling and support facility for women set up by the UN Population Fund, the UN agency dedicated to sexual and reproductive health. Sitting on the mud floor with a local female colleague as translator, I listened as a group of 24 women each told their personal stories of being gang-raped, being forced to watch as their husbands and young sons were killed in front of them, seeing their homes and fields set ablaze, and then being evicted at gunpoint towards the border areas. I met an 11-year-old cradling his severely malnourished 2-year-old sister in a UNICEF therapeutic feeding centre. He had walked for nine days to reach the camp. His mother had died on the journey, leaving him, still a small boy, in sole charge of his four younger brothers and sisters. At the press conference at the end of our visit, Tony showed crayon pictures some of the children had drawn in the facilities UNICEF was setting up for them. In rough lines and vivid colours, they depicted men shooting guns, burning huts, and children running away. Normally, when you visit refugees or displaced people, you see children smiling and playing, irrepressible whatever the circumstances. All we saw that day in Cox's Bazar was trauma, terror, and suffering.

———————————————

Muslims arrived in what was then the independent kingdom of Arakan (now Rakhine state in Myanmar) more than a thousand years ago. They were seafarers and traders from the Middle East. In the 17th century, thousands more arrived, captured from Bengal by Arakanese marauders and enslaved or forced to settle in the area. They were called Rohingya—people of Rohang, the early Muslim name for Arakan. For long periods, the different communities lived together in relative harmony. But ethnic tensions were inflamed during and after the Second World War, when the British armed Muslims to fight against the Rakhine, who had largely sided with the Japanese. In postwar Burma, military governments marginalised more than a hundred officially recognized minority ethnic groups, including the Rakhine, the Karen, and the Kachin. But even though the Rohingya had lived there for centuries, the state never recognised them as an indigenous ethnic group or granted them citizenship. They are stateless, a direct consequence of decades of systematic discrimination, persecution, and exclusion by Myanmar law, policy, and practice. (Bangladesh has not allowed the Rohingya citizenship, either.) António Guterres has called the Rohingya "the most discriminated-against community on the planet."

Discrimination against the Rohingya started to turn violent in the late 1970s. Some 200,000 were driven from Myanmar into Bangladesh in 1977–1978, though most were repatriated by 1979. (Of those who remained, some 10,000, mostly children, died after food rations were cut.) In 1982, a Myanmar citizenship law explicitly excluded the Rohingya. A junta established in 1988 increased the military presence in Rakhine, subjecting the Rohingya to compulsory labour, forced relocation, rape, summary executions, and torture. In 1991–1992, 250,000 were again forced into Bangladesh. With UN help, Bangladesh established camps for them in Cox's Bazar, but said there would be no integration with the local communities and the Rohingya would have to return home. Accordingly, some 230,000 were repatriated over the following years.

Tensions persisted in Rakhine, and intercommunal violence erupted between Buddhist and Muslim communities in 2012. Some 140,000 Rohingya were rounded up from their homes and put into camps lacking adequate food, water, shelter, and medical facilities. Their freedom of movement was severely curtailed. In 2014–2015, when the

Myanmar military had started to signal an intent to hand over control to a civilian government and the country was being rehabilitated into the international community, the Rohingya, then estimated to number 800,000, were excluded from the census. The UN published a report saying that crimes against humanity may have been committed in Rakhine. The Myanmar authorities expelled the outspoken medical NGO Médecins Sans Frontières. More than 100,000 Rohingya boarded flimsy boats attempting to reach neighbouring countries. Many drowned or starved. The Rohingya were again totally disenfranchised in the 2015 Myanmar election. A report by the US Holocaust Memorial Museum said the conditions were ripe for genocide.

In April 2016, Aung San Suu Kyi, an opposition politician and human rights activist who was awarded the Nobel Peace Prize in 1991 and had been held in military detention for the best part of 20 years, was installed as the head of a new government in Myanmar. Pulled in different directions from outside the country and within, she asked Kofi Annan to lead a commission to advise on concrete measures to improve the conditions for all people, Buddhist and Muslim, in Rakhine. In October 2016, a previously unknown Rohingya militant group attacked three police outposts in Rakhine, killing nine state security staff. Reprisals followed, triggering another exodus into Bangladesh, this time of 80,000 people.

All that was the context against which the horrors of 2017 unfolded. The Annan Commission issued its final report on 24 August. The commission recommended initiating a large-scale investment program to reduce poverty among all communities, as well as lifting restrictions against the Rohingya and reviewing Myanmar's citizenship law. The following day, the militants—now called the Arakan Rohingya Salvation Army—attacked 30 police outposts and killed 12 security officials. They claimed that they had launched these attacks as a response to protracted discrimination and persecution. Within hours of the attacks, however, the Myanmar army launched what it described as clearance operations. Estimates suggest that at least 10,000 people were killed. Well-evidenced reports described mass killings and rape and other extreme sexual violence on a huge scale. Returning from Cox's Bazar in November 2017, my colleague Pramila Patten, the special representative of the secretary-general on sexual violence in conflict, recounted horrific descriptions from Rohingya women and girls of the brutality they suffered. In addition to forced public nudity and sexual slavery in military captivity, many reported having been tied to rocks or trees before being gang-raped by soldiers. It was a concrete example of sexual violence being used as a deliberate tool of dehumanisation.

In the space of three weeks from August 2017, 600,000 people crossed into Cox's Bazar in the largest exodus yet. The world watched, with satellite images and other footage recording huge lines of people on the move and television crews filming their arrival and reception in the camps. Packing my final bags at home in London in late August, ready to head off to New York to start my new job, I watched the news reports with increasing foreboding.

——— ✦ ———

The international response to these atrocities was meek from the out-set. While António Guterres wrote a powerful letter to the Security Council on 2 September, it was a fortnight before the Council could agree to hold a meeting on the crisis and another 38 days before it is-sued a statement. (As we will see, this is a common problem: coun-tries with powerful friends can often stymie UN action, even when the majority wants it.) In early September, we held agonised meetings among the senior staff in New York, wringing our hands for any-thing we could do to stop the killings. On 11 September, UN High Commissioner for Human Rights Zeid Ra'ad Al Hussein issued a statement saying what was happening was "a textbook example of ethnic cleansing." The following week, world leaders meeting at the UN General Assembly proved unable to agree any collective response, with China protecting Myanmar from all the criticism and sanctions others thought appropriate.

The UN's own institutions were not immune from criticism. Staff from the NGO Human Rights Watch told Al Jazeera that "dealing with UN officials during this period was like dealing with members of a dysfunctional rich family who despise each other." There were divisions between the leadership of the UN team in Myanmar, who were heavily influenced by and wanting to sustain good relations with the government, and the humanitarian and human rights agencies who were appalled by what was happening and wanted a stronger reaction. The extent to which the UN actually could have prevented and curtailed the atrocities is moot, given that Security Council members China and Russia chose to protect Myanmar. Charles Petrie, a former UN resident coordinator in Myanmar, was, however, right to criticise the UN and some Western countries for their "refusal for a long time to let go of the fairy-tale view of Myanmar with Aung San Suu Kyi coming to power and the corresponding refusal to push back on some of her dogmatic positions."

If diplomatic and other pressure on Myanmar was ineffective, humanitarian efforts at least managed to provide some assistance to the refugees who had fled to Bangladesh. The bulk of the burden fell upon the Bangladeshis themselves, in their congested and developing but still poor country, and they were generous from the outset. They offered material help in the form of land to house the refugees as well as basic infrastructure and support services, and also spoke up loudly for the Rohingya and their plight in international fora. One consequence of Myanmar's subjugation of the Rohingya was that the Rohingya initially had few spokespeople of their own. From 2017, with assistance from NGOs like Amnesty International and BRAC (formerly the Bangladesh Rural Advancement Committee), that gradually changed.

UN agencies, the Red Cross, and Bangladeshi and international NGOs also mobilized support. One of the purposes of my October 2017 visit was to assess the progress of that support. In the six weeks after the influx began after August 25, the UN refugee agency, the World Food Programme, UNICEF, the UN Population Fund, and the International Organisation for Migration (IOM), with all their national and international NGO partners, combined to deliver 9 million food rations; water and sanitation support to 300,000 people; immunisation for 150,000 children; shelter kits to 150,000 people; and counselling and trauma support to over 50,000 people. That was a start. But there were inevitable difficulties. The situation on the ground remained chaotic and unsatisfactory, largely because of the scale and severity of the Rohingya's needs and the limitations of the cramped, hilly terrain of the refugee camps. There were also tensions among the agencies. Since this was a refugee crisis, the playbook suggested that the UN refugee agency should be in the lead, coordinating everyone else's contributions. The Bangladeshis, however, had strong relations with the IOM, a Geneva-based intergovernmental institution established in 1951 with responsibilities for nonrefugee migration issues, and they wanted it to be in the lead for the international partners. That demand predictably upset—and was resisted by—the refugee agency. In the initial weeks, these internal struggles complicated coordination between all the international agencies in Cox's Bazar.

We had sent an OCHA team, mostly from the Bangkok regional office, to support coordination efforts, working closely with the UN resident coordinator for Bangladesh. The OCHA team's proposal, which it wanted me to enforce, was that OCHA and the resident coordinator should take charge. I was sceptical. For one thing, both the IOM and the refugee agency would surely resist such a proposal. For another, I doubted we had the capacity to do the job well enough. But most importantly, the stance I wanted to adopt from the outset as ERC was to facilitate, enable, and support the agencies in the Inter-Agency Standing Committee, not try to control them. So I told the OCHA team that their job was to mediate a joint approach between the IOM and the refugee agency on coordination, with us providing services and support. After some huffing and puffing, that is what happened. The tensions did not fully evaporate, but collaboration between the agencies—which is of fundamental importance in a crisis situation—improved.

One issue on which I thought OCHA did have a major role to play was in the development and financing of a plan to cover the costs of the UN agencies and NGOs involved in the response. With the other agencies, we put together a plan seeking $434 million to meet the needs of 1.2 million people for the first 6 months—deliberately including both the refugees and local Bangladeshis burdened with the influx. We launched the plan on 3 October, and used the visit to Cox's Bazar that week to promote it across the media. We invited UN member states to a briefing meeting on 16 October. I chaired a fundraising conference, which the UN co-hosted with the EU and Kuwait, in Geneva on 23 October. By the end of the day, pledges totalled $360 million: a good outcome. Afterward, though, we needed to follow up to ensure that those who had made promises actually paid up. Fundraising of this sort absorbed a huge amount of my time as the ERC, and it is a topic to which I will return. When dealing with protracted crises, the cycle of developing response plans, holding fundraising events, and gathering pledges must be repeated every year. In the case of the Rohingya, whose plight touched the hearts of people across the globe, we raised nearly $700 million in both 2018 and 2019—more than 70 percent of what we sought. But by 2020, even though funding requirements for the Rohingya crisis remained similar, fundraising responses fell to below 60 percent of our requirements as the issue fell out of the headlines and other problems, above all the pandemic, dominated. Although some requirements, such as food, continued to be well funded, others such as education and special services for women and girls were much less so.

What was needed, obviously, was some sort of durable solution. For the Bangladeshis, that meant repatriation—a reasonable expectation both as a matter of principle and given the precedents after the outflows of the 1970s and the 1990s. This time was different. The

Bangladeshis made strenuous and extended efforts to negotiate safe returns, but both the military elements of the Myanmar government and Aung San Suu Kyi were obdurate. The limited, and mostly Western, international opprobrium they faced was insufficient to offset the widespread nationalist Burmese sentiment against the Rohingya. Over and over, the UN stressed to all and sundry that the causes of the problem were in Myanmar and the solution must be found there, too.

But to no avail. As the years passed, the focus shifted increasingly to the fate of the Rohingya inside Bangladesh. Facing growing domestic pressure over the strain that the refugees were putting on their own communities, government leaders felt more and more boxed in. Prime Minister Sheikh Hasina, who had been head of the government on and off since the 1980s, took personal responsibility for the issue. A diminutive, grey-haired woman in her seventies, she often adopted a conversational style that appeared meandering and slightly scatter-brained. But, as we learned in repeated discussions over the years, she was shrewd, stubborn, and determined. Having been a refugee from Bangladesh herself early in her life, she was visibly proud of having offered the Rohingya refuge. As the years passed, however, she became disenchanted by the international community's failure either to offer Bangladesh sufficiently generous financial support to provide for the Rohingya or to bring enough pressure to bear on Myanmar to accept repatriation. The indigenous population of Cox's Bazar, dismayed by the environmental impact of a million new people in their already congested district and frustrated by the pressure on local services, became vociferous in their opposition to the Rohingya's continued presence. Government circles also grew concerned over the rise in criminal activity and smuggling networks taking advantage of the refugees' presence. The Rohingya were denied freedom of movement, access to education, and employment opportunities.

Since 2015, the Bangladeshi government had mooted the idea that some of the Rohingya could be relocated to the island of Bhasan Char, nearly 40 miles into the Bay of Bengal. The island, which had been formed in 2006 by shifting Himalayan silt, was similar to other chars inhabited by millions of Bangladeshis across the delta that makes up the south of their country. But the unpopulated Bhasan Char was located so far out in the bay that it risked being inaccessible during the monsoon, and was vulnerable to cyclones. It had been rumoured that the government had spent hundreds of millions of dollars on infrastructure on Bhasan Char in a partnership with China, potentially for military motives that never fully came to fruition. In early 2017, the government ordered an initial resettlement programme for a first wave of Rohingya; by 2019, the infrastructure programme on Bhasan Char was expanding to meet the needs of 100,000 people. During that initial period, small groups of Rohingya visited the island to see its facilities, though it was not until 2020 that the first few thousand people were relocated. This all caused a good deal of nervousness and anxiety in the UN. Publicly, the line was that we were keen to understand the viability of the resettlement scheme and wanted reassurance on safety issues, not least during the monsoon and cyclone seasons, as well as guarantees that there would be no coercion. But the message that the Bangladeshis took was that the UN—under, they thought, influence from human rights organisations and Western donors—were trying to stymie a reasonable solution to the congestion and inadequate facilities of Cox's Bazar. The Bangladeshis felt badly used: the West in particular had preyed on their generosity in accepting the Rohingya, had provided only limited help to meet their needs, and now was objecting to practical measures to ease the strain.

When the UN refugee agency chief Filippo Grandi, IOM head Antonio Vitorino, and I visited Bangladesh together in April 2019, we had to navigate this complicated situation with Sheikh Hasina while at the same time seeking to ease some of the constraints on the Rohingya in Cox's Bazar. By that point, the physical conditions in the camps were better and the trauma of late 2017 had eased: we saw children laughing and playing, representatives of the Rohingya taking up roles in the management of facilities, and more of the semblances of a normal life. But the underlying air of tension and anxiety persisted.

The cyclone season was arriving again. Fire was a constant risk, as evidenced by a subsequent blaze that destroyed large areas of the camp in early 2021. Above all, the fundamental absence of a long-term solution hung like a cloud over the whole population. We tried to get all the decision-makers to focus on what the children in the camps, who were the majority of the population, would be like as adults if their conditions did not improve. As I said to the press at the end of that visit, "I think the world ought to worry about what this very large group of people will be like in 10 years' time if they don't get an opportunity to access education and a chance to develop a livelihood and have a normal life." It was hard to imagine a more radicalisable population anywhere in the world. None of these warnings really cut through: decision-makers, as so often is the case, could not lift their heads above the immediate to think about the longer term.

If it has been difficult to negotiate better conditions for the refugees in Bangladesh and secure resources to support them, and if there is no sign of the situation in Myanmar changing to make their return a realistic possibility, then seeking any kind of justice for the crimes perpetrated against the Rohingya has been even harder. Echoing what many believed, the *Economist* in 2018 said that the crisis "has all the hall marks of a genocide." The Gambia, with the backing of the 57 member countries of the Organisation of Islamic Cooperation, brought a genocide case before the International Court of Justice, the so-called world court which hears cases involving governments and UN bodies. To date, it rumbles on; in 2019, Aung San Suu Kyi appeared for Myanmar in oral hearings. There is a separate case before the International Criminal Court, the international tribunal set up to handle crimes against humanity, war crimes, and genocide. That case focuses on violations committed in part on Bangladeshi territory, because Bangladesh (unlike Myanmar) is a state party to the 1998 Rome Statute that established the International Criminal Court. The

UN Human Rights Council also set up an Independent International Fact-Finding Mission on Myanmar. None of these processes have yet gained much traction. Every time I hear an update on any of them, my thoughts turn to the woman in the pale-orange headscarf. I had asked her what she wanted. Her response was simple, clear, and eminently reasonable—but justice for her still looks a long way off.

TWO

The Stupid War in Yemen

A NORMAL WEIGHT FOR A 12-YEAR-OLD GIRL is 92 pounds. Abrar, though, weighed 28 pounds. She sat hunched on her hospital bed, her head resting on her spindly arm. Her skeleton was almost fully visible through her translucent skin. Abrar's organs were consuming what little remained of her flesh. Eight-year-old Yaqoob had been in the hospital more than a month. He barely made a sound, his brain sending the message that calories could be afforded for nothing other than keeping his essential organs alive. Fawaz, 18 months old, a few rooms down, had never developed the muscles that would enable him to walk. He had not had enough food for that. His skin was scarred by sores.

This is what happens when you starve. With no food, the body's metabolism slows down to preserve energy for vital organs. Hungry and weak, people often become fatigued, irritable, and confused. The immune system loses strength. As they starve, people—especially children—are likelier to fall sick or die from diseases they may have otherwise resisted. There is no shortage of diseases in Yemen that will prey on these weakened immune systems. They include cholera, COVID-19, other respiratory infections, malaria, dengue, and diphtheria. For those who manage to escape disease but still have nothing to eat, their organs will begin to wither and then fail. Eventually, the body starts to devour its own muscles, including the heart. Many will experience hallucinations and convulsions before, finally, the heart stops. It is a terrible, agonizing, and humiliating death.

Children like Abrar, Yaqoob, and Fawaz, who I met with their families in Aden in 2017 and 2018, are the real story of the war in Yemen. Every parent fears the same fate for their young sons and daughters. In September 2020, I spoke to Abdulrahman in Sana'a. He told me his six children came crying to him every day in hunger, and he had even less to give them than a few months previously because the aid he was receiving had been cut. The same day, Mohammed, who had fled with his family from the northern town of Sa'ada after war planes controlled by the Saudi-led coalition destroyed his house and the bus he used to drive, told me his family had had their aid cut, too. His children were now too hungry to go to school. Every night they asked him, "Daddy, where is the food. When is it coming?" He had no answer for them.

When you talk to people like this—and there are millions of them all over Yemen—and listen to their articulate, human, and emotional stories, the main thing you learn is they are just like the rest of us, except they are victims of people and forces over whom they have no influence or control. Their stories are hard to listen to, but they are a lot harder to live. Yemen is in the state it is because those with power and influence decided there were more important things than the fate of these people.

———————— ❖ ————————

Roughly the size of France and with a population of 30 million, Yemen is a land of spectacular mountains, wide plains, and expansive desert. Aden, the southern capital, is one of the world's great natural harbours, a regular port of call over the centuries for vessels travelling between Europe and Asia. The old city of the northern capital of Sana'a has been inhabited for more than 2,500 years. Built of tightly packed, multistorey, beautifully decorated rammed earth houses leavened by scattered green gardens, it is a UNESCO World Heritage Centre and one of the wonders of the world. It housed an early Christian cathedral and later became a major centre for the spread of the Islamic faith.

The human history of Yemen reflects its many tribes and clans, each fiercely independent and suspicious of others. Previously split between a northern republic and a southern communist state, formerly colonised by the British, Yemen was unified in 1990 after years of negotiations and an insurgency. Ali Abdallah Saleh, a military officer involved in a coup in North Yemen in 1974, became president, piecing together a fragile coalition of tribal leaders from across the country. Bankrolled by moneyed interests in Saudi Arabia, Saleh's 33-year rule was sustained by his ability to perpetuate a tapestry of complex alliances. He famously referred to ruling Yemen as an act of "dancing on the heads of snakes."

From early in the current century, the Saleh regime faced a string of rebellions fomented by the Houthi clan originating from Sa'ada, the northern region bordering Saudi Arabia. In June 2004, Saleh retaliated, and in the ensuing fighting the rebel leader Hussein Badreddin al-Houthi was killed. His younger brother Abdul Malik al-Houthi then took command. Sporadic fighting continued through 2005 and 2006, before a deal including an amnesty led to a brief pause, ended by further clashes in 2007 and 2008. In August 2009, Saleh's forces launched an offensive to end the rebellion, this time with military support from Saudi forces. Another cease-fire was agreed in early 2010. Meanwhile, the prevailing fragility and instability had opened space for al-Qaeda, whose Arabian Peninsula franchise gained effective control of part of the Governorate of Shabwah in southeast Yemen. With Western support, the government sought to root them out, besieging the area from late 2010.

And then came the Arab Spring. In early 2011, protests started in Sana'a. The grievances originated from economic hardship and corruption. Long the poorest country in the Middle East, Yemen's resource pressures had accumulated, exacerbated by rapid population growth. Yemen has significant reserves of oil and natural gas. Oil production peaked in 2001; it then fell substantially but still accounted for more than half the country's exports a decade later. The natural gas has never been fully developed, as potential investors have been put off by instability and attacks on facilities. Water shortages are a worse problem. Yemen ranks among the most water-scarce countries in the world. Experts expect Sana'a to be the first capital to run out of water completely, possibly within the next decade. Much of what remains is expensive to get to, requiring ever-deeper drilling and ever-higher fuel costs to pump it out. Yemeni commentators say that 70 to 80 percent of local conflicts are linked to competition over water.

Yemen historically had a vibrant agriculture, with a large livestock sector and beautifully terraced hillsides carved over the centuries across the northern highlands, which yielded coffee, fruit, and other produce. Much of that has now been lost to another uniquely Yemeni blight: qat. This leafy plant, a drought-tolerant, easily grown weed produced mostly in the mountains and plateaus of the north, plays a much larger role in the problems of Yemen than is commonly appreciated. The leaves are chewed in bundles and stored for hours inside the cheek, gradually releasing an amphetamine-like stimulant into the bloodstream. Qat produces a sustained buzz, a high that calms, chills, and generates confidence all at the same time. (It can also heighten the temper: experienced UN colleagues in Yemen tried to avoid sensitive meetings with counterparts after lunchtime, put off by frequently irrational and unpleasant behaviour from people who had been chewing for hours.) Qat stems the appetite, and frequently is bought ahead of food. Flying over the country in 2018, the only green I saw below was the qat fields.

In the past, qat was used exclusively by men, and in most cases on an occasional basis. Now it is ubiquitous, chewed every day by most men and by many women and children too. It is anaesthetising a nation against the pain of the war. One of the saddest sights I saw during my visits to Yemen was a pick-up truck carrying a group of young boys to the front. They looked 13 or 14, were dressed in rough fatigues and carrying guns. They were all chewing qat. It reminded me of a German army practice from World War II, where soldiers received methamphetamine- and cocaine-based stimulant pills so they would fight harder and worry less. The boys in the truck were paid maybe a hundred dollars a month by the backers of all the military forces, and much of their money went on qat. In the circumstances they face, why not dope yourself up if you can?

The limits to Yemen's own economy have historically led many Yemenis to leave the country for work elsewhere. The money they send home has become one of the main sources of income. In a country where nearly everything is imported, access to hard currency is a major factor in how much food and other necessities you and your family can afford. In 2014, just before the war started, Yemen's central bank estimated that nearly all the foreign exchange coming into Yemen was from two sources: oil exports (65 percent) and remittances (30 percent). Once the war started, oil exports collapsed, and remittances became even more important. By 2016, the Central Bank of Yemen estimated that remittances were used to pay for nearly 60 percent of imported goods. Notwithstanding all these elements of the formal economy, war has for years been the biggest business in Yemen, and the main employer.

<hr>

In the wake of the Arab Spring protests, and Saleh's crackdown that left up to 2,000 dead, Yemen's neighbours in the Gulf Cooperation Council (with US support) decided enough was enough. They wanted Saleh to resign in favour of Vice President Abdrabbu Mansour Hadi, a soldier-turned-politician from the south. Saleh's party, the General People's Congress, agreed to the deal, and in November 2011 Saleh handed over power to Hadi. The following February, Hadi was sworn in for a two-year term as president after an election in which he ran unopposed. There were hopes that Yemen would see a period of calm and recovery.

From 2013, a UN Special Envoy, backed by the Security Council, sought to facilitate a Yemeni national dialogue involving the participation of diverse civil society and political groups, including southern separatists and the Houthis. An outcome document was released in January 2014, extending Hadi's term for another year to oversee a transition to a broader-based government. But the deal did not hold. In August, after antigovernment protests erupted over high fuel prices, Hadi dissolved the government. Most of the few remaining foreign embassies shut up shop in Sana'a and left over the following months. (The Russians stuck it out for another couple of years, and I was able to talk to their well-informed staff when I visited in 2017.) The Houthis, who had continuously strengthened their military machine, took control of Sana'a following months of steady expansion across the north of the country. They moved south, taking the key Red Sea port of Hudaydah. In January 2015, Hadi resigned after being placed under house arrest by the Houthis. In February he fled to Aden, rescinding his resignation.

Up to that point, the effect of the political turmoil and (relatively) low-level conflict on most of the population, while bad, was contained. But now a much more violent and destructive war began in earnest. Houthi and General People's Congress forces, including important elements of the national armed forces, advanced rapidly into the south, threatening Aden. Hadi fled again, to the Saudi capital of Riyadh. A Saudi-led coalition, in which the Emiratis played a prominent role, initiated military operations, in particular large-scale air strikes. Western countries, primarily the United States and the United Kingdom, provided weapons. In April 2015, the Security Council passed Resolution 2216, which called for the Houthis to surrender, imposed an arms embargo, and promoted a return to UN-facilitated political talks. In July and August that year, the Hadi government and its loose coalition of tribal and other forces succeeded, with Saudi and Emirati support, in pushing Houthi-led forces out of Aden and much of the southern lowland zone. But in doing so, they displaced many ordinary people and caused substantial destruction, with large parts of central Aden being reduced to rubble.

In April 2016, the UN sponsored peace talks in Kuwait seeking an end to the conflict. US Secretary of State John Kerry made strenuous personal efforts to get the Yemeni stakeholders to some kind of a deal. But they were not ready. The talks broke down in August. The Saudi-led coalition escalated the air strikes and closed Sana'a airport. From this point on, Yemen was relegated from a poor country with an unstable polity to a humanitarian disaster. The deliberate, calculated choices of the belligerents and those arming them immiserated the population.

Front lines moved remarkably little in the next five years. In January 2017, government-backed forces launched an offensive to regain parts of southwest Yemen. They advanced slowly over the following year. Minor ports along the coast were taken, and government forces eventually closed in towards Hudaydah by the middle of 2018.

Consistent with Yemen's history, the conflict has also been marked by permanent turmoil within each of the leading alliances. In 2017 tensions mounted on the Houthi-led side, when their governing partner, the General People's Congress, was perceived to be reaching out to the coalition to end the war. That December, shortly after I had visited, armed clashes erupted in Sana'a. Among the casualties was former President Saleh, shot in his car apparently in the act of fleeing. The Houthis consolidated their grip across the north progressively in subsequent years, in particular assuming more of the functions of the state.

Meanwhile, on the other side, the Saudi and the Emirati positions began to diverge. The latter emboldened southern separatist forces who opposed both the Houthis and the internationally recognised government. In January 2018, the Southern Transitional Council, established with Emirati backing a few months previously, briefly seized control of Aden city. Much diplomatic effort over the following year was expended in trying to piece back together the fragile progovernment alliance. When I was in Aden in late 2018, an uneasy calm prevailed, with multiple militias across the city just about contained by Emirati forces. Their armoured personnel carriers protected the street where UN staff lived and worked, but did little about the small-arms fire that kept everyone awake through the night.

For years now, the Houthis have controlled the north and west of the country, where 80 percent of the population lives. The government holds larger but less densely populated areas across the south and east, with a few no-go areas under the sway of al-Qaeda- or ISIS-affiliated groups. But that is not to say the fighting and bloodletting has eased. The opposite is true. In 2021, there were still nearly 50 active front lines, with countless young men sacrificed along them for no apparent gain month after month. According to the independent Yemen Data Project, there were between 400 and 900 air raids every month from when the coalition started bombing in March 2015 until the first round of peace talks in April 2016. After those talks failed in August 2016, the air strikes ramped up again, before falling back from 2019. With the air strikes, the ground clashes, shelling, and other explosions, Yemen became progressively more violent. According to ACLED, another independent conflict monitoring group, there were about 7,800 violent incidents in 2017. In 2020, there were 9,200—an increase of 18 percent.

Most of the fighters have been Yemeni. On the government side, many were paid by members of the Saudi-led coalition, whose bills have run into billions of dollars. They are also believed to have financed mercenaries from elsewhere, including Eritrea and Colombia. The International Crisis Group reported in 2016 that the Sudan of then President Omar al-Bashir was being paid billions of dollars for its support. As many as 40,000 Darfuri paramilitaries are thought to have gone to Yemen—many of them, according to widespread reports, children. The *New York Times* reported that these child soldiers were paid "the equivalent of $480 a month for a 14-year-old novice to about $530 a month for an experienced officer." Lump sums were paid at the end of a six-month rotation—to those who were still alive. When Bashir was deposed in 2019, Sudanese troops were withdrawn, with just a few hundred left by early 2020.

Nor have Yemenis away from the front lines been spared by the guns and bombs. A series of atrocities have arisen from air strikes. In September 2015, 135 people were killed when planes dropped bombs on a wedding outside the Red Sea city of Mukha. In March the following year, a hundred people, dozens of them children, were killed at Al Khamees market in the western governorate of Hajjah. The UN could find no significant military objects within 250 metres. That October, in one of the most notorious incidents, 140 were killed and 600 wounded in the bombing of a funeral in Sana'a. In August 2018, 60 primary school children, out on a bus trip to celebrate their graduation, were killed and 56 wounded when their bus was hit. For years, children across Yemen would look up to the skies and wonder if they were next. The single deadliest air strike recorded (at least up to 2021) occurred on 31 August 2019, when 150 civilians were killed at a Houthi detention centre. Speaking live on television at the opening ceremony of a humanitarian conference in Riyadh in October 2017, I complained about an incident a few days earlier when, on the morning I arrived in Sana'a, the OCHA offices there were shaken—and the staff sent scuttling to the basement—by an air strike. It was apparently aimed at a munitions dump a few hundred meters from our premises. Those organising these attacks were, it seemed to me, careless of the fear they generated in people on the ground.

Arms suppliers, particularly from the United States and the United Kingdom, have enriched themselves with the permission of their governments in keeping the materiel flowing. From 2010 to 2015, US arms transfers to Saudi Arabia amounted to $3 billion. In the next five years, those sales rose more than twenty-fold to over $64 billion. The United Kingdom licensed the sale of at least $6 billion worth of arms to Saudi Arabia between 2015 and 2020. This was controversial on both sides of the Atlantic. Several resolutions passed in the US House and Senate in 2018 and 2019 called for an end to US support for the war. They were consistently vetoed by President Donald Trump. In the United Kingdom, campaigners took the government to court to try to block British sales, on the grounds that the arms would be used in a manner that infringed international humanitarian law. The Court of Appeal ordered a suspension of sales in June 2019. A year later, the ban was lifted, and over the following three months the British government approved another £1.4 billion of arms sales to Saudi Arabia.

———— ❖ ————

In an opinion article published by CNN in December 2018, shortly after my most recent visit to Yemen, I tried to describe the impact of the war up to then. Four years previously, Yemen had been a fragile country where millions of people struggled to make ends meet and many survived only with the help of foreign aid. But there was a functioning economy, infrastructure stretched across the country, and people received basic services from their government. The war had now decimated the Yemeni economy. National income was half what it was. Attacks on fishing vessels, destruction of farmland, and bombing of factories had destroyed production. The UN estimated that more than 600,000 jobs had been lost. Oil revenue, the main source of government income, was down by 85 percent. More than a million teachers, health care workers, and pensioners had barely been paid for years. Millions of families did not have the money they needed to buy food to survive. Air strikes and ground fighting, including artillery fire, had destroyed and damaged schools, water systems, clinics, and other health facilities. One consequence was a spate of killer diseases. There were more than a million suspected cholera cases in 2017, in an outbreak some experts thought the worst the world had ever seen.

The fighting also killed or injured tens of thousands of civilians and displaced well over three million more. The displaced were among the most desperate people I met. In late 2018, I went to a makeshift camp north of Sana'a where a few hundred families from all over the country were sleeping out under paper-thin sheets of plastic. It was cold, and there was no water, little food, and no health services. I asked the grizzled old man showing me round what there was to do all day. "Looking after dogs" he said, to the laughter of the watching crowd, and pointing at one. As we walked away, I asked my bodyguards why that had attracted such hilarity. "No-one looks after dogs in Yemen," they said. "They fend for themselves. These people have nothing to do." Except watch the sky for the next bomb.

Accompanying the military activity was an economic blockade imposed on Houthi-controlled Yemen by the Saudi-led coalition and their allies. It was ostensibly intended to curtail the flow of weapons and other military supplies to the Houthis. The Saudis in particular had a legitimate interest in preventing the import of rockets and components which were being used to attack their territory. These attacks started just weeks after the coalition air strikes began, with the Houthis firing mortars in early May 2015 into the Saudi border city of Najran. That attack reportedly killed three civilians and temporarily closed the local airport. It set off what became a steady stream of mortars, missiles, and other cross-border attacks into Saudi Arabia. US-supplied missile defences intercepted most of these attacks, and therefore they often were little more than a nuisance, but they occasionally killed or injured small numbers of people and damaged property. Over time, they became more intensive and sophisticated, reaching deeper into Saudi territory and targeting oil infrastructure and other important sites. Attacks of this sort cannot be tolerated by any country and preventing them was a proper objective. Starving millions of people through a blockade in the attempt to do so, however, was disproportionate and unacceptable.

A partial blockade was put in place in 2015, with Saudi and other warships stationed in the Red Sea seeking to restrict access to Houthi-controlled ports like Hudaydah. Hudaydah was of strategic importance. Yemen had always been heavily dependent on imports for food. Conflict and resource pressures had reduced domestic production to little more than 10 percent of national needs by this point, meaning that 90 percent of the food consumed in the country had to be brought in. Hudaydah accounted for the vast majority of this trade, both before the conflict escalated and more so after, when it became progressively difficult to transport supplies from other ports like Aden across the front lines to the bulk of the population who lived in the Houthi-controlled parts of the country. The UN established a verification and inspection mechanism in 2015, intending to facilitate legitimate commercial cargo getting to Yemeni ports but to prevent arms and other military supplies from doing so. The government and its allies were sceptical about the effectiveness of measures to block contraband. Preventing small dhows landing unseen somewhere along the thousands of kilometres of Yemen's coastline, much of it not controlled by the government, was obviously difficult.

In early November 2017, the Houthis launched a missile attack on Saudi Arabia's most important civilian airport, King Khalid International Airport in Riyadh. It was intercepted, but the Saudis were understandably furious. They believed the missile technology had been provided by Iran. Within days, they announced a total closure of all the air, sea, and land ports in Yemen—even banning UN flights. On 8 November, I told the Security Council, convened for an urgent private meeting, that while I condemned the missile attack, unless the blockade was lifted there would be famine in Yemen. And it would be the largest famine the world had seen for many decades, with millions of victims.

A week later, the secretary-general's media team told the UN press corps he thought the war was "stupid." Guterres repeated this comment during a CNN interview in December. He pointed out that the war was ultimately detrimental to the interests of Saudi Arabia and the Emirates. Even from the point of view of Iran, it was hard to see any advantage to it. Worst of all was the suffering imposed on the people of Yemen.

The rotten thread weaving together the story of Yemen is how little attention any of the main protagonists—those men controlling the guns, shells and warplanes—pay to the lives and wishes of ordinary Yemenis. The powerful have demonstrated that they could not care less about the fate of so many ordinary people—and that was the source of most of the problems humanitarian agencies in Yemen struggled against while I was the ERC.

The government of President Hadi was—in a competitive field—among the most venal and corrupt I have encountered. Hadi himself, old and suffering from health problems, was mostly based in the palace the Saudis lent him in Riyadh. He was rarely in Yemen. At the time I left the UN in 2021, he had not been there at all since 2019, when he went for a few hours for a meeting of a putative parliamentary assembly. Many of his officials were little better, ever angling for personal gain and frequently seeking to interfere with the work of aid agencies or putting barriers in the way of their ability to get help to people. There were exceptions. Prime Minister Dr. Maeen Abdulmalik Saaed, who had been appointed in 2018, genuinely tried to keep the economy as stable as possible, pay the salaries of key workers, and collaborate with the aid agencies. His was a lonely furrow. The motley mix of tribal and militia leaders who between them have more control across the south than the recognised government lacked any coherent vision or programme beyond narrow sectional interest.

The Houthis, meanwhile, established an increasingly repressive police state, clamping down on civil rights and the position of women and girls, and seeking greater administrative as well as security control. Their emergence as a power in northern Yemen in the 1990s was partly a reaction to growing Saudi financial and religious influence in their home area. The Houthis are Zaydi, a Shiite branch of Islam that is theologically and historically distinct from Iranian Shiism. Over the past 20 years, there have been increasing efforts to portray the Houthis as Iranian proxies. Knowledgeable people were initially sceptical about this. One US Embassy cable (which found the light of day through WikiLeaks) reported that they "did not find any evidence to support allegations of links between the insurrectionists and Iran." It would not be surprising if links had grown, given that Iran and the Houthis had a common antagonism towards the Saudis. One effect of the war, it seemed to me, had been to strengthen what were previously looser ties. But it is an exaggeration to portray Iran as the Houthis' puppet master. Iranian officials make good points when they comment now on the situation. The Houthis, they observe, have proved themselves a potent fighting force on the ground, and will inevitably have to have a prominent part of any future power-sharing government. Moreover, some of the tactics of the government and its supporters, especially the blockade, have added more to the misery of the population as a whole than the fighting itself.

It was difficult for the UN to play the role it was charged with. The UN can facilitate but not enforce. It can save lives and get help to ordinary people, but—to pick up a tune played too often—only when the men with guns and bombs will allow it, and only when someone is willing to foot the bill. The UN's political envoys worked hard to encourage the parties to find common ground to end the war. There were no thanks in that. One envoy found his car shot at, apparently by a sniper, during one of his visits to the north. His bodyguards that day later looked after me on one of my visits. It was not an assassination attempt, they said. Just a warning. If the Houthis had wanted to kill him, they would have done so. Aid workers—of whom there are many thousands with the UN, the Red Cross, and NGOs—suffered similar threats, hindrances, and harassment. Most of them were Yemeni. Some, both international and local, lost their lives.

UN lobbying contributed to a partial relaxation of the Saudi blockade of Hudaydah from December 2017, but the coalition continued to angst over smuggling through the port. Over the course of 2018, Emirati-backed ground troops, supported by the air campaign, clawed their way up the west coast, picking up minor ports along the way and beginning to encircle Hudaydah city. We began to fear a major attack displacing a lot more people and threatening cargo handling in the port. An Emirati amphibious assault was mooted; there was some doubt about their ability to pull it off, but regardless we did not see what in practice it would achieve. If the Houthis lost the port and city, they would still be able to shell it from the surrounding highlands and the coalition would still need to negotiate with them if grain was to be kept moving to feed the population further north. Nevertheless, with brief pauses, the stranglehold tightened, with heavy clashes through September.

On 2 October 2018, Jamal Khashoggi, a Saudi journalist and critic of the government, went to the Saudi consulate in Istanbul to sort out some paperwork. He was strangled and, probably once dead, his body was hacked and sawn into pieces. Unfortunately for those responsible, Turkish intelligence services had bugged the room where it happened. Within days, the tapes were being listened to in Washington, London, and elsewhere. Khashoggi was a columnist with the *Washington Post*; his assassination dominated the headlines for days. Many Americans, including Republican Senator Lindsey Graham, the powerful chair of key Senate committees, were incensed.

In the ensuing furore, criticism of the Saudi role in Yemen mounted. In mid-November, a pause in offensive operations around Hudaydah was announced. The parties agreed to go to talks in Stockholm, where the following month a deal was hammered out to establish a UN assistance mission for Hudaydah with a view to stabilising the situation and safeguarding humanitarian supply lines. The Security Council resolution setting up the mission included provisions giving the secretary-general a mandate to report regularly on developments on the humanitarian situation. That was important to me, but the United States resisted it for reasons I did not understand. Only the stubborn negotiation of Karen Pierce, then the United Kingdom's forthright and ebullient UN Ambassador, managed to secure the mandate.

Few things illustrate better the difficulties of solving problems in Yemen when I was ERC, and the frustrations the UN encountered, than the sorry saga of the *Safer* tanker. The *Safer*, originally a sea-going vessel, had for years been used as an oil storage facility in the waters off Hudaydah. It was more than 40 years old, corroding and in disrepair. It could easily be the source of a spillage through an explosion or leak. Such a leak occurred in May 2020 when sea water flowed into the engine room. The *Safer* carried 1.1 million barrels of oil. That was about four times as much as was discharged in the 1989 *Exxon Valdez* disaster off Alaska—a major environmental disaster the world still talks about 30 years later.

Fortunately, the 2020 *Safer* leak was relatively small, and divers were able to contain it. But the fix they applied was only temporary, and it was impossible to say how long it might hold. A spill would have appalling environmental consequences for Yemen and its neighbours. As well as destroying livelihoods of fishing communities along the Houthi-controlled western coast, it might also render the port of Hudaydah inoperable for weeks or even months. The risk from the *Safer* was therefore a direct and severe threat to the well-being, and potentially the survival, of millions of Yemenis in Houthi-controlled areas.

The Yemeni government and the Houthis first formally requested UN assistance with the *Safer* in March 2018. There was to be a technical assessment, in order to provide impartial evidence to guide next steps, which might include the safe extraction of the oil upon agreement from the involved parties. For much of 2018, the coalition-backed military threat on Hudaydah made it too dangerous to visit the site. But with the Stockholm Agreement in December of that year and the subsequent cease-fire in Hudaydah, safe access again became possible. The UN worked closely with the parties to secure the necessary clearances so the technical team could visit to carry out the inspection.

The government of Yemen agreed to the assessment and actively sought to facilitate access to the *Safer*. The Houthis also consistently agreed—in principle. They sent several letters to the UN and to the Security Council confirming their agreement. But they were unwilling to accept a mission in practice. Instead, they imposed preconditions and linked the *Safer* with other issues.

I gave the Security Council, in the course of nearly 20 briefings on the issue over three years, a running commentary on this protracted bureaucratic minuet of permissions to visit being sought, apparently being granted, and then turning out in fact not to have been granted. It was difficult to get to the bottom of why the Houthis did not take the opportunity to make the *Safer* safe. Up to late 2018, they might have reasoned that it had some defensive benefit against the risks of an amphibious coalition assault on Hudaydah. It was hard to see that after 2018, when the threat to Hudaydah lessened. Perhaps they did not believe the technical assessment that the tanker was dangerous and a large spill would hurt their interests.

As the war and the associated blockade progressively destroyed Yemen's social capital, institutions, infrastructure, livelihoods, and basic services, more and more people became dependent on aid. The number of people in need of humanitarian assistance grew from 15 million in 2014 to 24 million—80 percent of the population—in 2020. These were among the metrics by which from 2017 we judged Yemen to be the world's worst humanitarian crisis, worse even than Syria. But it was also the worst in terms of the numbers of people who may not survive.

In 2014, the UN humanitarian appeal amounted to $600 million, 60 percent of which (nearly $400 million) was raised. That amount allowed UN agencies and partnering NGOs to provide help to four million people. In 2019, we sought $4.2 billion and raised $3.6 billion, a ten-fold increase over five years. That meant we could help nearly 14 million people with food (or money and vouchers to buy it), health services, clean water, shelter, and other needs. It was the largest humanitarian relief operation in any country in the world.

Delivering assistance to people across all Yemen's 333 districts would be a significant logistical challenge in peacetime. It was much harder in the circumstances faced since 2014. More than 200 humanitarian organisations were involved in the UN-coordinated response in 2020. Their work was constantly impeded, especially through restrictions imposed by the parties on the ground on the movement of aid supplies and staff. The biggest risk, however, was that the aid effort itself would be caught up in the conflict.

Air strikes were a particular concern. In 2015 the UN, through the OCHA office, put in place a deconfliction system to assist the

Saudi-led coalition to fulfil its obligations under international humanitarian law to protect civilians and civilian infrastructure, as well as to facilitate safe humanitarian access. Aid agencies using the system give OCHA details of their planned convoys, premises, and staff movements, and OCHA passes them on to the Saudis. In 2020, the system processed 13,500 notifications, mainly for the transportation of humanitarian cargo like food. While most were for UN agencies; it also covered thousands of NGO activities. A small OCHA team in Riyadh processed the information through the coalition command centre there.

Unlike the similar system in Syria (see Chapter 3), this one was consistently successful. The coalition acted seriously on the information provided. Very few accidents or other incidents occurred. I had a number of opportunities to visit the coalition headquarters in Riyadh and was always pleased to express my thanks to them. I was well aware during my travels round Yemen that I too was relying on deconfliction working well. All my movements were notified in advance to protect me. Equally, one wondered why comparable care could not be taken to protect Yemeni civilians.

I spent a lot of time year after year trying to ensure continuing funding for the relief operation. Much of the money came from Western governments, voluntarily making grants to UN agencies, NGOs, and the Red Cross. But we were also able in 2018 and 2019 to put in place some of the most innovative and efficient funding arrangements I have seen in any international relief operation. Through contacts established via a well-connected staff member in my office, in early March 2018 at the Plaza Hotel overlooking Central Park in New York, I met Prince Khalid bin Salman. He was the younger brother of Saudi Crown Prince (effectively the national ruler) Mohammed bin Salman. Khalid was then the Saudi Ambassador in Washington. We pitched to him the idea that for 2018 the Saudis might make their contribution to the UN Yemen appeal in a single payment at the beginning of the year. He was intrigued enough to invite us to make a detailed proposal.

We went to see him again at his Washington residence shortly after. By then, we were promoting the idea that the Saudis might encourage the Emiratis to take a joint approach. Rather than agreeing a string of different grants with multiple UN and other agencies, OCHA could take delivery of a single payment and pass it on to the agencies on a formula agreed with the donors. This would be more efficient all round, and the UN could cut its normal overhead rate from 7 percent to 5 percent so more of the money could get to those we all wanted to help. (All the agencies, with the exception of the World Food Programme, eventually agreed to this arrangement.) We would also set up a dedicated reporting office to provide regular detailed information on exactly how the money was being used, corroborated with monitoring by independent third parties. The Saudis were looking for public relations opportunities for the Crown Prince's visit to the United States in late March. We managed to finalise the agreement, and Prince Mohammed handed over a cheque for $930 million in a photo call with Guterres at the UN in New York on 28 March. It took longer to clear the cheque than to negotiate the deal.[1]

The Saudis agreed to repeat their single payment through OCHA in 2019, this time for $500 million and without the Emiratis. That September, we organised an event at the General Assembly High-Level Week to mark the occasion. I suggested to the Saudis that this time perhaps an electronic transfer would be better. As the cameras clicked, they handed me another cheque.

A lot of people have questioned how the United Nations could, in good conscience, accept money to stave off humanitarian suffering from the very parties that were contributing to that suffering in the first place. My position was always that an end to the conflict was the only way to end suffering, but in the meantime, we had an obligation to save as many lives and reduce as much suffering as possible. Anyone wishing to contribute to that goal of reducing suffering was urged to do so. And high levels of predictable and sustained funding

---

1. When UN staff took it to our bank in New York on 29 March, the teller said they could not accept it because their computer system could not cope with a cheque with so many digits. Several weeks later, during which the cheque travelled from New York to Delaware, then to Texas, and then back to Riyadh, the funds were released.

for the humanitarian operation certainly reduced the misery. There was no respite from the conflict in much of the country, but humanitarian agencies nevertheless saved millions of lives. Large-scale famine, which had emerged as a clear and present danger, was averted. The record-setting cholera outbreak was mostly brought under control. Malnutrition cure rates exceeded global standards.

As well as funding the humanitarian operation, there was also a desperate need to avoid a total collapse of the Yemeni economy. In late 2018, despite a well-funded humanitarian operation, famine warning lights again started flashing red. At the time, agencies described the risk of famine as "income-driven." In other words, there was food in the country, but no one could afford it.

The economy had been declining for months, but things really unravelled from August to October when the Yemeni rial crashed, sinking in value from about 500 rial to the US dollar in August to about 900 rial by late October. Because nearly everything had to be imported, including almost all the food, millions more Yemenis suddenly could not afford to eat.

The rial collapsed because the government had run out of foreign exchange. How that happened reveals another dimension of the pain inflicted on Yemen. In 2014, the year before the war started, the Central Bank of Yemen had about $4.8 billion in foreign currency reserves. By August 2016, with the Central Bank still operating from Houthi-controlled Sana'a, reserves had dropped to about $700 million. The government was furious, claiming the Houthis had stolen the money for the war. That month, it abruptly fired the Bank's governor and announced that it would move the Bank to Aden.

Most of the world had warned against this. The former central bank governor was widely respected by diplomats and others for his efforts to insulate Yemen's economy from the war. That included continuing to meet Yemen's financial obligations—like salary payments, basic commodity imports, and essential services—despite revenues essentially falling to zero. The governor vigorously denied accusations of mismanagement and implored President Hadi to have the International Monetary Fund (IMF) commission an audit of the Bank's internal and external operations. President Hadi was not moved by this appeal, and the Bank moved to Aden a few weeks later, leaving behind much of its expertise in Sana'a. Now fully in control of monetary policy, the government quickly started printing more money to pay its bills, which compounded the downward pressure on the rial created by the rapid depletion of foreign reserves.

The Saudis, who had a political interest in ensuring that the Central Bank of Yemen made a successful transition to Aden, saw where this was heading. In early 2018, they announced a $2 billion deposit to help the bank strengthen the rial and finance commodity imports. As it turned out, the Saudis did not trust the Yemenis enough to hand this amount over as a single cheque. Instead, the Yemeni government drew down the deposit over nearly 40 instalments, each one reportedly signed off on by Saudi authorities.

When the rial hit 900 to the dollar in October 2018, the Saudis expedited a direct cash infusion of $200 million. It worked. By December 2018, the rial was again trading around 500 to the dollar. These periodic injections helped to contain the damage, but they were never large or frequent enough to keep the exchange rate at a level affordable for people trying to buy food (about 440 rial). And when the $2 billion deposit started to run out in the summer of 2020, the exchange rate started to unravel again. The idea of increasing the stranglehold of the blockade in an attempt to pressurise the Houthis had resurfaced. The previous failures of that strategy had been forgotten or ignored. Saudi support for the rial dried up.

The blockade on fuel tightened, too. In 2018 and 2019, the government introduced a series of new import regulations, some of which were intended to clamp down on suspected fuel smuggling from Iran.

The regulations—and the pressure by the Houthis on traders in the north not to comply with them—made it much harder to keep a reliable supply of fuel entering the ports in the north.

The UN brokered a solution to this problem in November 2019. It was agreed that commercial fuel ships serving Hudaydah would pay customs and fees into a special account of the Central Bank in Hudaydah. The parties would then work together to agree how to use the revenue to pay civil servant salaries and other expenses. For several months, fuel ships entered Hudaydah without problems. The shortages in the north stopped. But sometime in April or May 2020, the Houthis withdrew all the money from the special account and spent it. They say they spent it on salary payments, but there was no accounting to prove that. Incensed, the government abandoned the agreement in June. After that, they allowed fuel vessels to enter Hudaydah only on an exceptional basis. On average, the ships that got that exceptional clearance had to wait more than three months before being allowed in.

All this helps explain why, even with a well-managed and well-funded relief operation and efforts to help Yemen avoid complete economic collapse during 2018 and 2019, 2020 proved much more difficult. The COVID-19 pandemic took its toll. It understandably made most countries, even those with significant national interests in Yemen, focus on domestic issues. Gulf countries felt poorer as the oil price fell with the global economic contraction. Frustration both with the Houthis and with government intransigence over political talks weakened commitment to the aid effort. The Houthis attempted to raise resources from the aid agencies, including threatening a 2 percent levy on all their activities—which no aid agencies or their donors would ever accept. The Houthis also resisted the World Food Programme's attempts to introduce biometric registration systems to provide greater assurance that all the money was reaching the intended beneficiaries and minimise leakage risks. These things tarnished the atmosphere. Some donors, led by the Trump administration, wanted to threaten aid cuts as a response to Houthi pressure. I thought that amounted to the collective punishment of the starving, so it was not acceptable, and in any case it would not work because it assumed against the evidence that the Houthis cared what happened to ordinary people. In early March 2020, Guterres and I had a tense face-to-face meeting in New York with US Secretary of State Mike Pompeo, dancing around the issues. With Guterres' help, we resisted pressure to support aid cuts. Several weeks before, Guterres had issued a statement re-affirming "the importance of sustaining the humanitarian operation" and calling on everyone to "ensure that help reaches all those who need it, in accordance with humanitarian principles." This statement made it clear that the UN did not agree with the US push for major aid suspensions. But we still needed somehow to secure the necessary resources.

In June 2020, we held the annual fundraising conference for the humanitarian operation. We had agreed with the Saudis that they would co-host a video event on the basis that they would repeat their financing as in 2019. That undertaking was not kept. Other Gulf financing also failed to materialise. Overall, funding during 2020 was barely half the level of the previous two years. Out of money, agencies started cutting back. Most importantly, the World Food Programme reduced their number of recipients from a peak of 13.5 million a month in 2019 down to 9 million, by reducing ration provisioning from once a month to once every two months. The people who missed out got hungrier. Our data started to show famine indicators as bad or worse than 2018. With World Food Programme Executive Director David Beasley, I rang the alarm bell again in the Security Council in January 2021. David told them the current situation in Yemen was "a repeat performance" of the famine risk we saw in 2018, again putting the country on what he called a "countdown to catastrophe." We both tried that day to remind the world not just what was at stake—millions of people starving to death—but also that it was entirely preventable. Aid agencies could stop famine from happening, because we had managed to do so two years before.

But, as David told Council members, "in the two years since that time, so much of our good work [has been] wiped out." And that work had been wiped out in large measure because donors, mainly in the Gulf, had chosen not to keep paying for aid operations at the scale they had done in 2018 and 2019. The nature of humanitarian crises is that they need continuous funding until the emergency is over. Past contributions may have been extremely generous, and they certainly saved millions of lives, but that money had been spent. It could not save a single life tomorrow or the next day.

As I have emphasised, humanitarian assistance can keep people alive, but it cannot solve the problems which put them in need in the first place. As the years passed, frustration with the leading Yemeni protagonists grew. Everyone but them wanted the conflict to end. But each time enough pressure was put on one grouping of the Yemeni parties to make them ready to do a deal, their opponents used it as an opportunity to wriggle free and increase their own demands. There was no military victory available in Yemen. A negotiated peace settlement was the only way out and the only way to dramatically reduce humanitarian suffering. Yemen's leaders had to pay more attention to the needs and desires of their people.

In the dying months of the Trump administration, talk grew about increasing the pressure on the Houthis by formally designating them as a terrorist organisation. With others, I argued privately and publicly against that. We expressed scepticism that it would change Houthi behaviour and said the actual effect would be to freeze food and other essential imports. Yemeni traders told us that their international suppliers, shippers, insurers, and bankers would no longer do business with them if the terrorist designation was issued because they feared the impact of US regulatory action, which could lead to prosecution and jail time. Most of the food imported into Yemen came in commercially, and people bought it with vouchers or money they got from aid agencies. There was no chance that the agencies could replace what the commercial traders did. Our lobbying was in vain. In one of his last acts as secretary of state, Mike Pompeo issued the designation on 10 January 2021. Four days later I told the Security Council that unless it were revoked, the likely result would be a famine larger than anything the world had seen for 40 years. (I could not escape the sense of deja vu all over again: I had said the same thing about the Saudi blockade four years earlier.)

President Joseph Biden had stood in the 2020 US election on a campaign pledge to end US support for the war in Yemen. On 4 February 2021, a fortnight after taking office, he announced in his first major foreign policy speech the implementation of that pledge. He added that his administration would also prioritise dealing with the humanitarian crisis. The following week, the new secretary of state, Tony Blinken, announced the Houthi terrorism designation would be revoked with effect from 16 February.

The new US posture, which was welcomed notably by the leadership of Saudi Arabia, created the best opportunity since the war began for it to be brought to a close and the misery of the Yemeni people finally to be stemmed. It was then up to the Yemeni parties, not only on the government side but also the Houthis, the Southern Transitional Council, and their various allies and associates, to work out whether to take it. They had to decide whether they wanted finally to become statesmen rather than warlords. All the main entities could have a role in a future government. The alternative was the life-style of the pariah, skulking from safe house to cave, wondering if tonight was the night when the bullet or the missile would finally find them. Is that what they wanted indefinitely into the future? They did not get off to a good start. In early 2021, there were months of escalating fighting in and around Marib, the centre of Yemen's oil reserves.

In the meantime, on 1 March, Guterres and I, together with the Swedish and Swiss foreign ministers, convened the 2021 high-level pledging event seeking resources to sustain and avoid further cuts in the humanitarian operation. The appeal, at $4 billion, was again enormous. We secured promises amounting to $1.7 billion on the day, with the Gulf donors mostly resuming their funding under pressure from the United States. That was enough for the food relief operation temporarily to be increased again, once more pushing catastrophe further into the future.

As I left my post, I still hoped the rotten thread could be replaced—if not with a golden one, then at least with something slightly less rotten. Everyone could gain from peace. Restoring the battered economy and creating jobs and livelihoods, as well as basic health, education, and other services, to a point where Yemen could sustain itself would be the work of decades. It would take generations to piece back together Yemen's fractured society and overcome the anger and grievances the war had amplified. But nothing was going to get better until it stopped getting worse. There was still no progress on the underlying political issues. The stupid war raged on.

THREE

The Many Atrocities of Syria

OVER MY FOUR YEARS as the ERC, I spent more time on the Syria crisis than on any others. I made many visits there and to neighbouring countries—mostly Jordan, Lebanon, and Turkey—to which Syrians had fled. I attended dozens of Security Council meetings, multiple fundraising conferences, and countless discussions with humanitarian agencies and representatives of UN member states. One of the bloodiest civil wars in decades has now been raging for more than 10 years. The misery was endless. I had been following the issues closely for years before I joined the UN, because Britain (through DFID) was a major provider of humanitarian assistance to the region. I thought I had a degree of understanding of the crisis, but I soon learned that handling it in the UN was more challenging and complex than I had appreciated. Humanitarian agencies have been up to their necks in the horror. What have they learned from the experience, and how has it reshaped the work they do?

This is a complicated question, which is one reason why this is the longest chapter in the book. In order to understand the question, it is necessary first to remind ourselves of what has happened. In the first phase of the crisis, between March 2011 and August 2012, anti-government protests in Syria evolved into armed conflict. Under the leadership (from February 2012) of former UN Secretary-General

Kofi Annan, the international community began to engage in conflict resolution efforts, but it soon became clear that those efforts were not going to succeed.

Before the conflict began, Syrians held similar grievances to other Arab populations caught up in the tumult of the 2011 Arab Spring—unemployment and underemployment, unaccountable and brutal governance with little respect for human rights, corruption, and the capture by elites of a disproportionate share of the country's wealth and income. The Syrian conflict is sometimes simplistically presented as a confrontation between a ruling Alawite minority and an oppressed Sunni majority. However, the government of Bashar al-Assad could in fact rely on the support of an array of religious minorities and parts of the moneyed Sunni middle class.

The protests, which started in the southern city of Deraa and soon spread, were inspired by unrest that had already led to the fall of governments in Tunisia and Egypt. Determined to avoid a similar fate, the Assad government responded with beatings and bullets. Those reprisals, in turn, led the opposition to take up arms. By July 2011, dissident members of the Syrian Armed Forces had established the Free Syrian Army, and so unrest turned into civil war.

The international community's stake in Syria stacked up differently than it did in other countries rocked by the Arab Spring. The Russian Federation had long held a naval facility in the Syrian port of Tartus. Iran, meanwhile, had sustained a long-term alliance with Syria's ruling Assad family. Both Russia and Iran, therefore, had important stakes in the survival of the Syrian regime. Meanwhile, other key powers, including the United States, Saudi Arabia, and Turkey, hoped the Arab Spring might topple Assad and open the space for a government that would be more aligned with their interests. And thus, from the very outset, the conflict was internationalized.

Before the war, Syria was a relatively prosperous middle-income country with a gross national income close to $5,000 per capita. The UN's role there was focused on development issues and support for Palestinian refugees. But by summer of 2011, for the first time—and in recognition of what was now happening—the UN appointed a humanitarian coordinator in Damascus. At that point, the conflict was limited to a few cities and towns and was, relative to what followed, mild in intensity. But people were already on the move. The first waves of refugees were arriving in Jordan, Lebanon, and Turkey. The UN's first humanitarian and refugee response plans were developed in December 2012.

From the outset, Kofi Annan's diplomatic efforts were undermined by growing acrimony among the P5—the five permanent members of the Security Council, consisting of China, France, Russia, the United Kingdom, and the United States—over the NATO intervention in Libya. The Security Council had authorized that intervention in March 2011, in the same week as the peaceful protests started in Deraa. The objective of the Libya intervention was to protect protesting civilians against a violent crackdown by the government of Moammar Ghaddafi. However, within a few months, the NATO intervention under the guise of civilian protection had culminated in Ghaddafi's death and regime change. This chain of events led to a falling-out among the P5, with Russia and China (the latter of which has long-standing reservations about international interference in other countries' internal affairs) accusing NATO of overreach. Moscow and Beijing both feared that if the Security Council were to invoke Chapter VII of the UN Charter, which allows for enforcement action, it would be the start of a slippery slope towards regime change. In the decade that followed, Russia vetoed 15 Security Council resolutions on Syria, and received China's support for 8 of these vetoes. Three-quarters of the vetoes exercised in the Security Council in the decade after 2010 were on Syria.

It is likely that the Council's response would have fallen short of the steps needed to decisively alter the course of events on the ground in Syria even if Moscow and Beijing had been more accommodating. The United States was reluctant to get involved militarily in the region. It had been chastened by its experiences in Afghanistan, Iraq, and Libya, all of which had illustrated the difficulty of establishing and stabilizing a new order after enforced regime change.

In the face of a paralyzed Security Council, the United States and the EU imposed their own sanctions on the Syrian government in response to the continuing violent repression of the population. The EU sanctions, originally imposed in 2011, expanded over time to encompass travel bans and asset freezes aimed at specific companies and businesspeople tied to the Assad regime, a ban on the import of Syrian oil, steps to freeze the EU-held assets of the Central Bank of Syria, and export restrictions on equipment and technology that might be used for internal repression. Similarly, the United States—in addition to earlier sanctions imposed in 1979 when it declared Syria a state sponsor of terrorism—blocked property of the Syrian government and officials and imposed an investment ban and oil sanctions. Australia, Canada, Japan, Norway, Switzerland, Turkey, the United Kingdom, and the Arab League all also introduced financial sanctions, asset freezes, travel restrictions, and arms embargoes.

Kofi Annan was able to get rhetorical buy-in from the P5 for his six-point peace plan, which called for an inclusive political process, cessation of all violence, humanitarian access, release of people arbitrarily detained, access for journalists, and the right to peaceful demonstration. But the Security Council's backing extended no further. Frustrated by the lack of support for his efforts, Annan stepped down in July 2012. The Council has remained divided on Syria ever since. The onus increasingly fell on humanitarian organisations to deal with the consequences.

* * *

The failure of politics was reflected in, and set the scene for, a new phase of the crisis from mid-2012 to September 2015. This period saw a dramatic increase in the scale, intensity, and brutality of the fighting. Syria became not just the scene of the worst war on the planet but also the centre of its biggest humanitarian crisis.

Three factors drove this escalation. First, in light of Russia's veto power in the Security Council, Assad realized that he faced little risk of being held accountable for his actions. That perception of his own security, coupled with his government's existential survival imperative, led to a string of major and constantly repeated breaches of taboos, humanitarian law, and human rights law, which all set precedents for the years that followed. Year after year, the government of Syria committed unspeakable crimes against its own people on an industrial scale. One of the most important breaches was Assad's decision to use his government's chemical weapons against the opposition.[1] After deploying chemical weapons on a smaller scale in early 2013, the Syrian government, on 21 August that year, carried out a large-scale sarin gas attack against opposition-held suburbs of Damascus, killing some 1,400 civilians. The Obama administration had earlier declared that the use of chemical weapons would constitute a red line that could trigger a potential military response against the Assad regime. However, after the British Parliament defeated the Cameron government's plan to join mooted US-led military action, and the US Congress seemed likely to deny any authorisation for the use of force in Syria, President Barack Obama opted to change course. He decided instead to seek Russian cooperation for the destruction of Syria's chemical weapons arsenal through the UN. Assad knew that he had been let off the hook, and his sense of immunity grew.

The second factor fuelling escalation was the increase in military and financial support for the fighting parties from outside powers. Iran and Hezbollah (Lebanese Shia militia) in particular had boots on the ground in Syria. Starting in 2013, Tehran deployed thousands of Islamic Revolutionary Guard Corps and paramilitary personnel. Meanwhile, Hezbollah was so heavily invested that by 2016, it was thought to have lost some 1,500 fighters in battle.

The third factor in the conflict was the emergence of a huge number of opposition groups, and their growing success especially

---

1. The use of chemical weapons is banned under international law. Since the end of World War II, this taboo has been breached only sporadically: in the 1963–67 Yemen War, by Saddam Hussein in Iraq and Iran in the late 1980s, and by the terrorist group Aum Shinrikyo in Japan in 1995.

in eastern and northern Syria. The number itself was bewildering: at one point, OCHA counted more than 1,500 separate groups, all with constantly shifting agendas, alliances, and backers. Amorphous, highly localised, and often with weak chains of command and unclear and changing objectives, these groups added to the chaos. While the more moderate groups failed to unify, others like the Islamic State of Iraq and Syria (ISIS) were able to establish a strong foothold. Before long, Syria became the global centre for jihadi militancy.

The rise of nonstate armed groups was facilitated by some of the features of globalisation and modern technology. Illicit financial flows helped armed groups get their hands on money and guns. Effective manipulation of social media allowed ISIS to attract at least 30,000 foreign fighters from more than a hundred countries to the battlefields of Syria and Iraq, far surpassing the influx of mujahideen to Afghanistan in the 1980s. Syria became a theatre in which multiple global agendas were played out.

ISIS committed some of the most heinous crimes of the conflict. Its genocidal campaign against the Yazidi population of Syria and Iraq stands out in the wider horror. ISIS fighters abducted thousands of Yazidi civilians, summarily executed hundreds if not thousands of boys and men, and subjected women and girls to systematic sexual enslavement, frequently awarding them as spoils of war. ISIS even developed so-called theological justifications for these acts, including explicitly condoning child rape.

Syria became increasingly fragmented. One of OCHA's roles is to produce conflict maps showing the locations of people in need, the positions of front lines, and the powers controlling specific places. OCHA's Syria maps resembled densely formatted, multicoloured patchwork quilts. By September 2013, government forces controlled only 30 percent of Syrian territory. Much of the rest was under the sway of a plethora of armed groups, including ISIS and Kurdish militias—the latter of which were a force to be reckoned with in the country's northeast.

The consequence of all this conflict was a mushrooming humanitarian tragedy. Many civilians were killed, maimed, wounded, and traumatized by the fighting itself. But they fled in even larger numbers. In the summer of 2012, neighbouring countries had registered around 70,000 Syrian refugees, with an additional 300,000 internally displaced people (IDPs) within Syria itself. Just two and a half years later—by the end of 2014—the number of refugees had grown almost fifty-fold to 3.3 million. Most of them were in Turkey, Lebanon, and Jordan. In the same period, the number of IDPs had grown some twenty-five-fold to 7.6 million. Incredibly, at that point, fully half of Syria's population were no longer living in their prewar homes. Many had been displaced multiple times, exacerbating their misery.

The fact that the Syrian government no longer controlled most of the country's territory, combined with its refusal to allow the UN's Damascus-based aid operation to deliver aid across front lines to opposition-held areas, made it clear that special measures would be necessary to reach people in need. In July 2014, the Security Council adopted a resolution permitting the UN to carry out cross-border aid operations to non-government-controlled areas without the consent of the authorities in Damascus. My OCHA colleagues worked closely with the members of the Security Council on this. It enabled us in the following years to send life-saving aid from Iraq, Jordan, and Turkey to millions of civilians in opposition-held areas.

The resolution also allowed us to unify and coordinate two aid operations that hitherto had worked separately: the one run by the UN from Damascus serving government-controlled areas, and the one run by NGOs from southern Turkey, Jordan, and Iraq. Up to that time, the humanitarian agencies' operational setup was—as a contemporary study pointed out—"uniquely fragmented." Even after bringing the Damascus-based and cross-border-based operations under one roof, we struggled to join up the various parts of the humanitarian response. That reflected deeper challenges. One was the difficulty of coordinating an inherently fragmented humanitarian architecture in which each organisation is self-governing and cooperates with others only when and where it suits them. Another was the multiplicity of armed actors, and the individual negotiations with each that were required in order to reach people in need. A third involved the constraints imposed by the Syrian government, which remained opposed to the cross-border operations even after the Security Council endorsed them, and at the same time continued to block aid across front lines to people in opposition-controlled areas.

The expanding humanitarian operation on the ground was also expensive. There have been major international fundraising conferences every year since 2012, each attended by participants, normally at foreign minister level or above, from dozens of countries. The burden was initially shouldered by Kuwait, which hosted international conferences raising $11 billion between 2013 and 2015.

Over the summer of 2015, the refugee issue assumed much greater prominence, especially in Europe. Many of the refugees were living in severe conditions and were hungry. They were frustrated with their limited prospects for employment and education and increasingly feared ISIS and other extremists. Supported by the facilitation efforts of international organised criminal groups, they began an exodus to Europe. A million new people, most of them originally from Syria, arrived in the EU that summer. Though the refugees' fate initially generated an outpouring of sympathy and solidarity in parts of Europe—what the Germans at the time called *Willkommenskultur* (welcome culture)—it quickly turned into a hardening of borders meant to deter new arrivals.

In the face of all these developments, the focus of the international response shifted in practice from resolution of the conflict to mitigating its fallout. The policy focus was on three areas—chemical weapons, terrorism, and humanitarian assistance—around which there was a degree of unity among the P5.

In terms of chemical weapons, the decision of the United States and its allies not to instigate a military response opened up the space for a Security Council resolution to deal with the August 2013 sarin attacks. The resolution directed the UN to remove and destroy Syria's remaining chemical weapons. Although the resolution fell short of enforcing penalties for the use of these weapons, it nevertheless was one of the few instances in which the Council was able to muster a unified response in Syria. Over the next two years, a joint mission of the UN and the Organisation for the Prohibition of Chemical Weapons destroyed 1,300 tons of chemical agents—the entirety of Syria's declared chemical weapons stock—along with the 12 chemical weapons production facilities that were known at the time.

In June 2014, ISIS sent shockwaves through much of the world when it declared that it had formed a "caliphate" and proceeded to occupy large swathes of Syrian and Iraqi territory. For Western countries and their Middle Eastern allies, dealing with ISIS became the most important policy objective in Syria, even at the expense of tolerating Assad for a while longer. That September, a US-led coalition began mounting air strikes against ISIS inside Syria. Over time, that campaign would grow in scale, especially in the wake of the ISIS-linked attacks that killed 130 people in the Bataclan concert venue in Paris in November 2015. They were believed to have been planned from inside Syria.

The resultant refocusing of the West's Syria policy to counterterrorism and efforts to combat ISIS inevitably distracted from the goal of finding a political solution to the conflict. It also helped the Assad government regain a degree of legitimacy, by giving some credence to its narrative that it was fighting a counterterrorism campaign—though in fact it was instability that had fuelled the rise of jihadism, rather than the other way around.

Humanitarian assistance constituted another area of consensus in the Security Council. But it also increasingly served as a fig leaf to cover—and compensate for—the failure to bring an end to the conflict.

A third phase of the war is discernible between September 2015, when Russian military forces formally intervened on the ground, and the summer of 2018. By the end of that period, the government had re-established control over much of central and southern Syria, in no small part thanks to Russian and Iranian support. The US-led coalition against ISIS had largely achieved its objective of dismantling the caliphate. International diplomatic efforts, including the work of Kofi Annan's two successors as the UN's Special Envoy, Lakhdar Brahimi and Staffan de Mistura, proved largely fruitless in this period, though they helped slightly to ease the scale of the humanitarian suffering.

By this time, siege warfare of the sort characteristic during the medieval period had become the government's tactic of choice to reconquer opposition-held towns. Initially deployed to devastating effect in Homs in 2014, the number of sieges grew over time. By the end of 2016, around a million Syrians lived in areas besieged by their own government. Between 2016 and 2018, the government used these sieges, in combination with indiscriminate aerial bombardment, to coerce dozens of communities in places like Darayya, Madaya, el Waer, eastern Aleppo, Douma, and East Ghouta outside Damascus into surrendering. (One of my own more bizarre experiences in early 2018 was listening to the thunder of jets over the skies of Damascus on their way to bomb the people of East Ghouta while I was in a meeting failing to persuade the government to agree a humanitarian cease-fire.) Sieges inflicted huge suffering on civilians, in particular women and children. They normally ended in agreements, frequently brokered by the Russian military on the ground, through which the government regained the towns while allowing their armed opponents to leave with their families to other areas. Most went to Idlib, the opposition-controlled region in northwest Syria. Sometimes courageous and knowledgeable staff from my own office would be involved in negotiations on these agreements, not least to provide confidence to the opposition groups that if they came to meetings with Syrian and Russian military officers they would not simply be killed then and there. These "starve or surrender" tactics re-established government control in much of central Syria, while putting off the challenge of dealing with other areas, including Idlib and the northeast.

There were a number of surrender agreements within so-called de-escalation zones in western and southern Syria. These zones had been established in May 2017 by the Astana agreement between Iran, Russia, and Turkey. On paper, these de-escalation zones were designed to advance the cessation of hostilities, protect civilians, and facilitate humanitarian access. In practice, Syria and its allies used them mostly as cover to roll up the opposition with intense military attacks.

Meanwhile, US-led coalition forces, working closely with ground troops from Kurdish militias, were increasingly successful in displacing ISIS from northern Syria. This campaign culminated in the liberation of Raqqa—the city ISIS had chosen as its headquarters—in late 2017. But the by-product of the fighting was the complete destruction of the city and the displacement of tens of thousands of its citizens. According to US journalist Anand Gopal, who visited Raqqa shortly after ISIS was evicted from the city, the decimation was "unlike anything seen in an American conflict since the Second World War."

April 2018 saw further chemical weapons attacks on Syrian citizens. UN investigators subsequently concluded that the Syrian government had conducted the attacks. This finding exposed the limitations of the previous UN-led efforts to rid Syria of these weapons. However, it also attracted a different response. This time, unlike in 2013, the United States (under the Trump administration), together with France and Great Britain, responded with air strikes against Syrian military targets. The reprisals partially restored the taboo against the use of chemical weapons and increased the price likely to be paid if they were deployed in future. The United States' "red line," in other words, was re-established.

This period also saw continued cooperation among key powers on humanitarian issues. In November 2015, foreign ministers from 20 countries, including the United States and Russia, met in Vienna to form the International Syria Support Group and a Humanitarian Task Force. Humanitarian organisations were at the time encouraged by this development, because the task force applied pressure on Damascus to enable relief workers to send dozens of aid convoys across front lines inside Syria in order to provide life-saving food, medicines, water supplies, and shelter equipment to civilians in opposition-held territory. As the Damascus government gradually regained control of more of the country, it became more capable of resisting pressure for cross-line convoys, and by 2017 the convoys became much less frequent.

With humanitarian needs on the ground expanding, efforts to mobilise resources also increased. Building on the Kuwait conferences, the UN, together with four donor governments, organised the Supporting Syria Conference in London in July 2016. The preparations for that conference were one of my main responsibilities in my then role as permanent secretary of the UK DFID. We raised $12 billion in pledges for both the immediate and longer-term needs of affected Syrians: the most ever raised in a single day at such a meeting.

The London event was then followed by a series of annual conferences in Brussels, cochaired by the EU and the UN. They raised billions of dollars to meet ongoing humanitarian needs in Syria and even larger amounts for Jordan, Lebanon, and Turkey. Those countries generously continued to offer safe haven for Syrian refugees, even as they were reeling under the economic impact of the war next door. The EU granted Jordan preferential access to its markets in 2016, with the objective of helping create 200,000 jobs for Syrian refugees and Jordanians. The United States and Egypt also lowered tariffs on Jordanian exports. In a similar vein, the World Bank invested heavily in Lebanese infrastructure projects, particularly in the transport sector, also trying to generate jobs for Lebanese and Syrians.

From the second half of 2018, the situation was more peaceful across most of Syria—as I found when I visited Damascus in late summer of that year. But there was still no meaningful political process towards a lasting solution to the conflict. And there was an ongoing struggle, mostly between Syria and Russia on the one hand and Turkey on the other, over control of the two main areas that at that point remained outside government control: Idlib in the country's northwest and the Kurdish-dominated areas in the northeast.

The underlying dynamics of the standoff between these powers were fairly straightforward. Russia was—and remains—keen to help the Syrian government re-establish state authority over the entire country. Turkey was—and remains—keen to keep up pressure on Assad, to protect Syrian civilians under threat from their own government without incurring a further huge influx of refugees into Turkish territory, and to ensure stability in the buffer zones on its border with Syria as part of its strategy for dealing with its Kurdish antagonists. In the case of the northeastern region, in October 2019 Turkey launched an operation into areas that had been under the control of Kurdish forces for several years and had developed de facto Kurdish autonomy. The operation, which established a 30-kilometer-wide Turkish-controlled "safe zone" inside Syria, displaced over 200,000 people. The Kurds nevertheless retained control of most of the northeast, with US support.

In the case of Idlib, Turkey and Russia had agreed in Sochi in September 2018 to establish a buffer zone that would be monitored by Turkish troops. Despite that agreement, Syrian and Russian forces renewed their offensive in 2019, leading to a military escalation that saw some of the most intense fighting in nearly a decade of conflict. It directly pitted the forces of a NATO member—Turkey—against Russia. The ensuing fighting displaced another million people, many of them Syrians who earlier had fled to Idlib to escape fighting in other parts of the country. Finally, in March 2020, after military clashes in which the Turks were believed to have inflicted significant damage on Syrian forces and suffered their own (lesser) losses, Russia and Turkey brokered another cease-fire agreement. Opposition forces, with Turkish backing, continued to control territory populated by over four million people. The situation remained fragile.

Meanwhile, the last remnants of collaboration among key powers on humanitarian issues broke down during this period. In December

2019 and July 2020, the Security Council, faced with Russian and Chinese vetoes, consecutively reduced from four to one the number of entry points through which the UN could provide cross-border aid.

Syria in 2021 was a picture of economic despair, with heightened humanitarian needs and still no meaningful political progress. Violence had reemerged (albeit on a smaller scale than at the peak of the fighting) in several parts of the country, including from ISIS-affiliated groups. The economy, ravaged by a decade of war, was teetering on the edge. By 2020, it had shrunk to less than a third of its prewar size. The country had become a narcostate, producing hashish and Captagon, an amphetamine pill sometimes called the "poor man's cocaine," which is smuggled into the Gulf States. People had to wait in line for hours to get gas for cooking and for home heating. They faced daily power cuts. The Lebanese financial crisis further pulled down the Syrian economy. The Syrian pound lost half its value against the US dollar in the second half of 2019, and prices for basic food items skyrocketed. The economic devastation meant that over 80 percent of Syrians were now living in extreme poverty, compared with 35 percent before the war. More than nine million people were food insecure: a greater number than at any other time during the crisis. The UN estimated that 34 percent of children under age five in northwest Syria suffered from stunting. Meanwhile, the United States continued to tighten sanctions with the adoption in 2019 of the Caesar Civilian Protection Act, titled in recognition of an anonymous individual code-named "Caesar" who secretly documented the Assad regime's torture of civilians. The act expanded restrictions to include non-US-registered companies doing business with the Syrian government.

On top of all that came the COVID-19 pandemic, which seems to have spread rapidly throughout Syria. Precise numbers of cases remain unclear because of low levels of testing and apparent concealment of cases by the authorities in some areas. Though the direct health impact of the virus was less severe than was originally feared, the secondary impacts on the economy were grave.

The UN expanded humanitarian operations to reach on average 7.4 million people each month in 2020 and 2021, up from 5.8 million in 2019. The UN's 2021 response plans for the Syria crisis—both for people inside the country and refugees in neighbouring countries—amounted to $10 billion.

Meanwhile, the costs of reconstruction were estimated at around $400 billion. But there was no start on that. In the absence of progress towards a viable political future for the country, Western donors—who controlled the purse strings—were unwilling to invest in rebuilding the country. And while Russia provided significant bilateral aid to Syria, for instance in the form of wheat shipments, it lacked the resources or will to make a meaningful start on reconstruction on its own.

The human toll the war in Syria has wrought—all the death, destruction, and human suffering—is mind-boggling. The number of deaths became so high that the UN reached the point where it could not keep track. It stopped counting the bodies years ago. Others calculated that more than 500,000 Syrians died in the war. That makes it the deadliest conflict so far in the 21st century. By 2017, there were already 1.5 million Syrians living with permanent disabilities as a result of injuries suffered during the war. There are now many more. Countless Syrians were arbitrarily or unlawfully detained, held without due process, and subjected to brutal torture. Tens of thousands of the detainees were disappeared. Many may no longer be alive. And the conflict caused the world's largest displacement crisis since World War II, with some 13 million Syrians—60 percent of the country's prewar population—forcibly displaced.

Amid these mind-numbing figures, the suffering of individual Syrians and the lifelong trauma they will carry often gets lost. On my visits to Syria and surrounding countries, I met many Syrians who told me what had happened to them, and shared the hopes and needs they now had. People frequently wept and shook as they told their stories, unable to recover from their trauma and still terrified for what lay ahead.

Ten-year-old Khaled, for instance, who I met in Homs in 2018 and who was displaced with his family from Palmyra, said he just wanted to get back to school. Khawla, a 36-year-old woman from Aleppo, told me how she fled with her husband and four children after the war reached their home. They had spent the next six years living in a refugee camp in Kilis in southern Turkey, where she felt, as she put it, "isolated from the outside world." Fatima fled with her husband and three children to the countryside from her home in Aleppo when bombs started raining down on the city. But, deprived of income and faced with the widening war, they entrusted their fate into the hands of a people smuggler who led them through a journey to Turkey, which she described to me as "torture." When I met her, she was making a determined effort to learn Turkish in the hope of one day finding a job to support her family. Naima, a 40-year-old mother of nine, described her family's escape to Turkey from her village in the Aleppo countryside, where one of her children had fallen seriously ill as a result of the mental trauma caused by constant shelling.

I have not visited Syria since 2018, because the Syrian authorities made it clear that I would not receive a visa. They were annoyed, like their Russian friends, by what I found it necessary to say in my monthly briefings to the Security Council. The closest I came to visiting the country again was in 2019, when the Syrians got wind of the fact that I was about to visit southern Turkey along the border with Syria, and they suggested that they would let me visit Damascus if I called off that trip. It was neither right nor feasible to do that. I continued, however, to talk over video-link to Syrians in different parts of the country about what they were experiencing and what they wanted.

Some of the nastiest incidents occurred during the 2019 assault on Idlib, launched by the Assad government and its allies. The tactic of choice appeared to involve targeting civilian facilities like hospitals to terrorize the civilian population into concluding they had no alternative but to flee towards Turkey if they wanted to survive. I spoke in July 2019 to Dr. Mohammed Abrash, a surgeon at Idlib Central Hospital. As we talked, he tended to a nine-year-old girl, Dalia, who had been brought to the hospital two days earlier by emergency ambulance along with her two younger sisters, Rawan and Tuka. Their house had been hit by a bomb dropped by a war plane, and their mother and five-year-old sister had been killed in the attack. Rawan, only three years old, had clung on to her baby sister Tuka's T-shirt to stop her falling to her death off the precipice that the bomb had made of the upper stories of their home. Though Tuka survived, brave Rawan died of her injuries the day after the attack. When I asked Dr. Abrash if he had a message for the world, he said: "We are afraid. Please help us. Make it stop." I heard the same things from many people I talked to, especially children.

So, standing back, thinking about what has happened, what have humanitarian agencies learned from all this and what are the implications for the future? I offer seven conclusions. They arise amidst a great tragedy. There is a lot that remains uncertain. Lesson learning is incomplete. More evaluation and analysis is needed. We do not know what the future holds. But I do believe it is important to try to take stock, not least so that humanitarian agencies can aspire to do better in future, however difficult the challenges.

The first and one of the most important points is that despite all the obstacles, humanitarian agencies have been able to save hundreds of thousands of lives by bringing aid to people in severe need.

In the light of the war's human toll, some people might be inclined to question humanitarian engagement as the futile endeavour of ensuring that people are not hungry at the time they are killed or maimed. That is wrong. The truth is that while humanitarian organisations could only offer a Band-Aid rather than a cure, the human costs of the war would have been a great deal worse without their efforts.

When the war started, and throughout 2011 and 2012, the humanitarian system was slow in getting the relief operation off the ground. Like others, many humanitarian agencies failed to prepare adequately for the war's massive escalation. They were hobbled by a plethora of restrictions, imposed especially by Damascus. But by 2014, operations had been scaled up, and the Security Council authorisation for UN cross-border aid allowed us to expand assistance to opposition-held areas. In the years that followed, the UN sent more than 30,000 trucks of food and other relief supplies across the border. By 2019, they were reaching three million people every month in northwestern Syria alone. None of this could have been done without the support of the governments of Turkey, Jordan, and Iraq.

Even after Russian and Chinese vetoes in 2020 reduced the number of border crossings from four to one, we continued to dispatch a monthly average of 1,000 aid trucks, allowing aid to reach at least 2.4 million of the 3 million people in need every month. Assertions that cross-border aid could be replaced by deliveries crossing military front lines within the country were simply false. Ending the cross-border operation would have amounted to the collective punishment of millions of trapped civilians. In July 2021, after months of negotiations, the Security Council decided that the remaining crossing could be used for another year.

Though the cross-border operation was important, even larger volumes of aid were delivered to government-controlled areas, where needs were often equally or more severe. The Damascus government insisted that the UN and NGOs operate largely by giving supplies to the Syrian Arab Red Crescent—the Syrian component of the worldwide Red Cross family—and leaving it to organise the distribution. That approach attracted a good deal of criticism from human rights groups and consternation at various points from the (overwhelmingly Western) donors who voluntarily financed the operation. These groups asked legitimate questions about the extent to which those receiving help were really the neediest, rather than those who demonstrated loyalty to the government, and whether assistance was getting through or being siphoned off. In my visits to Damascus and in other private discussions with the Syrian authorities, I told them that we would raise more money for things they wanted us to do if they allowed more access and freedom of movement for UN staff and responsible international NGOs. They were not persuaded by that argument: to them, control remained of crucial importance. Proven allegations of fraud and abuse were limited, though that may also reflect limitations on access. In my own interactions with the leadership of the Syrian Arab Red Crescent, I found them to be courageous, committed people determined to help the most vulnerable. They also suffered more casualties among their own staff during the conflict than any other humanitarian organisation. But it would be naïve to think they were never fettered by the government in what they could do.

Most of the people who worked on humanitarian operations inside the country have been Syrians helping their fellow citizens. Syrian aid workers have paid an outsized price in terms of blood and lives, with more than 250 of them killed since 2011. Many worked in opposition areas. Some of their heroics have been well captured, including in documentary movies like the Oscar-nominated *The Cave*, a heart-wrenching portrayal of the work of Dr. Amani Ballour. A gentle, softly spoken paediatrician, she treated children and other war victims in her underground hospital in Eastern Ghouta, the cave constantly shaking and rumbling from the explosion of the bombs dropped by their own government's jets above. When Eastern Ghouta fell, Dr. Ballour moved to Idlib to do the same work. I was privileged to meet her and thank her for her courage and humanity.

So, notwithstanding all the savagery, there have also been acts of humanity on a vast scale. And while the Syrian conflict created sky-rocketing needs, it also bred new capacities, with hundreds of local NGOs springing up all across the country and tens of thousands of volunteers serving on the aid front lines. In turn, the UN got better at finding and working with these local organisations and supporting their efforts to save lives in their communities. That shift in operational approach reflected both the principle that local groups should be supported wherever possible and the practical reality that some places were inaccessible to UN agencies. We need to draw on these lessons as we try to empower local humanitarian groups in conflicts around the world.

My second takeaway is that the Syria crisis exemplifies the challenges that humanitarian organisations face in today's geopolitical realities. More explicit rivalry among the leading powers and the willingness of others to interfere militarily (often through proxies) in regional issues has created a greater politicisation of the humanitarian realm and forces humanitarian organisations to engage much more actively in the political arena. We can decry this trend and invoke the humanitarian principles of neutrality, independence, and impartiality all we want, but we still have to deal with it.

Indeed, calling the Syrian conflict just a civil war is misleading. More than 30 countries were engaged on different sides in direct military action in Syria, many of them with planes in the air and boots on the ground. The participants included all the permanent members of the Security Council other than China, as well as Iran, Turkey, and Israel. Not since the Vietnam War has there been a military conflict that involved both the United States and Russia as active combatants. Numerous other regional powers added fuel to the conflict by giving the belligerents arms and money. This dynamic not only undermined conflict resolution efforts but also led to a highly politicized environment in which a number of key powers tried to instrumentalise humanitarian action for their ulterior goals. Put simply, Syria's allies wanted to ensure that humanitarian action reinforced Syria's sovereignty and state control. Conversely, those paying—voluntarily—for most of what humanitarian agencies were doing harboured a sympathy for the protesters and the moderate opposition.

I will come back to some of the implications of these dynamics. But one key takeaway is that in this new reality, and for all the frustrations it brings—which I know something about, having spent more than 30 mornings or afternoons during my tenure as ERC in frequently unproductive meetings on Syria in the Security Council—humanitarian leaders will need to engage more rather than less with the political sphere. While divisions in the Security Council run deep, humanitarian action constitutes an area of potential convergence among its members. And when we engaged the Council, as we did on the cross-border resolution, it did pay off—at least for a while. The same is true for our engagement with the Humanitarian Task Force established in 2015, which included the P5 in addition to influential countries like Turkey and Iran.

The third conclusion I have drawn is that we need a more honest and nuanced debate about the difficult trade-offs humanitarian agencies face when trying to save lives in a context like Syria.

The trade-offs result from a basic dilemma. On the one hand, humanitarian action anywhere requires the consent of whoever is in control of the relevant territory. Humanitarian agencies can never force their way in. For the UN, the provision of humanitarian assistance also requires the consent of the affected country, even if that country's government is not in control of all its territory. Failing that, it will need the permission provided by a Security Council resolution. In Syria, however, the government not only tried to manipulate humanitarian aid at every turn, but was also responsible for the lion's share of the atrocities committed during the war.

This dilemma has made aid organisations' engagement in Syria a perennial walk on an ethical tightrope. Humanitarian agencies, not least OCHA, have taken quite a bit of flak from some human rights NGOs and others for the compromises they say the situation has forced us to make. As they see it, we have been too accommodating to Damascus, we have allowed the government to rig humanitarian assistance in return for access, and we have sacrificed humanitarian principles on the altar of consent. Some even accused us of unwittingly helping to finance the government's war effort.

I think elements of this criticism disregard some basic realities. But I want to engage with it because it is important to have an honest debate about the issues. Yes, we were willing to accept a greater degree of intrusion by the Syrian government than in other conflict zones. Yes, we agreed to having a national organisation—the Syrian Arab Red Crescent—oversee much of the distribution of humanitarian aid. And yes, we never threatened to pull out over the countless restrictions and hurdles that were put in our way, from delays in granting visas for our staff to the denial of requests to carry out needs assessments.

Sometimes, we were pushed to take on tasks we would rather have avoided. Take the sieges, for instance. On a number of occasions, conflict parties or trapped civilians asked us to observe the evacuations of cities following "starve or surrender" tactics. These requests confronted us with the unpalatable choice of either denying demands for assistance from civilians in need or exposing ourselves to the accusation that we were helping to legitimise ethnic cleansing.

And we were never really in a position to extract any quid pro quos from the government. The case of Deir-ez-Zor, a town in the Euphrates Valley in northeastern Syria, illustrates the point. In 2014, the town was under government control, but the surrounding areas were dominated by ISIS, which had laid siege to it. By 2016, the humanitarian situation was dire and the government urged us to provide assistance to the town's civilian population—at the same time as it denied us access to the many towns that government forces held under siege. Ideally, we would have made a deal with the government. We would have told them, "We're happy to help out in Deir-ez-Zor if you in turn let us in to Daraya, Aleppo, Ghouta and all the other places you're trying to starve into submission." But they would not have agreed to any of that. So what were we to do? Deny help to the nearly 100,000 civilians of Deir-ez-Zor? Instead, with encouragement and financial help from Western countries, the UN mounted a complex and expensive operation involving hundreds of airdrops between April 2016 and April 2017. To evade artillery fire, aircraft dropped food, medical kits, and other relief items from extremely high altitude onto a very small area where local organisations could pick up the packages without getting shot by ISIS fighters. Was it fair that we organized airdrops in Deir-ez-Zor but not in other sieges? No, it was not. But was it the right thing to do?

Alas, these types of choices have no simple answers that offer the comfort of moral clarity. But the tendency of humanitarian agencies to err on the side of providing assistance wherever possible reflected the dilemma they faced. Saving tens or hundreds of thousands of lives through the provision of assistance outweighed the damage done by accommodating government restrictions. Moreover, there is zero indication that we would have generated any leverage on the Syrian government by withholding assistance or suspending operations. And those financing the operation, primarily Western donors, wanted it to be sustained despite the difficulties and dilemmas.

What this boils down to is the hard truth that humanitarian agencies can only do what the decision-makers who control the places where the needy civilians live will let the agencies do, and what others are willing to pay for.

The fourth point comes from the opposite end of the spectrum. The emergence of extremist groups who do not even pretend to meet the basic norms of humanitarian action—to which all UN member states notionally subscribe—and who regard aid workers as legitimate targets of attack, has major implications for established humanitarian agencies. We have yet to find an adequate way of handling this problem.

ISIS not only denied humanitarian groups access to the hundreds of thousands of people living in the places they controlled, but they also actively targeted humanitarian personnel as well as foreign journalists. ISIS fighters abducted and killed their chosen targets, sometimes by beheading them, and proudly broadcasted their vile deeds in a sickening cinema of terror. The violent deaths of brave aid workers like Kayla Mueller, Peter Kassig, Alan Henning, and David Haines sent shockwaves through the humanitarian world. Areas controlled by ISIS consequently often became no-go areas for humanitarian agencies. In a few cases, humanitarian agencies were able to deliver help in areas controlled by the most extreme jihadists. One instance involved a large-scale polio vaccination campaign in ISIS-controlled territory in eastern Syria in 2016–18. But that was an exception to the general experience.

My fifth conclusion relates to the UN's particularly important responsibility to try to protect the innocent against atrocities and other abuses in conflicts. In no other crisis over the past 30 years has that been as challenging and disheartening as in Syria. The level of brutality and taboo-breaking there over the course of the past decade has no recent parallel. It tells us something about a wider erosion of respect for humanitarian norms.

In 2011, the UN Human Rights Council established a Commission of Inquiry on Syria. This commission has produced 21 reports documenting the extent of this norm-busting. The indiscriminate bombardment of cities and towns. The medieval siege warfare. The countless summary executions and massacres. The enforced disappearances. State-sponsored torture on an industrial scale. The systematic use of rape and other sexual violence. The widespread recruitment of child solders. The arbitrary mass displacement. And the repeated use of chemical weapons, even though international law absolutely prohibits them.

On a personal level, what I found particularly hard to stomach were the systematic attacks on medical facilities. According to the WHO, over 250 such attacks took place between 2018 and 2020 alone. Around a thousand health care workers were killed over the decade after the start of the crisis. As well as being acts of pure cruelty, these attacks also lastingly devastated the Syrian health system.

My predecessors and I used our appearances before the Security Council to call out violations and plead on behalf of people trapped in the fighting. Some speakers in the Council sought to deny the facts of what was happening. The huge amount of the real-time footage of indiscriminate attacks, posted on YouTube, Twitter, and elsewhere by Syrian activists and citizens and the international groups that supported them, made such denials the subject of considerable ridicule.

As the war escalated from 2013 onward, humanitarian leaders grew increasingly worried about the threat not just to civilians but also to aid workers on the ground. We needed to establish more robust systems to protect them. To do so, in 2014 we set up a so-called humanitarian deconfliction mechanism under which the UN gave the United States, Russia, and Turkey details of planned aid convoys and the coordinates of humanitarian sites such as hospitals and health centres to help protect them from attack. That protection is required under international humanitarian law. (The implicit expectation was that the Russians would inform the Syrians.) For a while, this system worked well enough, and attacks on sites included on the deconfliction list were rare. One exception was an attack in September 2016 on a joint UN–Syrian Arab Red Crescent aid convoy in Big Orem, not far from Aleppo City. Some 10 aid workers were killed and 22 wounded. A subsequent UN Board of Inquiry pointed to the Syrian government as the likely culprit, though it did not exclude the possibility that this was an unintentional attack. I rather suspect it was: these things sadly happen in the fog of war.

Unfortunately, in the following years, attacks on aid workers grew and our efforts to protect them faltered. From 2018 onward it became increasingly obvious that the Syrian government and some of its allies no longer bought into the deconfliction arrangements. In 2018, more aid workers were killed in Syria than in a single year in any other conflict over the previous 20 years. On 18 July 2019, I strongly condemned violations in Idlib, highlighting deliberate attacks earlier that month on specific health facilities, hospitals, schools, water stations, bakeries, ambulances, and a street market. That summer, we sent notes verbales (diplomatic letters) to parties to the conflict in respect of six different attacks on deconflicted locations, mostly health facilities in northwest Syria, over the previous few months. We never received a response from the Russians. The government of Syria wrote to the Security Council, claiming that there were no hospitals or ambulances in that region: "All health care facilities in Idlib Governorate have been rendered inoperative since the terrorist groups overran them. . . . The ambulance network has been completely knocked out." Their position was essentially that every target they wanted to hit was a legitimate target because it was supporting or was used by terrorists. Yet, in our estimation, there were a hundred civilians for every terrorist in Idlib. In espousing this view, the Syrian authorities stripped the core international humanitarian law principle of proportionality of any meaning. The Russian stance, meanwhile, was subtly different: there may have been hospitals in northwest Syria, and somebody may have been bombing them, but it was not them.

I told the Security Council that in spite of our efforts to work with parties to the conflict to prevent attacks on civilian objects and humanitarian workers, I had come to the conclusion that deconfliction was not working. We began cautioning humanitarian organisations on the ground about the risks of continuing to provide information on new sites or humanitarian movements. I had come to believe that air strikes were actively targeting sites on the UN's deconfliction list. Subsequent evidence suggests I was right. In October 2019, the *New York Times* published an exposé in which it used video evidence, flight logs, witness reports, and thousands of Russian Air Force communications to tie Russian pilots to the bombing of four hospitals on a single day in May 2019. Separately, the *New York Times* compiled a list of 182 deconfliction sites and, based on its investigations, concluded that of those facilities, 27 had been damaged by Russian or Syrian attacks since the previous April. All were hospitals or clinics.

At the request of 10 members of the Security Council, the secretary-general set up another Board of Inquiry to investigate five attacks in mid-2019 on sites in Idlib covered by the deconfliction system. (These five were the tip of the iceberg.) The board confirmed that the five sites had indeed been attacked and that the correct information on their location had been provided to the parties. They concluded that it was "highly probable" that four of these attacks were "attributable to the Government of Syria or its allies." (For some, the board even identified the weapons that were probably used.) In the other cases, it found it was merely "probable." Shortly after the Security Council received the board's findings, the Russian government decided to quit the deconfliction system.

The fundamental conclusion is that deconfliction mechanisms of this sort only work if the main conflict parties want them to work. And that, sadly, was no longer the case in Syria by 2019. The UN's ability to influence the battlefield behaviour of the belligerents was ultimately limited. We could not replace the potential strength of a unified Security Council. And in the warring parties' deepening battles over truth, and the thickening fog of information warfare, the facts feeding our advocacy were sometimes falsely dismissed as fake news.

But that is no excuse for cynicism. Advocacy remains hugely important. Ultimately, facts tend to prevail. There is therefore an ever-greater premium on our ability to gather, assess, and present truthful information. Fact-based advocacy remains vitally important for the simple reason that it reinforces the validity of the norms UN member states all profess to support. However much they dodge and weave, no one likes to be shamed on the world stage for grave misdeeds. The good news is that the Syrian war has been very well documented. Thanks to the efforts of Syrian activists, international NGOs like the White Helmets and others, and professional journalists from many countries, we have better evidence of war crimes in Syria than anywhere since the 1945 Nuremberg trials. The bad news is that in 2014, Russia and China vetoed a Security Council referral of the Syrian crisis to the International Criminal Court.

That veto left us relying on criminal proceedings in national courts on the basis of the principle of universal jurisdiction. In a farsighted move, the General Assembly established a mechanism in 2016—the International, Impartial and Independent Mechanism, or IIIM—which collects and analyses evidence of atrocities in order to facilitate national prosecutions. The IIIM's work will be relevant in a number of European countries which have opened at least two dozen court cases against suspected Syrian war criminals.

Many of these cases are in Germany, including a trial which started in April 2020 in Koblenz against the head of the investigations unit at a notorious torture prison in Damascus. On 16 September 2020, Christoph Heusgen, the German Ambassador to the UN, relayed some of the truly horrific evidence heard at that trial. He cited a witness, an undertaker in Damascus from 2011 until 2017, who had recounted how the Syrian government had recruited him to transport victims of torture killed in prisons, security branches, and military hospitals to be buried in huge mass graves outside Damascus. Heusgen summarised the undertaker's testimony in the open chamber of the Security Council:

> The van of the witness had no license plate, but the front and the rear carried large pictures of Assad. The convoy of the witness consisted of three trucks. All the trucks had between 300 and 700 corpses. Their route went from military hospitals to two huge mass graves, one in the north and one in the south. The convoys

arrived in the morning hours between four and five o'clock. The witness described what happened there. As men climbed into the trucks, they dragged corpses out, put them into digs and dispersed them with bulldozers. The digs were six meters deep, 100 meters long. And the witness said that they were many of these digs. To fill one dig, it needed about 50 convoys. . . . The witness was asked if the corpses had traces of torture. Yes, he said. They were all naked, had bruises, ripped out fingernails and toenails, and faces were un-recognizable, as if they were covered with acid. One corpse had his penis cut off. The witness spoke straight, almost without interruption for three hours until the end, when he described the worst moment. Under a mountain of corpses, he detected a mother with her newborn baby in her arms—and the witness in Koblenz collapsed.

Processes like this mean that—notwithstanding the bone-chilling horrors they unearth—there is a ray of hope that in coming years, we will see at least some of the perpetrators of atrocities being held accountable for their crimes. In the absence of a commitment to accountability, miscreants elsewhere will draw the lesson that serious crime pays. They will use tactics like siege warfare as the blueprint for future collective punishment campaigns against battlefield opponents and the innocent men, women, and children in the areas they control. What is not punished is incentivized.

My sixth takeaway from a decade of humanitarian operations in Syria is about the experience of raising the resources which have paid for the relief effort. Together with the UN refugee agency, which mobilizes resources for the refugee response, this fundraising responsibility falls largely on OCHA.

Between 2013 and 2019, we raised a total of $30 billion to cover humanitarian needs in Syria and for Syrian refugees in neighbouring countries. That amounts to close to a third of global humanitarian funding managed by the UN over that period. The United States, Germany, the United Kingdom, and the European Commission account for over two-thirds of all these contributions. A group comprising Canada, Norway, Kuwait, Japan, Sweden, Denmark, Switzerland, the Netherlands, and Belgium contributed another 21 percent. Some other countries that might be expected to share some of the financial burden, in light of both their means and their political responsibilities with regard to Syria—including three of the P5 (China, France, and Russia), as well as Saudi Arabia—are conspicuously absent from the list of significant donors.

How and why were we able to raise funds at that scale? I think three factors are at play.

First, thanks to the courage, determination, and grit of Syrian and Western journalists, Syria consistently featured prominently in the news headlines in donor countries. This publicity reminded everyone of the scale and extreme nature of the civilian suffering, and helped sustain taxpayers' support for their governments' humanitarian investments. Atrocities like the 2013 sarin gas attack; the sieges in Homs, Aleppo, Eastern Ghouta, and elsewhere; and the 2015 refugee crisis sickened people around the world and they wanted something to be done about it. Powerful photos putting a human face on the crisis in Syria—like those of the limp, dead body of three-year-old Aylan Kurdi, the little boy fleeing with his family who washed up on a beach in Turkey while trying to get to Europe—touched people's hearts.

Second, donors were afraid of contagion: that problems would spread if not contained in the region. Without humanitarian aid, the situation in Syria would have been far worse. Donors were also keen to bolster the stability and economic health of Syria's neighbours, strained by the costs of hosting millions of refugees.

Third, relief agencies were largely able to convince the donors that most of their money was reaching the people in need. Agencies displayed a lot of innovation and creativity to ensure that aid ended up in the hands of those needing it most. The cross-border operation in particular became one of the most closely scrutinized aid efforts in the world. As is the case with aid distributions in government-controlled areas, it was not UN staff who managed the final distribution to individual families. But the movement and delivery of aid under the cross-border mechanism was monitored at four distinct levels: at the border, at warehouses inside Syria, at distribution points, and after distribution.

Under the United Nations Monitoring Mechanism, UN staff of 15 different nationalities verified the humanitarian nature of the cargo being shipped. The monitors, who I met on several visits, climbed into every truck. They opened boxes, cut into bags of rice, and inspected vehicles before clearing them to cross the border. When aid arrived at warehouses inside Syria, it was examined by UN-contracted third-party monitors. They were separate and independent from the organisations doing the distribution, and they checked the offloaded items against the waybill. These monitors also observed the direct distribution to affected people, and deliveries of aid to schools and hospitals, and interviewed beneficiaries. Their monitoring did not identify any evidence of systematic aid diversion.

Agencies also used new technologies to monitor the delivery of aid. Through video, and time-stamped, geotagged photos, the delivery process can be monitored every step of the way. Commodity tracking systems, using barcodes on each box of aid, allowed assistance to be followed from the border, to the warehouse, and on to the individual beneficiary. Those same boxes had phone numbers printed on them to allow beneficiaries to report back by phone or WhatsApp if anything they were expecting was not delivered, or if they needed other things. Through a call centre, anyone with questions about aid deliveries could get in touch with the providers.

It would be a step forward for these sorts of systems to be used elsewhere—including in those parts of Syria under government control. Apart from anything else, that would help sustain donor financing. The UN knew what was going across the border under its programme and where it was going. We knew that help was reaching the civilians who needed it. It would be good to be able to say the same with equal confidence elsewhere in Syria and far beyond.

———————◆◆◆———————

My last conclusion relates to sanctions. The Syrian government and its allies point to sanctions as the main culprit for humanitarian suffering and the sorry state of Syria's economy. They also decry sanctions as illegitimate because they lack Security Council endorsement. Western countries, in turn, claim their sanctions target those responsible for atrocities and are crafted to avoid any humanitarian impact. The question of sanctions has been one of the most contentious issues in the UN in New York in the later phases of the Syria crisis. The debate enjoys a great deal more heat than light, but some things are clear enough.

First, the Syrian authorities' repeated attempts, whether in the UN or elsewhere, to blame sanctions for all of the problems their country faces or to claim that the underlying intent of sanctions is to maximize the suffering of their people should not be taken seriously. For one thing, it glosses over the impact of a decade of war; the physical destruction of infrastructure; the paralyzing psychological effects of mass death, displacement, and injury; the government's own corruption and mismanagement; the economic and health impact of the COVID-19 pandemic; and the effect on Syria of the Lebanese banking crisis. For another, why is the West providing billions of dollars a year in life-saving aid if the overarching goal is to maximize the suffering of ordinary people?

Equally, the point of the sanctions is to harm. That is what their instigators are trying to do. The measures may be aimed at the Syrian government, human rights abusers, and beneficiaries of the war. But are they really the only people affected? The World Bank has noted the dampening impact of sanctions on Syrian exports and on the country's manufacturing, banking, and energy sectors, and has suggested that the effect is being felt by ordinary Syrians in employment, wages, and the cost of living. The truth is that it is difficult to disentangle the socioeconomic and humanitarian impact of sanctions from other war-related and economic factors. More dispassionate and robust analysis might theoretically provide a stronger basis for a more constructive discussion. But the issues probably remain too toxic for better analyses, even if they were available, to have much effect.

One thing we know from elsewhere, notably Somalia, where the impact of sanctions has been documented more dispassionately, is that they can complicate the delivery of humanitarian assistance in ways those imposing them say they do not want. This is particularly true for NGOs, who do not benefit from the same immunities and exemptions as the UN. They struggle to find banks willing to channel funds into Syria to pay local staff and suppliers. They are forced to use informal channels instead, including carrying banknotes into the country informally. They also chafe under the cumbersome, costly, and time-consuming process of applying for exemption licenses to allow them to export certain humanitarian goods to Syria. As in a number of other countries, the problem is further exacerbated by UN and other counterterrorism sanctions against ISIS and al-Qaeda, which increase the risks to banks. The reluctance of banks to offer services to humanitarian organisations arises partly out of fear they will fall foul of counterterrorism measures. What that means is that the UN will need to continue to explore—with the countries imposing sanctions, NGOs, and other parties, including banks—how the system of sanction exemptions can be improved to support the efficient delivery of humanitarian assistance.

Looking at the situation in Syria at the end of my time as ERC, I found it difficult to be optimistic. While there had recently been less fighting, the conflict was far from resolved. Outside powers continued to vie for influence and control of territory. More than half the population remained displaced. Poverty and hunger were worse than ever. A resurgence of ISIS, which benefitted from the widespread desperation, was a real risk. Progress with recovery and reconstruction was negligible. It was hard to see how that would change without movement towards a political settlement, which did not look imminent. To my mind, Syria would need humanitarian assistance for a long time to come.

FOUR

The Looming Catastrophe
of the Sahel

MY FIRST VISIT AS ERC, in early September 2017, was to Niger. In the small village of N'Gagam in the region of Diffa, in the southwest of the country, I met a 30-year-old woman named Achaitou. She had fled Nigeria with her four young children. She was surviving under a plastic sheet by the side of the main road with the help of the UN and NGOs. N'Gagam had a pre-crisis population of 1,000. When I went there, it was hosting 13,500 people from both Niger and Nigeria. Overall, there were a quarter of a million displaced people in Diffa. They lived in 140 informal settlements alongside vulnerable host communities, who were themselves feeling the strain of the influx. The displaced had all fled unspeakable atrocities and violence. I was struck by Achaitou's dignity. She said she retained hope of a better future for her children. But she was terrified of violence and abduction, and for that reason took her children into the bush at night, risking disease and snakebites. She wanted to go home to Nigeria. But she said she would only do that when it was safe for her family.

Niger was then the poorest country in the world. Diffa was the poorest region in the poorest country. Niger, and Diffa in particular, has suffered from years of underdevelopment. This endemic poverty, combined with climate shocks, meant that many of its people frequently did not have enough to eat. And, for the past eight years, they had suffered the violence and barbarity of armed groups like the Islamist terrorist movement Boko Haram. By late 2017, 400,000 people needed humanitarian assistance in Diffa. Niger rarely got the international attention—or the donor funding—it deserved. It was a forgotten crisis.

Achaitou's story and the broader story of Diffa exemplified the successes of the humanitarian system as well as the challenges. In Diffa, humanitarian aid was keeping people alive, but at the same time struggling to tackle the complexities of the crisis.

Nowhere scares me more than the Sahel. I fear the region is very close to a tipping point—and so by extension are its African neighbours. A preventable tragedy is looming. Most public policy efforts, at both national and international levels, have been treating symptoms rather than their causes. That is a sure-fire recipe for failure.

Geographically, the Sahel is loosely defined. Most of the problems are concentrated in the six countries of Burkina Faso, Cameroon, Chad, Mali, Niger, and the northeast of Nigeria—in other words, the central Sahel and the countries of the Lake Chad Basin. West Africa and the Sahel historically have been home to great and powerful empires. Mansa Musa, a 14th-century Malian ruler, gave away so much gold when he passed through Egypt that he left them with a major inflation problem. Sahelians have contributed their ample share to the world's artistic, musical, architectural, and scholarly heritage. Timbuktu was home to the world's first university and one of its oldest libraries. All six of these countries host UNESCO World Heritage Sites. The region is rich in natural resources, not least through its massive renewable energy capacity.

But when I went to Niger, people who lived in the six countries (which are all different but have plenty in common) found themselves at a true epicentre of conflict and insecurity, weak governance, chronic underdevelopment and poverty, demographic pressures, and climate change.

Conflict in the Sahel is complex. The causes and perpetrators of violence are many and they only seem to increase. There is conflict between farmers and herders, mostly arising from competition over increasingly scarce water, land, and pasture resources. There is conflict instigated by terrorist and extremist groups seeking to undermine states and control territory, like the campaigns being waged by Boko Haram, the Islamic State in West Africa, and others. Torture, brutality, abductions, sexual slavery, killings, and other flagrant human rights abuses are their stock in trade. Then there is the violence of organised criminal groups, who run trafficking networks, stage kidnappings, loot assets, and steal natural resources for profit.

State security authorities have sought to combat all this, spending an ever-greater share of scarce public resources doing so. But too often they have exacerbated the problem and driven citizens into opposition through their own violent excesses or failures to protect civilians. Sahelian countries have always fared poorly on the World Bank's governance effectiveness indicators. State authorities offer few services, are neither accountable nor responsive to their own citizens, are too often led by people who think the purpose of public office is self-enrichment rather than serving the community, and frequently reinforce rather than address legitimate grievances. Crucially, they behave in ways that leave people feeling excluded. Justice is elusive, and that also reinforces grievances.

All this makes it hard to address poverty and underdevelopment. Sahelian countries consistently rank at the very bottom of human development indices, reflecting high poverty, low life expectancy, high infant mortality, and low levels of access to education. Only 9 percent of girls across the region complete secondary school. Traditional livelihoods are undermined by resource pressures, and it is expensive to improve infrastructure in these large countries with dispersed populations. That applies to hard infrastructure like roads and power and water systems, but also to schools and clinics.

Meanwhile, fertility rates in the Sahel are the highest in the world, with annual population growth of 3 percent on average. In Niger, the average woman has seven children, resulting in a doubling of the population every 17 years. Globally over the past 200 years, population growth generally has fuelled development, especially during the period of the demographic dividend when countries have a low proportion of dependents—young children and older people—compared to workers. But that dividend is not guaranteed. There are examples, like Ireland (where many of my forebears were from) in the first half of the 19th century, where rapid population growth in the absence of economic diversification proved a recipe for catastrophe.

One of the striking things about the Sahel is that there is little dispute about the analysis or the challenges. There certainly has been no lack of diagnostics or "strategies." As ERC, I counted well over 20 international donor or multilateral strategies, including the UN's own, that covered the region. I also saw that some regional leaders were doing their utmost to help their citizens. But despite the potential and all the effort, things continue to get worse. It is important to try to understand why that is. Why were we seeing skyrocketing numbers of displaced and hungry people? Why was conflict spreading? Why did we see an increase in terrorist and militant attacks and influence across the region? And why was the response, nationally and internationally, so ineffective in turning the tide?

I have been travelling to some of these countries for nearly 30 years. In recent years, I have become more convinced than ever of two things. First, humanitarian aid is a crucial lifeline for millions of people across the region. The humanitarian system is effective at getting help to many of the people who need it most. Without aid, millions more would die each year. For the six countries I am talking about in this chapter, humanitarian organisations raised more than $1.3 billion in 2020 and provided help to 22 million people. In 2019, humanitarian agencies ensured nine million children were vaccinated against measles, nearly three million children were treated for malnutrition, and four million got food. And the vast majority of that support was delivered by local and international NGOs. But second, humanitarian aid can only be a sticking plaster on a much deeper wound, and the wound in the Sahel continues to grow in size. No one really wants to live in a camp for displaced people, or receive food rations from a humanitarian organisation. They would rather buy or grow their own food and cook dinner for their children themselves.

The first decade of the 21st century was characterized by relative political stability and security across the Sahel, especially compared to some other parts of the continent. From 2000 to 2010, we saw slow but steady improvement in indicators of human development across most countries of the Sahel, alongside improvements in governance indicators and macroeconomic growth.

But then things deteriorated. Lake Chad, the historic source of livelihood for many across the region, was visibly shrinking and competition for grazing land was increasing. And from around 2010, an opposition group that had been quietly growing and evolving over the previous decade emerged from the shadows, and started conducting terrorist attacks, bombings, kidnappings, and abductions in the areas around the lake. The world became conscious of Boko Haram. In 2014, they attracted global attention by kidnapping hundreds of girls from a Nigerian secondary school—the Chibok girls. The following year, they abducted even more in Damasak.

With the exception of Burkina Faso, every country in the region had experienced some degree of internal violence since the end of colonial rule, whether civil war, insurrection movements, or terrorist activity. But this time the situation was different. Suddenly, arms were streaming across the region's porous borders in the wake of the disintegration of Libya in 2011. And 2012 marked the overthrow of the Malian government by rebel soldiers.

Before 2012, only one militant Islamist group, al-Qaeda in the Maghreb, operated in Mali. But as ISIS' strength and territorial control grew in Iraq and Syria after 2014, extremist groups in the Sahel drew lessons from their ambitions and tactics. By 2018, more than 10 groups were active in Mali, Burkina Faso, and Niger, in addition to groups like Boko Haram in the Lake Chad Basin. There were more violent episodes in 2018 alone than in the whole of the 2009–15 period.

And then came climate change. Since the 1970s, the Sahel has warmed twice as fast as the rest of the world. Environmental assets have been literally evaporating, with increasingly erratic rainfall undermining access to water, fisheries, livestock, and agriculture. The water crisis fuelled intercommunal tensions, and governments failed to establish fair and transparent land and resource management strategies to contain the situation.

The symptoms of these problems became increasingly visible after 2010, in the form of large-scale displacement and growing hunger. A major drought in 2012 affected 18 million people across the region. This was the moment when humanitarian agencies started to become heavily engaged in the region on a continuous basis. There were previous humanitarian problems, including food shortages in 2006 and 2010. But at the start of the last decade, many humanitarian agencies were still operating on the basis of one-off responses to what seemed to be short-term disasters. By 2014, there was a chronic, sustained, and growing humanitarian problem affecting all six of the countries in the Sahel. Humanitarian agencies started to set up shop for the long haul.

The international community's wider engagement in the region at this time was mostly supporting security interventions. They ranged from international efforts like France's anti-insurgent Operation Barkhane and the UN's peacekeeping mission in Mali, to regional efforts like the G5 Sahel and the Multi-National Joint Task Force in the Lake Chad Basin. The focus was on remedying the shortcomings of military responses implemented by the security forces of the countries themselves. But international support for development efforts, though vital, have (in relation to the needs) been piecemeal, underfunded, and lacking in coherence.

In March 2019, just over 4 million people were displaced across the region, just under 10 million were food insecure, and more than 22 million needed humanitarian assistance. By the end of 2020, displacement had increased by 25 percent, food insecurity by 40 percent, and the numbers in need of humanitarian assistance by 50 percent. Burkina Faso, Niger, and some parts of Cameroon saw sharp deteriorations, and other areas like northeast Nigeria and Chad saw no improvement and increasing hopelessness. Burkina Faso, which until recently had been a peaceful and developing country, now had one of the fastest-growing displacement crises in the world. Some 700,000 more people needed help in late 2020 than eight months previously. In Niger, the number of extremist attacks continued to increase and more people were displaced. Political instability in Mali, which in 2020 experienced its second coup in less than a decade, threatened to undermine efforts to tackle violent extremists in the north of the country and thereby to drive humanitarian needs higher. In northeast Nigeria, where I went in 2017, 2018, and 2019, a record 11 million people needed humanitarian assistance in 2020. The people of this region had become trapped on all sides. Violent extremist groups and criminal gangs were attacking and robbing them. State security forces struggled to protect them, and in some places they were just as mistrusted as extremist groups.

We also saw another effect of climate change: unprecedented flooding forced people from their homes and deprived them of their livelihoods. Flooding in 2020 had a greater impact than in any previous year for which we have data. Across West and Central Africa, nearly two million people in 13 countries were affected. Altogether, there were now more than 30 million people in need of humanitarian assistance across the six Sahelian countries I am focusing on here, double the number of 2015. The sharp increase in so little time is what alarmed me the most—it was a sign of things ahead.

It was also getting harder to ensure aid reached those who need it most, for two main reasons. First, funding for humanitarian response in the Sahel was always chronically short. The funding gap was consistently larger than elsewhere in the world. Second, even if you had the money, it was difficult to get help to people. There were all sorts of impediments. Sometimes they were bureaucratic, sometimes logistical, and sometimes related to huge distances with poor infrastructure and harsh terrain.

The region had also become an extremely dangerous place to be an aid worker. The year 2019 saw a record 85 attacks against aid workers, twice the number of the previous worst year. Getting help to people meant facing the danger of being attacked, abducted, or killed. And although in many conflict situations, humanitarian organisations manage to negotiate access with the protagonists, terrorist groups like Boko Haram or the Islamic State simply reject the role of humanitarian agencies. For them, murdering aid workers is a tactic of choice.

It is not difficult given recent trends to imagine what the Sahel might look like by 2030. The basic point is that none of the responses or interventions over the past decade have improved the underlying situation or altered the trajectory. At best, they have merely stemmed the flow. First, there are the demographic pressures. In 2010, the population of the region was 240 million people. In 2021, it was more than 310 million. By 2030, it will be well over 400 million. Some projections envisage almost a billion people in the wider region by 2050. Second, the Sahel is truly the epicentre of accelerating climate change, a canary in the coal mine of our warming planet. The consequences are already visible. But by 2100, worst-case estimates say that the region could be up to eight degrees hotter than now—and average daily temperatures already reach 35°C. One wonders how in those circumstances life could continue in any way close to how it is lived today, where three-quarters of the population depend on rain-fed agriculture because the region lacks much in the way of irrigation or water storage capacity.

Of the world's 15 countries most vulnerable to climate change, 10 already have chronic humanitarian problems, for which the UN has been mounting responses every year for most of the past decade. And yet, these 15 countries—which include Chad, Niger, and Mali—

receive less than 6 percent of all global multilateral funding for adapting to climate change.

Heat also has more subtle consequences. To quote American journalist David Wallace-Wells, "heat frays everything." An increase in conflict, domestic violence, and crime rates has been documented as temperatures have risen. Experts predict that for every half-degree of warming, societies will see a 10 to 20 percent increase in the likelihood of armed conflict. Some projections imply crop yields reduced by over 30 percent by 2080, and that rain-fed agriculture could be unviable in Chad and Niger by 2100.

Violence and extremism in the region continue to grow. Illicit networks have solidified their footholds, and efforts to stem them have failed. So one can only imagine that if nothing changes, violence will increase, and the average Sahelian citizen's sense of security and safety will fall even further.

In short, the Sahel in 2030 will be home to many more people, who will probably live in much hotter and more violent conditions. In all likelihood, they will be hungrier and sicker. Fewer, especially among the girls, are likely to complete secondary school. That is a huge problem, because we know that finishing secondary school means that girls earn more, marry later, have fewer children, and are more likely to send their own children to school. Generations of uneducated boys and underemployed young men—including many who did complete school—are likely to be increasingly disaffected. The pressure on them grows as they get older: families rely on them to bring in an income. They often want to marry, but need money to support a family. The region's demography risks becoming a curse rather than a dividend. As a former child soldier told one of my UN colleagues, "lack of hope, at a certain point, pushes humans into the devil's arms." Criminal groups often lure unemployed young men to join them with the promise of money and a sense of purpose. Only months later do some realise they have unwittingly joined Boko Haram.

Accounts from some of those who have fallen into that trap are revealing. They may experience a sense of belonging. But many are also beaten as part of their indoctrination. Some are used as human shields. Others are given drugs, often winding up as addicts. And some are forced to commit horrible acts of violence. All this often leads to profound psychological trauma. Many find it difficult to leave a group that they did not even intend to join, for fear of violent retaliation against themselves or their family. Those who do escape may face stigma and rejection and potentially violent community reprisal. And so they are back at square one, searching for economic opportunities where there are so few.

The consequences of failing to address all of these concerns more effectively in the next decade and beyond will be enormous and far-reaching. The people of the Sahel, who deserve a better future than the one in front of them, are the most important consideration. But the problems facing the Sahel will affect others, too. Political instability can be contagious. Some of the extremist groups behind the current violence and displacement have bigger ambitions. Countries that have been relatively stable, like Côte d'Ivoire, Benin, Togo, and Ghana, are on the front lines. Extremist groups have already appeared in northern Benin.

The countries neighbouring the Sahel will also be the first port of call for the region's economic migrants and refugees. But the world beyond Africa will not be immune from consequences. Illicit trafficking and smuggling organisations in the Sahel, peddling drugs, guns, and people, already target other regions, above all Europe. More extremist groups, with more entrenched footholds, nearly unchecked and left to grow, will not take long to start planning and instigating attacks further afield. These problems are large and deep-rooted. It will not be easy to turn the tide.

So what is to be done?

The most important point is that public policy has to address the causes, not merely respond to the symptoms. The second most important point is that the leading role and main responsibility must be taken up by decision-makers in the region itself, above all legitimate national and local authorities. Unless both of those things happen, the situation will not improve.

Then there are four pillars of necessary action. First, the state authorities in each country have to ensure control of their own territory. That means prosecuting a military response against the extremists and the organised criminals. Those extremists do not offer a better life for people under their control. The people who suffered under ISIS bear witness to that. But the military response needs to be conducted in a way that protects, supports, and wins the backing of local communities. This is about countering insurgency, and no counter-insurgency effort in history has succeeded without the engagement of the people it is supposed to be protecting. At the moment, the military response often is too small and too badly managed to do more good than harm. It is unrealistic to expect national or regional authorities to manage this on their own. More and better international help is essential. In 2019, more than $2 billion was spent on multilateral security initiatives in the Sahel. On top of that comes the even larger expenditure on bilateral military assistance from powerful countries like France and the United States to individual Sahelian nations. But let us not delude ourselves that this is a lot of money in relation to the size of the problem. It is not. More, not less, spending is needed, but the money needs to be better spent as well.

Second, more comprehensive, longer-term, and larger-scale humanitarian support is needed. Donors contributed $1.5 billion to UN-coordinated humanitarian appeals for these six countries in 2019. We needed a billion dollars more than that. In 2020 and 2021 the costs were higher still, especially because of COVID-19. Humanitarian action—food, shelter, education, protection, and medical services—matters not just because it saves lives, but also because it sends the message that people elsewhere do care about what is happening.

Third, the countries of the Sahel need much more investment in basic services, especially education, health, clean water, sanitation, and family planning. Healthier, better-educated people can do much for themselves, which is greatly to be preferred to relying indefinitely on external support. The international community will have to foot much of the bill for this. But national authorities should focus more of what resources they have on these priorities and be willing to allow organisations that can deliver programmes efficiently and effectively—not least community-based organisations and NGOs—to do so, particularly while many national institutions remain as weak as they are now. It is important that the needs of women and girls are explicitly prioritised and invested in. Gender inequality is more pronounced in this region than almost anywhere else in the world. Looking at any country that has prospered over the past century or more, one constant element is that the status of women has been enhanced. That is not only a symptom or a consequence: it is a cause.

Fourth, it must be clear that the region's traditional livelihoods, especially nomadic pastoralism or subsistence farming, will not be able to support populations of the size that will soon be living across Sahelian countries. That is the brutal consequence of climate change, resource pressures, and demographic trends. The process of development over recent generations in every region of the world has been a process of improving agricultural productivity and urbanization to develop new livelihoods. Development efforts in the Sahel need to be larger scale and more cognizant of the region's current underlying problems. Infrastructure, agriculture that is viable in the prevailing conditions, the generation and distribution of electricity, and well-planned urbanisation are among the priorities.

The bad news with this agenda is that it will be very difficult to do all these things to the necessary scale and standard. The good news, though, is that many countries have done them. A few started more than two hundred years ago. Many, particularly across Asia and Latin America, have made these advances over the past 50 years. There is no reason why, with help, the Sahel could not do so, too.

Right now, however, solutions being tried are inadequate in scale. They are also lopsided in composition: too much of the effort has focused on security and humanitarian need and too little addresses the underlying causes of the problems. Yet the answer to that imbalance is not to reduce spend on security or life-saving humanitarian help. Doing that would just make things even worse.

The only way the international community is going to invest heavily in solutions to the problems of the Sahel is if they have a higher degree of confidence in national and local leadership than they currently do. That may be the biggest hurdle of all.

FIVE

Conflict, Displacement, and Famine in the Horn of Africa

IN JANUARY 2018, I WENT to the annual African Union heads of government summit in Addis Ababa, and I took the opportunity to catch up on humanitarian problems in Ethiopia. On the outskirts of the capital, I visited a secondary school that had just been repurposed to house people displaced by fresh ethnic clashes on the border between the Somali and Oromia regions of southeast Ethiopia. The previous day, I had flown with UN Development Programme head Achim Steiner to the hot, dry, drought-prone interior of the Somali region. There we had met rural communities displaced by a combination of drought, water shortages, poverty, and conflict, with clashes often instigated by competition over natural resources. The people we met were entirely reliant on food aid. They told us they were sceptical that their previous livelihoods, based on nomadic livestock farming, were viable any longer given the pressures of people and the impact of climate change on rainfall patterns. They were like displaced people I have listened to in many places: caught in a poverty trap where development progress cannot get ahead of environmental and other resource pressures. The displaced people I met the next day in Addis Ababa, though, were different. They were educated, mostly town dwellers, had had homes and in some cases professional jobs. A few had even had cars. But they had had to flee ethnic fighting. They were victims of a failure of politics and governance to deal with tensions and grievances. They saw no alternative but trying to rebuild their lives somewhere else. If the life prospects of people like this are so fragile, I wondered, what is in store for this region?

------ ◆◆◆ ------

When I was young, many people—including researchers and scientists—thought famine was a permanent feature of the human experience. Famines are shocking, scarring events, the most extreme form of humanitarian disaster. They involve large-scale loss of life with a slow but visible prelude, a tipping point beyond which prevention is no longer possible, and then an explosion. As an undergraduate, I went to Amartya Sen's lectures on poverty and famine, and I wrote a master's dissertation on the use of food grain prices as an early warning of food crises. For many of my friends and me, the Ethiopia famine of 1984 was a lightbulb moment. In previous eras, famine was a feature of the fragility of agriculture against the ever-increasing pressure of higher populations. In 1968, Paul Ehrlich published *The Population Bomb*, in which he predicted that by the 1980s, four billion people would have been killed by famines. His opening sentences set the scene: "The battle to feed humanity is over. In the 1970s, the world will undergo famines in which hundreds of millions of people are going to starve to death." Ehrlich predicted that England would cease to exist by 2000 because the country would be consumed by hunger. Historical experience gave these dark warnings a degree of credence. Researchers think that famines may have taken more lives than war over the course of human history. More than 120 million people are believed to have died in famines in the hundred years after 1870, a larger number even than those killed in that period's uniquely bloody wars.

The doom-mongers, though, were wrong. In fact, in the past 50 years, famine has become much rarer and much less lethal. In the 20 years before I became ERC, there was only one certified famine in the world. That was in Somalia in 2011, when a quarter of a million people died.

As I said in the early pages of this book, I believe we can eradicate famine from the human condition. If we are going to do that, though, we need to understand what accounts for the progress made over the past few decades and then understand the nature of the remaining problem. Because famine is now back. The dangers are greatest in the Horn of Africa.

Three main factors have combined to produce unprecedented advances in reducing large-scale loss of life through starvation over the last 50 years. The first factor is an exponential increase in agricultural output and productivity. Improvements in plant breeding, protection, storage, irrigation, harvesting, transporting, and marketing have contributed to a 300 percent increase in food grain production, using only 12 percent more agricultural land around the world. The global spread in the use of nitrogen-based artificial fertiliser and the development through the Green Revolution of improved seed varieties for major crops explain most of the improvements.

Second, a spectacular reduction in global poverty has increased people's ability to afford food. In the 60 years after 1960, the extreme poverty rate globally dropped from more than 50 percent of the total human population to less than 10 percent. In particular, the 25 years from 1990 to 2015 saw a reduction from 35 percent to less than 10 percent, even while the global population continued to grow dramatically. So not only was there a lot more food available, but most people now had enough income to be able to buy it. Food security has been enhanced by the entitlements created by social safety net schemes established in dozens of the poorest countries over the past 20 years, including ones I have seen myself in countries including Bangladesh, Ethiopia, Ghana, India, Kenya, Malawi, Pakistan, Uganda, Yemen, and Zambia.

Third, when famine does threaten, the response is now much more effective than it was 30 years ago. My first job was on the famine in Ethiopia in the mid-1980s. Then, the overwhelming focus of the relief effort was on food, water, and shelter. Now we understand that in a famine, starvation is not the main cause of death. The real killers are the diseases that a healthy person can generally fight off but a starving one cannot: measles, diarrhoea, cholera, and a host of viral infections from COVID-19 to the common cold. As a result, today's famine responses include comprehensive immunisation programmes, primary healthcare, and nutrition interventions as well as food and clean water.

The result of all this scientific, technological, and economic progress is that modern-day famines are manmade. That was true to a degree in the past: Mao Zedong's Great Famine in China in the 1960s, generally believed to be the worst famine in history in terms of the total number of lives lost, arose largely from the authorities' policy choices. And the famine that some people claim took three million lives in North Korea in the mid-1990s—a repetition of which remains a risk, as I saw during a visit to Pyongyang and the south of the country in 2018—could have been forestalled had the regime been willing to receive more international help offered on reasonable terms. But in the 21st century, neglect and ignorant policy choices are not what is generating famine threats. Deliberate, concerted attempts to prevent help reaching the starving, as part of the military or political strategy of states or armed groups, are now the only explanation for the failure to have eradicated famine from the human experience.

<hr />

The 2011 famine in Somalia was the result of the behaviour of al-Shabaab, the al-Qaeda-linked extremist group which has in recent years dominated much of the south of the country, and the Western (mostly US) attempts to counter them. Al-Shabaab obstructed aid agencies running food convoys into areas made vulnerable by repeated seasons of failed rains. On occasion, its fighters also looted trucks and stole food. Between 2008 and 2010, it was designated a terrorist organisation by the United States and other Western countries. That stigma chilled the ability of aid agencies to operate in areas al-Shabaab controlled because it put agency staff at risk of being prosecuted under drastic counterterrorist legislation. (When the UN finally gathered enough data to formally declare a famine, the Obama administration exempted aid agencies from prosecution. However, this did not happen until after the death toll had already peaked.) In 2017, when famine threatened Somalia again, the memory of 2011 remained fresh, and agencies were more alert and ready to respond. Al-Shabaab was on the back foot militarily. Technology also had improved: as part of the 2017 relief effort, 600,000 families were sent text messages which they could present to redeem for food in local markets, making aid agencies less reliant on food convoys. As was often the case, local private markets could sustain themselves in ways that international public agencies sometimes could not, with commercial operators willing to take unusual risks to make a buck. Famine was prevented.

Humanitarian agencies were, however, all too aware of the repeated cycle of famine scares in Somalia. Often, they were staved off, but sometimes, as in 1992 and 2011, they were not. What was needed was a concerted effort to reduce the country's underlying vulnerability. That first required containing the conflict and stabilising government. Joint military and political initiatives by the African Union and the UN have contributed to a degree of progress on that front over the past decade. Similar efforts have been made over the same period to normalise Somalia's international economic relations, notably through debt relief from the World Bank and the IMF. Promoting debt relief was a main focus of the visits I made to Somalia in 2017, 2018, and 2019. On two of these visits, I went with Mahmoud Mohieldin, then senior vice president of the World Bank, as part of an effort to improve collaboration between our institutions. Formal debt relief finally was agreed in 2020. Dealing with Somalia's historic debt has opened the way for new financing for the country, provided it remains on track with the economic programme agreed with the international community. In an optimistic scenario, resources could be available for improving the governance of the country, including in justice and law and order, and more investment in infrastructure and public services. These improvements might give Somalis a chance of keeping ahead of climate change, which appears poised to imperil the agricultural economy as far into the future as can be seen.

Whether the optimistic scenario plays out will be determined by politics. Domestically, it depends on whether Somalia's diverse ethnic and clan-based structures can hold together under a view of a single nation. Internationally, it depends among other things on whether foreign powers, in particular from the east African and Gulf regions, can be persuaded to desist from interfering as some have done in recent years. The situation remains on a knife edge, as I was reminded during my last visit in 2019. On that visit, a prolonged attack by al-Shabaab prevented us from visiting the president in his Mogadishu compound. We sat instead in a grassed recreation square at the UN complex, where the staff showed us, with a bravura verging on enjoyment, unrepaired damage from recent mortar attacks.

If the issues look intractable and progress is slow and sporadic in Somalia, things are worse in South Sudan. I was first in Juba, now the capital of South Sudan, in 1983. That was shortly before what was then Sudan disintegrated into nearly 30 years of civil war, finally ended only with South Sudan's independence in 2011. Contacts in Khartoum told me when I visited that year that independence would simply open new fissures in the south. The fact that they had an obvious axe to grind did not make them wrong. South Sudan has oil (albeit in limited quantities), timber, and plenty of agricultural potential. But it is hard to think of a new country with greater problems at its birth. When I visited Juba again in 2011, it was a city with no tarmac. Indeed, there were no paved roads anywhere in the country—which is bigger than Kenya, and 50 percent larger than California. The country's institutions were equally weak, with hardly any trained staff in any of them. But the biggest problem of all was that the only thing that held the leaders of South Sudan together during the war was their enmity with Sudan; when it ended, the intensity of ethnic and tribal divisions inside the new country were rapidly exposed. Outside actors, including neighbouring countries and the UN—which established a peacekeeping mission with thousands of blue-helmeted troops from 2011—were unable to contain the internal strife. A newly born country, which already had some of the world's worst human development indicators, collapsed into war with itself.

The ensuing conflict, and especially the way it has been conducted, left huge swathes of South Sudan basically in a vacuum populated by hundreds of groups of 25 or 30 armed men, each with a Kalashnikov, who are permitted and often instructed by their leaders to pillage, rob, and rape as they please. More than six million people—60 percent of the population—have suffered crisis-level food insecurity, and the UN-led aid operation has supported five million of them. In 2016, UN reports described ethnic clashes in the oil-rich Unity State pitting the national army, dominated by Dinka tribesmen, against the Nuer population under rebel leader Riek Machar. The UN also reported the South Sudanese government blocking food aid to Unity State. In 2017, a localized famine, affecting tens of thousands of people, was declared. It was almost entirely manmade, the result of the conflict and the flagrant violation by the belligerents of the obligation to protect civilians. The UN concluded that government forces were pursuing a deliberate strategy of depriving people of any form of livelihood or material support—to cause a famine, in other words.

When I went in May 2018 to what had been South Sudan's breadbasket, the southwestern region of Equatoria, people there told me how the men with guns had cut them off from their livelihoods, their livestock, and other food sources. Marauders obstructed access to fields, looted food stocks, and damaged and destroyed essential infrastructure. Banditry, cattle rustling, and rape were the principal occupations of many young men. People were forced to flee, and many were hungry.

Later that month, and following long discussions in the wake of the four possible famines which had preoccupied humanitarian agencies the previous year, the Security Council, on the initiative of the Netherlands (then serving a term as one of its elected members), passed Resolution 2417. It required the secretary-general and the Secretariat to tell the Council when we thought a conflict was going to cause massive food insecurity, so that the Security Council could meet and decide what to do.

Two months after the resolution passed, we concluded that the rapid deterioration of the food security situation in South Sudan made it necessary to inform the Council. In the briefing I gave when the Council met in August, I called on them to support efforts to facilitate aid access and put greater pressure on the parties to avoid harming civilians. Thanks to the efforts of the UN teams on the ground and support from Western countries led by the United States, enough pressure was brought to bear to scale back the conflict and allow aid agencies to reach the most vulnerable.

In late 2018, a peace agreement and power-sharing deal was signed. Hundreds of thousands of displaced people began the process of returning to their homes, even though many more still could not go home. The situation eased slightly, yet more than half the population remained unable to survive without humanitarian assistance, including most of those who were still displaced. But acute problems returned in late 2019 and early 2020, caused first by heavy rains and flooding, and then by the pandemic. Like many others, the government of South Sudan closed the country's borders and shut down internal air travel in the second quarter of 2020, limiting economic activity and significantly impairing the aid operation. The numbers of people in need of assistance rose to seven million, including four million displaced. Many of those affected were South Sudanese refugees in neighbouring countries.

The situation could have been contained below the famine threshold, but by late 2020 localised famine, this time in Jonglei State in the east of the country, became a serious risk. Once again, ethnic clashes and displacement were the tipping point. World Food Programme head David Beasley, UN Food and Agriculture Organisation Director-General

Qu Dongyu, and I wrote jointly to the Security Council, once more citing the provisions of Resolution 2417, warning of a risk of famine in South Sudan as well as in Yemen and parts of western Africa. It proved difficult amid the pandemic to attract additional donor resources for South Sudan. The draconian aid cuts announced at the same time by the UK government, which had previously been a generous responder to acute needs there, also did not help matters. But aid agencies did just enough to stave off the heaviest loss of life.

Many of the problems of the Horn of Africa over the past 30 years were exacerbated by the poisonous regime of Omar al-Bashir in Sudan. Bashir came to power through a military coup in 1989, and subsequently oversaw a war in the western region of Darfur that displaced more than two million people and, on the best estimates, probably took several hundred thousand lives. The displaced in Darfur and nearby South Kordofan, some of whom I met during visits in 2017 and 2018, were among the most dispirited and dispiriting people I met as ERC. Their plight was grim: stuck in camps supported by humanitarian organisations for years on end, fed but unoccupied, and deprived of their agency and any ability to improve their own circumstances. Meeting them persuaded me that we needed new initiatives to try to find solutions to problems of long-term displacement. With the support of more than 50 UN member states, and working closely with the UN refugee agency and the IOM, we set up a Secretary-General's High Level Panel on displaced people in late 2019. The panel's work was delayed by the pandemic, but they submitted a detailed report in late 2021. It remains to be seen whether, in the midst of so many other global challenges, enough political energy can be generated to find solutions for the ever-growing numbers of displaced people.

In 2008, the prosecutor of the International Criminal Court accused Bashir of genocide, crimes against humanity, and war crimes. His regime, presiding over the progressive impoverishment of the people of Sudan and their ostracisation from the international community, nevertheless clung on until 2019. He was finally forced out as a result of prolonged street protests, another military coup, and then—when further civic protests made clear another military dictator would not be accepted—the installation of a temporary new civilian-led government. A respected former UN economist, Abdalla Hamdok, took charge as prime minister. The new government promoted peace deals with rebel groups, reintegration of displaced people, and Sudan's rehabilitation with the international community. While I was ERC, like lots of senior staff in the UN, I visited Hamdok to offer support and tried to persuade others to back him. We pressed for faster and more generous material support, including relief of the unsustainable debt Sudan had accumulated during its decades as a pariah state. The response was timid, with only modest steps forward. The jury is out on whether Sudan can get onto a path of economic growth, poverty reduction, and stable, accountable government. But it has at least stopped digging itself deeper into the trough, and started playing a more constructive role in the region.

Before the pandemic, I thought there was a fair chance, particularly given developments in Sudan, that the Horn as a region could get onto a positive path. But the coronavirus and catastrophe in Ethiopia may have put paid to that.

Ethiopia's rise from famine state to a regional beacon of relative prosperity and stability is one of the more remarkable national success stories of the modern era. Over the course of 30 years, the economy, led by agriculture, grew faster than almost anywhere else in Africa. The country developed a national road network and power system. Almost every child got to school. The newly created health system oversaw a reduction in the proportion of children dying before the age of five from 25 percent to 5 percent. Factories and railways started to appear. The population grew rapidly from 40 million to 120 million. Many people remained on the margins of survival, and the country suffered regular severe droughts over the period. But the government built an effective safety net, administered by one of the developing world's most competent disaster management agencies. Poor harvests were never allowed to lead to large-scale loss of life through hunger. Visiting the country every few years from 1986 to 2019, and comparing Ethiopia's progress with other developing countries, I (like many others) marvelled at what was happening.

But there was a hidden weakness. It was not, as some have said, so much the dominant role of the state in the development process—in previous decades, other countries including Korea, China, and Vietnam successfully adopted a similar approach. Rather, it was the political model. Ethiopia is a country of many nations and ethnic groups, which have competed for power and influence for much of the last century and the centuries before that. The Tigrayan-dominated government of Meles Zenawi, the medical student turned revolutionary soldier turned statesman, who was president and then prime minister from 1991 to 2012, failed to deal with the implicit danger. It is said that Nelson Mandela tried to persuade Meles he needed to build a country in which everyone saw themselves as Ethiopian first and foremost, subjugating their tribal or ethnic origins, just as Julius Nyerere had done in Tanzania after independence in the 1960s. But that is not what happened. Meles was able to contain internal tensions by delivering real and continuous improvements in the lives of most Ethiopians, which made many accept the limitations his government imposed on personal and political freedoms—and enabled him to continue wielding the heavy hand of the security state against dissenters. But the coalition he presided over was ethnically and regionally organized. And after his premature death in 2012 at age 57, tensions gradually overflowed in many parts of the country. I saw the consequences of that tension in coffee-growing regions of southern Ethiopia in 2019, visiting people displaced by ethnic clashes. Other parts of the country faced similar problems, often arising from competition over land and other resources.

Meles' successor, Hailemariam Desalegn, came from one of the smaller ethnic groups, as a compromise candidate. He was unable to hold things together and resigned in 2018. His replacement was Abiy Ahmed, who as an Oromo came from Ethiopia's largest ethnic group. Abiy hoped that his wide-ranging reforms would placate ethnic tensions, but instead they had the opposite effect. In particular, in the process of resolving a long-running dispute with Eritrea—for which the Nobel committee prematurely and unwisely awarded him the Peace Prize in 2019—he inflamed relations with the Tigrayans. Eritrea borders the Tigray region, and Ethiopia and Eritrea had gone to war over boundary issues in 1998. The Tigrayans thought Abiy had sold them out, creating an existential threat to them by allying with Eritrea. They tried to distance themselves from the Addis Ababa government. In a terrible strategic blunder, Abiy thought he could bring them under control by cutting funding and, in November 2020, sending the Ethiopian defence forces in. Even worse, he invited the Eritrean military to help subjugate the Tigrayan opposition.

From the outset of the military operation, many people familiar with Ethiopia saw catastrophe ahead. In an opinion piece for the *Washington Post* in early December 2020, I warned that Ethiopia was in danger of losing everything it had achieved over the past 30 years: "Conflicts like this are hard to stop once they get out of control—the lives they extinguish cannot be brought back and the grievances they create are long lasting."

For the next six months, Tigray was subjected to massacres, mass rapes, and the looting of farms, crops, livelihoods, businesses, infrastructure, and communications systems. The economy was destroyed, thousands killed, and millions displaced. Aid agencies trying to provide assistance were blocked and hindered, with staff detained, interrogated, assaulted, and killed. It was clear from the information available to me—and I said publicly—that the Eritreans in particular were using starvation and famine as a weapon of war. For months, Abiy repeated to everyone he met the fantasy that the situation was being brought under control and the law-and-order operation was succeeding.

For months, he denied the presence of the Eritreans in Tigray; when the weight of evidence finally made that claim untenable, he switched to saying that they would leave soon. In fact, it was the Ethiopian forces who had to leave—pushed out of Mekelle, the regional capital, in late June 2021 by Tigrayan soldiers, who were energised by the belief that they were fighting for the survival of their families and communities.

The start of the crisis coincided with the 2020 US presidential election and then the transition to the Biden administration. The Security Council could not agree to hold an open meeting on the crisis, with African members, under pressure from Ethiopia, and backed by China and Russia, objecting. Three times over the first six months of the conflict, I was asked to describe the humanitarian situation in closed meetings of the Council. (The material we presented in these meetings was consistently and, until we corrected it, sometimes inaccurately leaked.) In May 2021, I again invoked the provisions of Resolution 2417 to send the Council a formal note warning them the humanitarian situation in Tigray was approaching catastrophic levels. I told journalists it was reasonable to fear a rerun of the 1984 famine in which a million people are believed to have died. In early June, a week before I left my role, new data revealed that hundreds of thousands of people were indeed now in famine conditions. The Ethiopian government disputed the facts and tried to block publication of the data. It continued successfully to oppose a public discussion in the Security Council. In public events convened by others and in press interviews in my final few days as ERC, I was blunt: "There is famine now in Tigray."

One might say it is a huge step forward in the human condition that the only circumstances in which famines can arise now are ones in which they are caused deliberately—as in Somalia, South Sudan, and Ethiopia. The fact that agricultural production, poverty reduction, social safety nets, and responses to severe crises have improved so much over recent decades is indeed a huge boon, transforming the lives of millions of people in vulnerable countries. But one conclusion I drew from my experience as ERC is that, given that famines now arise only as a result of deliberate and often government-backed decisions, the international system for preventing them is no longer fit for purpose.

The main tool humanitarian agencies use to identify famine risks and provoke responses to prevent them is the Integrated Phase Classification system, or IPC. The IPC is run by a consortium of UN agencies, NGOs, and analytical groups. IPC reports are issued regularly on countries at risk of food insecurity, using tried-and-tested methodologies and data-gathering techniques, to summarise the current situation and make future projections. The IPC has five levels, from Phase One, which means no significant food insecurity, to Phase Five, meaning catastrophe or famine. A formal famine declaration, however, requires not just the identification of people now in Phase Five but also the assent of a review committee that has looked at the data and assessed whether a defined area has passed three thresholds: (1) at least 20 percent of households face an extreme lack of food, (2) at least 30 percent of children suffer from acute malnutrition, and (3) 2 people in every 10,000 are dying each day due to outright starvation or the interaction of malnutrition and disease.

Because everyone knows that famines are now avoidable, and because they are such extreme events that rightly attract global opprobrium, governments hate being told they risk presiding over famine. They typically have two responses: denial and blame shifting. Given that the IPC is led largely by UN organisations, who are accountable to their member states, countries have plenty of scope to delay or obfuscate and sometimes block the release of data in order to prevent or delay a declaration of famine. The authorities in South Sudan and in Ethiopia have both done that. Ultimately, the data tend to come out; but delay is deadly. Advance sight of IPC findings also gives governments opportunities to pick holes in them—part of the denial tactic.

Even more seriously, because one of the criteria relates to the death rate already observed, famine can only be officially declared once it has taken place. What is needed is a universal, high-profile system to identify places at high risk of famine *before* it happens, and then apply overwhelming pressure on those responsible for the problems, so those who can prevent famine are able to do so.

SIX

Natural Disasters: Earthquakes, Volcanoes, Storms, and Cyclones

ALONG WITH THE INCREASE in conflict-related humanitarian emergencies in the early years of the current century, the same period saw an unusual spike in natural disasters. On 26 December 2004, the deadliest tsunami in history struck South and Southeast Asia. More than 230,000 people are believed to have been killed, mostly in Indonesia. In October 2005, a massive earthquake rocked Pakistan-administered Azad Kashmir. The death toll was estimated at around 100,000, with 3.5 million left homeless. Even more people, about 20 million according to some estimates, were affected in 2010 when monsoon floods hit 20 percent of the land mass of Pakistan. And in January that year, one of the deadliest earthquakes in history killed between 100,000 and 300,000 people in Haiti, including many people working for the UN Stabilisation Mission there.

This slew of large disasters in the space of just a few years created the impression that disasters were becoming more common and more deadly. In fact, neither of those things are true. Since 1995, the number of people affected by natural disasters globally has decreased. That year, 222 million people were affected; by 2019, it was down to 95 million, even in a larger global population. Despite major events like the 2004 tsunami, the average annual death toll has fallen dramatically as well.

Mega-disasters have been few in the past decade. In some places that are vulnerable to earthquakes and volcanoes, they are probably overdue. But preparedness, early warning, and investments in resilience have reduced death tolls—especially in Asia, the most disaster-prone region. Weather-related events, in particular floods but also cyclones, hurricanes, and other major storms, are the most common form of natural disaster. Between 1995 and 2015, EM-DAT, the international disaster database, recorded roughly 6,500 weather-related events. They killed more than 600,000 people. But the proportion of the global population affected by weather-related disasters fell from 1 in 25 across the planet from 1995 to 2004 to 1 in 41 from 2005 to 2014.

The figures calculated for the economic impact of natural disasters vary widely from year to year, largely depending on whether developed countries see major events, like Hurricane Katrina in the United States in 2005, and the 2011 Tohoku earthquake and tsunami in Japan, in which case published loss figures are high. Average annual losses over the period 2009–18 were estimated at $187 billion, compared with $147 billion over the 30-year period 1989–2018. But this apparent increase obscures the huge expansion in wealth and infrastructure over the period, which means that a storm these days finds more in its path to damage than did one 20 years ago. In this light, overall, natural disasters do less damage now than in the past. Whether that will be reversed in the coming decades by climate change is one of the challenges policymakers need to address.

One of the first things I did on waking up every morning as the ERC, wherever I was in the world, was to check for messages on natural disasters that either had happened overnight or were thought to be on the way. We always had to make quick judgements on whether the UN and other humanitarian agencies would need to respond, or whether the national authorities, sometimes with help from their neighbours, would cope without international assistance.

In the event of a significant event in a country needing help, we had to make decisions on the scale and nature of the international response. For major natural disasters like earthquakes and volcanoes, there is often a need for international assistance with search and rescue, especially for people in urban areas buried under fallen buildings. Few countries choose or can afford to maintain a standing capacity of search-and-rescue teams big enough to deal with all conceivable events, and many plan on the possibility of help from experts from elsewhere. Japan and New Zealand, for example, both did that when dealing with the earthquakes they experienced in 2011. I was involved in organising British teams from the fire and health services to help in those cases when I was head of DFID.

International collaboration on search and rescue is organised mostly through OCHA, following a UN General Assembly resolution in 2002. Through its management of the International Search and Rescue Advisory Group (INSARAG), OCHA certifies national teams to accredited standards, and then channels requests from countries hit by disasters to those with the capacity to help. Search-and-rescue efforts normally last just a few days: after that, it is rare to find survivors among the ruins of a collapsed building, for instance. Speed is of the essence in these cases, and increasingly countries rely on their neighbours, who can reach them fastest, to support national responses. Many of these collaborations are facilitated through regional organisations in Europe, the Pacific, Southeast Asia, and elsewhere. They are therefore often the first port of call. The UN through OCHA has played a role in building the capacity of such regional organisations in recent years. Teams from China and South Africa which had been accredited by INSARAG went to Mozambique when Cyclone Idai, one of the deadliest cyclones on record in Africa, battered the coastline in March 2019. And INSARAG supported the deployment of 13 search-and-rescue teams from 10 countries to Beirut when ammonium nitrate being stored in the port exploded on 4 August 2020. That response, coming in the middle of the COVID-19 pandemic, was unusually challenging.

For major earthquakes, volcanic eruptions, and extreme weather events, longer-lasting international responses are frequently needed. These events cause large-scale loss of life not just from the immediate consequence of the disaster but because the resulting destruction leaves people struggling to find food, shelter, clean water, and life's other essentials, Learning from the lessons of the 2004 Indian Ocean earthquake and tsunami, where relief agencies were too slow and poorly coordinated, the response system was modernised. The UN established a central emergency response fund, aiming at annual voluntary contributions of $500 million. The idea was that responses could begin as soon as disaster struck, rather than being delayed by the need to launch appeals and raise money. During my tenure as ERC, we provided $240 million from the central emergency response fund for relief efforts in the wake of more than 50 earthquakes, volcanic eruptions, floods, and storms across five continents. The fund aims to be the first and fastest responder, and can often take action before other resources are available. Decisions on the size of the response were normally made within a day or so of the event, but consistently it took too long after that to decide which agency would do what, procure the necessary supplies, and then get help to the people who needed it. (I will return to this issue in Part Two.)

Making money available faster is one issue. Another is identifying quickly enough exactly what help is needed in each case and then providing it in a coordinated way. In light of the problems exposed during the 2004 tsunami, the Inter-Agency Standing Committee established more formal and professional coordination systems, with clearer divisions of responsibilities. Under the not-very-glamorous name of the cluster system, humanitarian agencies have been given enduring responsibilities in the areas of their international mandate and capabilities. Food security is led by the World Food Programme and the UN Food and Agriculture Organisation. The UN refugee agency and the International Federation of Red Cross and Red Crescent Societies are responsible for shelter. The WHO takes the prime role on health. UNICEF and Save the Children lead on education. The IOM and the UN refugee agency share responsibility for camp coordination if people displaced by disaster are housed in camps. Because emergencies often disrupt logistics, transport, and telecommunications, the aid agencies have standing arrangements, led by the World Food Programme, to establish temporary arrangements when national systems are disabled or nonexistent. They include the UN Humanitarian Air Service, which has become one of the world's largest airlines, servicing places and people no-one else can or will reach. In each disaster, the UN's resident coordinator, the most senior UN official in the affected country, will make decisions in discussion with the national authorities about which clusters need to be mobilised. The relevant agencies then bring in the necessary specialist staff and supplies.

For the biggest problems threatening large-scale loss of life, I convened meetings of the heads of the Inter-Agency Standing Committee agencies to ensure top-level engagement in the response. Sometimes specific international appeals were launched when it was clear that resources in the central emergency response fund or already available to the leading agencies were insufficient. The Inter-Agency Standing Committee also had long-standing protocols to secure enhanced responses for such cases, known as Level 3 (L3) emergencies. These responses could include the appointment of an experienced senior humanitarian coordinator, supported by additional OCHA staff, and would cause the agencies to prioritise the response to this problem over other ongoing work. The idea was to facilitate a rapid expansion of assistance in the crucial early phases of an emergency when large-scale loss of life is most likely.

When I took up the position, this system had fallen into disrepair: major crises like those in Yemen and Syria had been designated L3s for years, because political pressure especially from donors meant they could not be downgraded. The L3 label had become a political signal, not an operational concept. In one of the few system changes I put in place, we replaced the L3 system with two categories. One was for scaling up for new problems, where the label automatically expired after six months, or in extreme cases nine months; and another was for sustaining high levels of operational engagement in protracted, invariably conflict-related emergencies. During my tenure, we used the first category five times: twice in the Democratic Republic of Congo, including for the 2018 Ebola outbreak; for the 2019 Mozambique cyclone; for the

COVID-19 pandemic in 2020; and for the conflict in Tigray in 2021. On each occasion, the declaration supported stronger action by humanitarian agencies.

In my first few weeks in the job, I found myself dealing with a series of natural disasters. The 2017 Caribbean hurricane season was one of the worst on record. In the first week of September, Hurricane Irma crashed through many small low-lying islands, including Antigua and Barbuda and dependent territories of the United Kingdom and the Netherlands like Saint Martin and the Turks and Caicos Islands. It then moved on to Puerto Rico, where a state of emergency was declared on 4 September. Less than a fortnight later, Hurricane Maria, the deadliest Atlantic storm for nearly 20 years, devastated Dominica and inflicted huge damage in Puerto Rico. An official estimate commissioned by the governor there suggested that nearly 3,000 people lost their lives, and the Trump administration was criticised for the federal government's poor response to a disaster in a US territory. Total economic losses from Hurricane Maria were estimated at more than $90 billion. That compared with $2 billion from Cyclone Idai in Mozambique, which killed more than a thousand people and affected three million more. But there was much less infrastructure and other assets in the path of Idai, and the people it affected were much poorer than in the Caribbean. The risk of loss of life was accordingly larger, and it was important that humanitarian agencies managed to get assistance to more than a million people in the weeks after the cyclone. The prompt response saved many lives.

For both Irma and Maria, we triggered preplanned contingency arrangements, with the UN supporting the Caribbean's own regional emergency agency and sending staff to the islands likely to be affected ahead of time in order to be able immediately to prepare damage and needs assessments. World Bank staff were caught on Dominica; the UN was able to help extricate them. (World Bank President Jim Kim went out of his way to thank me afterwards.)

Some of the countries and territories most affected in the 2017 Caribbean storm season were the responsibility of the rich world—like British and Dutch overseas territories, as well as Puerto Rico. Realistically, those countries, with their naval vessels, helicopters, and other capabilities in the region, could do much more for their protectorates than we in the UN could do. But we still got requests for help. Nikki Haley, then the US Ambassador to the UN, called Guterres to ask if we could help in Puerto Rico. Within a few minutes, I and a senior colleague were despatched across the road from the UN Secretariat building to the US embassy to meet her. We managed not to point out that we could not think of anything the UN had that the United States did not have in much greater quantities—planes, ships, money, generators, logistics capability. Haley thought this was an opportunity to send a positive message in the United States about the UN. We ended up providing a consignment of water purification tablets which we happened to have in stock, and nothing more was said.

Just after 1 p.m. on 19 September 2017, a large earthquake—magnitude 7.1 on the Richter scale—struck central Mexico, toppling buildings, cracking highways, damaging water and gas supply systems, and leaving millions without electricity. A fortnight before, an even bigger earthquake had struck, but the epicentre then was off the southern coast and, because there was no major tsunami, the loss of life was restricted to double figures. The 19 September event, though, was close to Mexico City, and it occurred on the anniversary of the huge 1985 earthquake, in which 10,000 people in the city were believed to have been killed. That disaster had led to the fall of the Mexican government, whose reputation was irrevocably damaged by what was perceived to be a poorly organised rescue and recovery effort. There had been commemorative events for 1985—and practice drills in case it should be repeated—earlier on the morning of 19 September.

That week was coincidentally High-Level Week at the UN General Assembly, when world leaders come to New York for their annual meeting. In the middle of the afternoon of 19 September, I received an urgent call from the Mexican Ambassador to the UN asking if I could talk straightaway to his foreign minister. We need help with search and rescue, the minister said, but we do not want to make a public appeal—out of fear, it was clear, of domestic criticism for being unable to cope again. Can you help? I said I thought he could get help directly from those of Mexico's nearest neighbours with good search-and-rescue teams, including the White House. I explained how he could contact their best people directly, cutting out the UN middleman to speed things up. I said we would mobilise the OCHA system to explore the possibilities of teams that would come from further afield but could nevertheless get there in time to be useful. The OCHA office in Geneva—on call late in the evening—quickly identified the best candidates for these particular circumstances.

Over the next several hours, some of the strengths and weaknesses of the system were exposed. Passing up an invitation to an evening drinks reception hosted by President Trump and his wife Melania, who were in New York for the UN leaders gathering, I made a series of calls seeking help for Mexico. I spoke to a senior minister in one country who said they could help but only if the UN had a formal public request from the Mexicans, a position that proved rigid even when we explained why that was difficult. In another case, a highly capable team with all their equipment was put straight on a plane to Mexico City.

By the end of the month, more than 500 rescue workers from over 27 countries, with their dogs, equipment, and supplies, had contributed to the relief effort. Nearly 400 people died and more than 6,000 were injured, but many others were rescued. I thought the Mexicans had managed a difficult situation well. And they had been grateful for OCHA's agile and flexible help; the Mexican foreign minister wrote a fulsome letter of thanks to the secretary-general.

The deadliest earthquake during my tenure struck Sulawesi in Indonesia on 28 September 2018. It created a seven-metre-high tsunami in the Makassar Strait, which rolled through the coastal town of Palu, sweeping away houses, the main hospital, and other buildings along the coastline. The local airport and many roads were put out of action, and the earthquake caused soil liquefaction—essentially, turning the ground into a liquid floating mass—which submerged entire buildings and the hundreds of people in them. Because many visitors had come to Palu for a festival to celebrate the town's 40th anniversary, its population was abnormally high on the day of the disaster.

Following the 2004 tsunami, Indonesia had created one of the world's better early warning and response systems. Vice President Jusuf Kalla had also been the chair of the Indonesian Red Cross Society, which played a key role in responses to frequent disasters. But this time, Indonesia's national response capacity was already struggling to cope with an earthquake that had struck Lombok in the southeast of the country just a month previously. Hundreds of thousands of people had been displaced and needed help. After trying for the first couple of days to handle the Sulawesi disaster themselves, the Indonesian government reluctantly decided to accept offers of international assistance. I understood their reticence; not all the offers would be useful, and coordinating them was always a nightmare. Nevertheless, the provision of military transport aircraft from neighbouring and Western countries that could operate on the rapidly patched-up runway of the Palu airport, along with search-and-rescue specialists from the region, certainly helped speed up the relief effort. Following consultations with the government, on 3 October we announced a $15 million grant from the UN's central emergency response fund to finance the work of UN agencies on the ground to cover any needs that others were not meeting. Many clinics and hospitals were put out of action; there were 40,000 pregnant women in the affected area, and many were wondering who would now provide antenatal and delivery care. Staff from the

UN Population Fund, who had reached Palu, started emergency support programmes.

About a week after the earthquake, I visited the affected area with Guterres and Vice President Kalla. We talked to hospital patients who were lying in beds in the open air outside the destroyed town hospital, and children who were being looked after in safe spaces run by UN agencies. We also saw the extraordinary sight of semiburied houses flipped onto their roofs as a result of the liquefraction. We drove along the devastated shoreline. It transpired that the early warning system had not worked to inform people of the tsunami before it reached the shoreline, and many going about their business unaware along the commercial strip by the Palu beach were simply swept away. At least 4,000 people died in the disaster, and 10,000 more were injured.

In January 2019, my wife Julia and I went for a long weekend in Nassau in the Bahamas to escape the New York winter. The Bahamas is one of the richest Caribbean countries. We chose it for its beautiful azure ocean, white sands, and warm wet air, and because I thought there was no chance that I would ever have to go there for professional purposes. On 1 September that year, Hurricane Dorian, a powerful Atlantic storm with winds of up to 185 miles per hour arrived over the Abaco Islands, one of the northern island groups in the Bahamas archipelago. Unusually, the storm stayed parked over the Abacos for several days rather than passing through it in a matter of hours. Wind and water destroyed homes, roads, ports, and airports, and knocked out the electricity and telecommunications systems. This was, coincidentally, a quiet news period. Many wealthy Americans had second homes in the Abacos. CNN ran wall-to-wall coverage, and it was picked up around the globe. I went to Nassau on 4 September to talk to the prime minister and his Cabinet and check to ensure that the UN was doing all we could to help. The truth was there was not that much we could do: the affected communities were accessible only by helicopter, with airports and seaports having been put out of action. The UN did not have helicopters in the area. The US Coast Guard, who did, were the first to reach many of those affected. I advised the Cabinet to be fully transparent with their population on what they knew and did not yet know about the people lost or missing, and what they could and could not do given such an unprecedented event affecting the country. I said one mistake I had seen other governments make was overpromising. I offered to provide $1 million from the central emergency response fund as a signal of the UN's solidarity.

I also explained how I thought they could realistically expect the world to react: they would have a few days in the spotlight, receive limited immediate financial help from friendly countries, and receive payouts on any insurance policies taken out by private individuals, corporations, and the government. But there would not be much beyond that. Everyone at the top of the government had friends and family members caught up in the disaster. The press was panning the authorities over flaws in the relief effort. I advised the government to counter the impression that the hurricane had devastated the whole country. That was not true—Nassau was unaffected—but if it was widely believed, the tourist industry, on which the country depended, might be damaged through the following season. The economic impact of that could be greater than the destruction wrought by the storm. I also promised we would be back on vacation the following season. (Which we were, in January 2020.) After a few hours of talks, my special assistant Sofie Karlsson (who had come with me to the meeting) and I had done all we usefully could. We went for lunch at a beach restaurant looking over white sands and pristine turquoise ocean, feeling a bit of a fraud. Then it was back to the airport for half a dozen media interviews before getting on a plane back to New York. Guterres made his own visit a few days later, partly out of solidarity but also to draw attention to yet another example of climate risk.

Natural disasters are a fact of life. Most countries cope with them better now than in the past. Better-off and middle-income countries can minimise loss of life by investing in early warning systems, upgrading building standards to improve the resilience of infrastructure, maintaining emergency response capacities like search and rescue, and improving public awareness through education and practice drills. We can already see that climate change will mean more extreme weather events. Californian wildfires, Australian droughts, flooding in the United Kingdom, and a host of other examples all speak to that. Few countries are investing adequately in ways to mitigate them.

In the less-developed countries, humanitarian agencies have done a good job in recent years in helping limit the loss of life from natural disasters. That said, there have been surprisingly few really big ones in the last decade. At some point, that will change.

For smaller economies for which big-weather events, volcanoes, or earthquakes can have a national economic impact—as Dominica found—greater investment in regional collaboration and insurance-like mechanisms is a particular priority. The payouts that Dominica, the Bahamas, and others have received from their insurance policies, normally within days of the event, have justified the investment. I will say more about all these issues in Part Two.

(*top*) I briefed the Security Council more than a hundred times between 2017 and 2021.

(*bottom*) The woman in the orange headscarf, Cox's Bazar, Bangladesh, November 2017.

(*opposite page, top*) With (*left to right*) Mia Seppo, the UN Resident Coordinator; Antonio Vitorino, head of the International Organisation for Migration; and Filippo Grandi, UN High Commissioner for Refugees, Cox's Bazar, April 2019.

(*opposite page, middle*) Cox's Bazar, April 2019.

(*opposite page, bottom*) "This child cannot survive": Aden, November 2017.

(*above, top*) Displaced people in a makeshift settlement north of Sana'a, November 2018.

(*above, bottom*) Complaining live on Saudi television about bombs being dropped near the OCHA headquarters in Yemen, November 2017.

(*opposite page, top*) The Saudis hand over a cheque for $500 million, September 2019.

(*opposite page, middle*) A Syrian boy protects his baby sister from the war planes.

(*opposite page, bottom*) Khaled had fled with his family from Palmyra to escape Islamic State: Homs, January 2018.

(*above, top*) Getting briefed by the Jordanian military commander on the northern border with Syria, January 2020.

(*above, bottom*) The stories of women who had fled Boko Haram: Diffa, Niger, September 2017.

(*opposite page, top*) Visiting people who had fled ethnic conflict in southeast Ethiopia with (to my right) UN Development Programme head Achim Steiner, January 2018.

(*opposite page, middle*) People in crises want the same things as everyone else: makeshift school in camp for displaced people, Juba, South Sudan, May 2018.

(*opposite page, bottom*) UN peacekeepers provide protection as we visit opposition areas in Equatoria, South Sudan, May 2018.

(*left, top*) The earthquake and tsunami turned everything upside down: Palu, Sulawesi, Indonesia, October 2018.

(*left, middle*) With Guterres in Davos, January 2019. World Food Programme chief David Beasley is in the background.

(*below*) With Guterres in Palu.

(*top*) With the staff of Heal Africa, Goma, Democratic Republic of Congo, April 2019.

(*middle*) Listening to women in Kassala, eastern Sudan, November 2019.

(*bottom*) With Filippo Grandi visiting displaced people near Kabul, Afghanistan, September 2018.

PART TWO

SEVEN

Coordination

HOW SHOULD YOU BEHAVE if you are a coordinator but have no power over those you are supposed to be coordinating? I described in the introduction how the international humanitarian system, not through grand design but as a result of discrete decisions over decades, comprises an array of UN, NGO, and Red Cross bodies. They share common goals but are independently governed and funded, and they focus on different specialisms. The rationale for the coordinating function, when the UN General Assembly established it in 1991, was to try to make all this work as coherently as possible. I had expected that I might have to take up the reins within a few weeks after my appointment was announced in April 2017, but it turned out that I had three months to prepare. That proved beneficial, because it meant I was able to talk to lots of people about what I should be trying to do. They were invariably fulsome, and in some cases, unable to contain their delight, in sharing their critique of what, despite all the good work humanitarian agencies do, they saw as their many failings. It did not take long to work out that I was inheriting plenty of problems. It was not merely that humanitarian needs were escalating because their causes were not being addressed. The system was straining at the seams. OCHA was not very popular—or very happy.

As part of his manifesto when he was campaigning to become UN secretary-general, Guterres had set out a vision for management reform. When he took office, he joked (though it was not really a joke) that the thing that kept him up at night was the bureaucracy: red tape, byzantine procedures, fragmented structures. He thought the multi-lateral system had to change if it was to remain relevant and effective. And he invested significant political capital in moving a reform process forward. "The goal of reform," he said, "is a 21st century United Nations focused more on people and less on process, more on delivery and less on bureaucracy. The true test of reform will be measured in tangible results in the lives of the people we serve—and the trust of those who support our work."

The UN is widely criticised for being bureaucratic and inefficient. It is. Many of the causes, though, come from decisions made by member states in their governance of it. They frequently micromanage what the secretary-general can do, down even to detailed job descriptions of junior staff members. Most member states would like the UN to be more effective and efficient, and so they support reform efforts, but a minority do not want the UN to improve at all. The truth is that the UN—right from the principles set out in the Charter adopted in the mid-1940s—is largely a Western liberal construct, promoting human rights, equality between men and women, and individual freedoms, as well as peace and security and collaboration on shared problems. Many staff members, from every corner of the globe, join and stay because they believe in those values. But every year in the budget negotiations, a small minority of member states—led by the Russians—resist proposals that would make the UN more effective and efficient. That would advance the Western liberal agenda, they fear, so from their point of view it is rational to oppose it. Because decisions on the use of budget contributions that every country makes by dint of their membership are taken by consensus, they have significant blocking powers. (By contrast, there are no such constraints on the use of voluntary contributions outside the main budget, which is the source of most humanitarian aid. Only those who contribute have a real voice there.)

Not all the UN's problems can be put at the door of member states. The UN pays well, carries prestige, and pursues goals many people find attractive. It is able to hire highly intelligent staff from all round the world. But that is not to say they are always effective or productive. David Malone is a distinguished Canadian diplomat and author who is currently the head of the UN university in Tokyo. He was always one of the more interesting contributors when I attended meetings of the UN Chief Executives Board, the six-monthly meeting of agency heads chaired by the secretary-general. He put it well when he talked to the American journalist Linda Fasulo for her 2021 book on the UN: "40 percent of the Secretariat staff are movers and shakers and carry the full burden of action. About 30 percent do no harm and no good, and about 30 percent spend their time making trouble. Which means that the 40 percent who get the work done are fairly heroic and they exist at all levels of the system." (My experience in OCHA was that the proportion of movers and shakers was higher, and that of troublemakers lower. But I recognized the categories.) Many of the troublemakers are easily identifiable from their complaints about being underpaid (which they are not) and underappreciated (also untrue). They tend to be older, male, and "stale," and are expert in both blocking other people's good ideas and milking the UN's personnel rules and procedures to their advantage, especially those relating to benefits and terms and conditions. Their attitudes frustrate talented younger staff and competent senior executives who are brought in from outside and want to make a difference.

Promoting reform in these circumstances requires guile and persistence as well as determination, and the fact that Guterres was up for it was one of the things that attracted me to the job. All his reform priorities were relevant for the humanitarian sector. First, he wanted to streamline and improve peace operations. Strengthening the UN's capacities on mediation, conflict prevention, and peacebuilding would help with humanitarian objectives. Too often, humanitarian agencies end up subsidising the human and financial costs of the failure of politics. Doing more to stop conflicts from breaking out in the first place, resolving the ongoing conflicts, and acting to avoid relapse would go a long way to reducing the humanitarian caseload to a more manageable level.

Guterres' second area of reform was to make the UN development system more field-focused, better coordinated, and more accountable. A key aspect of that area was to strengthen the links between humanitarian and development work, especially in protracted crises. I agreed with that principle, and made a number of joint trips with UN Development Programme head Achim Steiner to promote the cause. But as I will discuss in more detail in the next chapter, it proved increasingly difficult as the humanitarian system became more and more overwhelmed between 2017 and 2021. The way some aspects of the development reforms were pursued in practice, with a lot of time on process and an underlying mindset of central control, was unpopular with many UN agencies and the intended benefits have been hard to realise.

To me, the most important reform priority was the third one: management. Guterres' smartest move, I thought, was to try from the outset to build a senior team of collaborative people with executive skills and experience and to invest in encouraging them to work together. Again, David Malone describes this situation well: "What's striking about the current crop of agency leaders is that they're very much focused on the task and they're personally low key. . . . Today it's about keeping the agencies running in businesslike ways and much less about individual big personalities at the top. And I think that's healthy."

Guterres created an Executive Committee of the senior staff, which acted like a cabinet in many governments, meeting weekly to discuss and agree on a way forward on key issues. I enjoyed and learned a lot from these meetings, which were always well-prepared and well-run even if the UN's actual ability to influence the topics being discussed was often limited. I admired the skills of many of my colleagues on the committee. The political affairs team always knew what every influential country thought and wanted on every subject, and had identified opportunities for progress. The soft-spoken peacekeepers had a tough, resilient, and worldly-wise core, and were experienced enough to understand that even if you can't solve a problem, there is still a lot to be said for stopping it getting worse. The (omnipresent) lawyers were brilliant at deflecting and navigating reputational threats, not least the large numbers of them created by friendly fire from naïve colleagues. Those responsible for managing the UN's precarious finances and antediluvian personnel systems (of which more below), who I sometimes thought should take more risk in pushing reform, nonetheless displayed a lot of integrity in keeping everything moving forward.

One of the main reform priorities was to do something about the UN's byzantine procedures and fragmented structures. Some people in the Department of Management in New York resisted efforts to decentralise and delegate authority, as well as simplify procedures, because they were worried about job losses and did not want to give up powers that they enjoyed. I signed OCHA up as a pilot department for greater decentralisation, and a degree of progress was made in giving people in field operations more autonomy and control over resources to solve their own problems. The biggest potential gains in terms of management reform were in personnel management, but Guterres' ambition in that regard was ground down over time by a combination of resistance from member states who did not really want the UN to function more efficiently, and people in the Department of Management who were wary of taking on vested interests in the staff unions. This agenda will have to be reinvigorated in future.

The overall reform agenda going on in the UN was highly relevant for OCHA. But the fact that there was a central impetus for reform also provided cover for dealing with a deeper set of problems specific to the office. In 2015 and 2016, OCHA had begun an internal review process in response to a set of internal and external pressures. The organisation had grown in recent years, but in an ad hoc rather than planned way. It had run into financial difficulties when expenditures started to exceed income—95 percent of which was provided through voluntary annual grants from donor countries, rather than through the regular assessed budget contributions from UN member states. By 2017, overspending had nearly exhausted OCHA's reserves. In addition, recent annual surveys of organisations in the sector were critical of the role OCHA was playing, with complaints that it was trying to impose its will on others rather than supporting their efforts.

The review process itself then started to become part of the problem: external consultants were brought in, challenges were described, solutions were mooted but not agreed or acted upon, and unrest grew. Internally, the management was divided and operated in silos; staff enjoyed describing their bosses' failings to a rolling series of outside experts; and the dysfunction communicated itself to outsiders, especially those expected to pay the bills. By early 2017, the donors, led by the Americans and the Swiss—who were generous financiers and thought OCHA's role was important and wanted it to be doing better—were frustrated by inaction. They were demanding that a formal change programme be adopted and implemented. They wanted it to include budget cuts, restructuring, reductions in the size of bloated and confused headquarters teams, more priority for field operations, and refocusing the work of the office on a few core responsibilities. They threatened funding cuts if these changes did not happen. With this impetus, a detailed blueprint was developed, with help from McKinsey consultants and a senior WHO official who was brought in to help the management team drive the work inside the office. The plan was titled *Creating a Better OCHA*. The idea was that it would be presented to the OCHA donors at their regular meeting in June, and they would endorse it and confirm funding. Some senior staff, however, preferring prevarication to implementing unpopular decisions, suggested when my appointment was announced that perhaps I should have the chance to reconsider things rather than being presented with a fait accompli. Consequently, Yasser Baki, the smooth and shrewd OCHA chief of staff who would head my personal office when I started the job and who was devoting a lot of personal energy to moving the change programme forward, contacted me after my appointment was announced and informally asked me what I thought of the plan.

I was not particularly enamoured by everything in the plan. I wanted to see more emphasis on streamlining internal processes that looked inefficient and disempowered junior and mid-level staff, and the plan did not address that issue at all. But I knew a lot of work had gone into it. I thought delay would make things worse. I duly told Yasser I thought the best approach was to adopt and begin to implement the *Creating a Better OCHA* programme. I added that I expected all the senior management team, composed of around a dozen people, to sign up publicly to it. On that basis, the United States hosted the June donor meeting. (I did not attend, though I was given a running commentary by a few people who were there.) The discussion was somewhat fraught, but the programme was endorsed, including a 15 percent funding cut for 2018.

I made a couple of visits to New York with the family in July and August to find and equip an apartment.[1] While there, I took some time to meet some of OCHA's staff informally. They included many of the people who would work in my personal front office. The team was bigger than I thought we needed, so some moved on, but many of those who stayed supported me through most (in some cases all) of my time as ERC. As well as the Anglo-Egyptian chief of staff Yasser, who I knew from an earlier life, there was Rania Abdulrahman, a Sudanese who had grown up in Saudi Arabia and who, as the person in charge of my schedule, had possibly the hardest job in the office. Sofie Karlsson, a polymath fashionista Swede; Daniel Pfister, a tech-savvy, problem-solving Swiss; and Natasha Geber, a nature-loving bibliophile Canadian between them took on the burden of accompanying me on trips and to meetings. They were all clever, hardworking, and emotionally

---

1. One of my ambitions was to be able to walk to work, which I had not done since we moved out of a small flat in central London when we first moved to Africa in the 1990s. We were able to find a great little apartment with views of the East River 10 minutes from the UN buildings on First Avenue, and it proved a good base for the next four years.

intelligent. But they also shared other desirable attributes: a reliable deadpan, necessary when sitting through the ERC's sometimes scratchy interactions with people responsible for creating human misery; a sunny disposition; and excellent banter. Every working hour was consumed with combatting human misery, and private humour was essential to dissipate frustrations and get through the day.

On those same visits, I also had a series of about 20 listening sessions on my own (that is, without any of the managers present) with small groups of staff from all round the world, mostly people from the junior grades of support staff and younger professionals. I explained that I wanted to know the main problems they encountered in doing their jobs and what they thought I should focus on. I said that I would not say anything during the meetings, but they could say whatever they wanted, and I would not be telling anyone. I did not promise I would necessarily act on what they said, but I did want to know what they thought. Hundreds of people showed up for these sessions. (On my last day four years later, when I held an event to say goodbye to all the staff and thank them for what they had done, one recalled these meetings and said that it was the only time that he, as a long-serving OCHA staffer, had been invited to talk to the ERC.) For me, it was a revealing experience. Most people were convincingly passionate about their work and wanted to make a difference; many were frustrated by too many processes that added too little value and took up vast amounts of time. The majority were sceptical that anything would come of the *Creating a Better OCHA* initiative, and they were startlingly scathing about their senior managers. From the staff's perspective, the managers were mostly interested in themselves and the silos they ran, and were psychologically incapable of acting as a team in leading the organisation as a whole. A similar picture came out of the various review exercises OCHA had been through. The McKinsey consultants told me the management situation was worse than they had seen anywhere else. I thought the consultants needed to get out more, but clearly there were significant problems.

One conclusion I drew was that I would need to spend more time than I had anticipated on management issues, and on personally overseeing the change programme. Another was that too much of the reform effort was being done *to* OCHA rather than *by* OCHA. We needed to appoint a change director, someone from inside the organisation who would need to be credible to the staff as genuinely passionate about humanitarian issues and someone I was confident could drive through painful decisions. A third conclusion was that most, if not all, of the senior headquarters staff would have to go. Because the change programme replaced the previous structure with a new one, we would be able to advertise most of the top posts. Existing staff could apply to the openings if they wished, but depending on the circumstances, we might not have to appoint them. In one-to-one meetings with the incumbents over my first few months, I repeatedly emphasised that just as Guterres had decided that the UN as a whole needed new leaders, so too, in my opinion, did OCHA. The more able and mature of the incumbents—several of whom I professionally admired even though they had, often through frustration, contributed to the problems we were trying to solve—saw the need for that change. I was happy to devote time to helping them find new jobs. Inevitably, some were less happy. (One of them told me that although he had put his signature on *Creating a Better OCHA*, he did not agree with it. *Are you really telling me that?* I thought. *Why would I believe anything this person tells me in future?*). Though the UN's archaic personnel systems generally provide employees with a very high degree of protection regardless of their competence, by a series of manoeuvres I was able to get a good new senior team in place over the course of my first year.

On my first paid day in the job, I held a town hall meeting to which all OCHA's 2,300 staff across 50 countries were invited. As well as talking about the global humanitarian situation and what I thought we could do about it, I told them I had been struck by what many of them had said about the state of OCHA while I was preparing to take up the job. *Creating a Better OCHA* had not been my idea or my plan, but I said that I would take responsibility for implementing all the decisions in it, without exception. That included cutting the budget and staff so that we could live within our means. I expected that OCHA would emerge from these reforms a stronger, better-run, and more highly regarded organisation, capable of making a bigger contribution to easing the suffering of people caught up in crises. We would be more accountable, agile, decentralized, effective, and transparent. Above all, though, we had to be more collaborative: both among ourselves inside the office and in our dealings with the rest of the humanitarian system. I tried to address head on the control-freakery problem some of those agencies complained of in OCHA. A good coordinator in our system, I said, has to support, enable, facilitate, and build trust. We are not in a position to tell the larger and more powerful agencies what to do. We have to listen more and talk less. When we are doing more of what the agencies value from us, then we will be more influential.

I also thought it was important to speak publicly about the reform effort we were undertaking—partly to try to shore up donor support and financing, which remained in a parlous state, but also to reinforce inside the office that I was serious about implementing the reform programme. I detected that plenty of people were still hoping the bad news would go away. In the early autumn, I gave a speech in Washington summarizing what I intended to do:

> In OCHA I have inherited an organization full of brilliant, passionate, capable and committed people. We are determined now to build an organization in which they can all do their best work. Based on the reform plan I inherited, we are restructuring to focus on five core functions. Advocacy, coordination, humanitarian financing, information management and policy development. We are building an organizational culture that is collaborative. Our role is to

offer a coordination service. We are not an agency. We are not operational, in the sense that we don't and won't implement programmes ourselves. We also need to be financially sustainable. For too long OCHA has spent more money than it receives in income. Our generous donors—whose voluntary contributions pay for 95 percent of what we do—are clear about what they can provide. We need to adjust to that. This is not about doing more with less. It is about doing less but doing it better. We will become more focused on the things that we do well, the things that our partners want us to do. And let me be clear about one thing. Given the structure of the humanitarian system, OCHA's role is not optional—it is indispensable.

I ended up spending a lot of my first year on internal issues. As a result, my working hours at OCHA were for a while longer than in any other of my 35 years of working life so far. After a short process to identify candidates, we appointed Reena Ghelani, an Australian of South Asian descent and a long-standing OCHA manager who had served in Africa and the Middle East, as the change director. She proved an outstanding choice, and I subsequently appointed her to the most important director job in OCHA, responsible for operations. Reena led an OCHA-wide exercise to explain and establish the new operating model, essentially how different parts of the organisation would interact and collaborate with each other. This exercise was vital to dealing with the entrenched silos. To support her, we established a team of nearly 40 change agents: staff from all levels and all locations who wanted to make a contribution to improving the office. We also benefitted from some high-quality pro bono advice from McKinsey, which had been frustrated by its previous experience with OCHA but now saw a chance to do (and be associated with) something that might work. We set up a small Organisational Development Unit, whose job was to review processes and functions and instil a culture of continuous improvement in office operations. One thing the unit did was to look at the size of the office staff supporting senior managers. It turned out that

10 percent of all headquarters staff were in these front offices, mostly operating as gatekeepers. We cut them all back, starting with mine. Another exercise reviewed the processes by which documents—like draft statements to the Security Council, or briefing notes for meetings with visitors or other senior UN staff—were prepared for senior managers. We discovered that drafts started by junior professional staff passed through more than a dozen other people before reaching the intended user. They often got worse along the way, which was frustrating and morale-sapping for the originator. We cut the chain down to three steps.

The reforms also envisaged OCHA playing a stronger role on humanitarian financing, a point of particular interest to me. As the director, I chose an experienced, capable, and collaborative American, Lisa Carty, who had had a wide-ranging career with the US State Department and the Bill and Melinda Gates Foundation before joining the UN. We established a new humanitarian financing team and began to hire finance professionals, economists, data analysts, and statisticians. We also started to build better links with academics working on these issues and people with experience in banking, insurance, and development finance institutions. (In the next chapter, I will explain what this talented and energetic group of people set about doing.)

The original idea had been to phase in a revised OCHA structure over the course of a year. However, in my first few months we had to finalise a new, smaller budget for 2018, and I concluded the best way to do that was to move straight to the new structure from the start of January and fix any problems that emerged after that. This decision created stresses late in the year and into the first few months of 2018 as the consequences for staff became clear, but it also conveyed the message that we were serious about implementing the change plan.

Another of the internal tensions that needed addressing was the relationship between the OCHA offices in New York and in Geneva. ERCs traditionally had been based in New York, in order to be available to the secretary-general and the Security Council, even though as a practical matter they often spent most of their time travelling. Many agencies with humanitarian responsibilities, including the Red Cross family, the UN's refugee agency, the IOM, and the WHO, were headquartered in Geneva. Having previously run a large organisation with a single headquarters split between two cities—the UK's DFID had headquarters in both London and East Kilbride outside Glasgow—I was familiar with this organisational model. But the OCHA culture had created competing centres of gravity that consumed too much unproductive nervous energy. We moved additional senior staff from New York to Geneva as part of the OCHA change programme, and started a process of decentralizing staff from Geneva to locations like Istanbul, which were better connected to the field operations they were supporting. I was frequently asked who was the head of OCHA in Geneva. No-one, I said: OCHA has one head (me) who worked in many different places. It has a single headquarters in two locations. For some functions, like humanitarian financing, the director is based in Geneva; for others, like human resources, the director is based in New York. I was pleased to be able to appoint an experienced OCHA manager, Ramesh Rajasingham from Sri Lanka, as the director of the coordination division based in Geneva. Gently, but with determination, he worked hard to implement the reforms there. I also made sure I was in Geneva at least once a month throughout my tenure, and we often held major events there, including the launches for flagship reporting products like the annual *Global Humanitarian Overview*.

I tried to get the office to focus on things the wider humanitarian system needed that no-one else could provide. The first was taking responsibility for identifying and quantifying humanitarian need, through both annual exercises for protracted crises and rapid needs assessments when new problems arose. The second was the coordination of costed response plans, which brought together the planned activities of all the UN agencies and the main NGOs. (The Red Cross family ran their own systems, but we tried to ensure informal coordination and shared planning with them wherever possible.) The third area where OCHA had a comparative advantage was on fundraising. We were able to increase the size of the funds OCHA managed, both the central emergency response fund and 19 country-based funds. From a starting point of $1.3 billion in 2016, the money we raised increased to $1.9 billion in 2019. (I will return to how we achieved that increase in the next chapter.) It was disbursed as grants to UN agencies and dozens of NGOs. It represented a significant source of revenue for many agencies and therefore was an important part of OCHA's offer to the members of the Inter-Agency Standing Committee. The other element of our fundraising role, on which I also spent a lot of time, was in organising pledging events seeking resources for particular crises, as described at various points in Part One of the book.

Another service OCHA provided that other agencies valued was in advocacy on behalf of people affected by crises, and negotiations with belligerents to get permission to reach those people. This effort typically involved calling out constant attempts by both malign governments and violent opposition groups to prevent aid reaching people in areas controlled by their opponents. Operational agencies often did not want to stick their heads above this parapet, for fear that their operations would be closed down even further. The agreed division of labour often meant that OCHA and the ERC in particular had to be the one to speak out. We also hired additional staff, often with a military background, to liaise with armed groups (both state forces and others).

One of the best pieces of advice I received before starting the job was that being the ERC was not a popularity contest. If the ERC did not speak up for the interests of people caught up in crises, no-one would. I quickly learned how important the best media organisations were as allies in that part of my job. Many journalists wanted to cover humanitarian stories. I tried to make sure I was always available to talk to the New York–based UN press corps, including staff writers for Reuters, Associated Press, and the other leading news agencies whose copy found its way into hundreds of newspapers in almost every corner of the planet. One of the best investments I made in preparing to become ERC was a day's coaching from an experienced television news anchor, kindly paid for by the Soros Foundation, to improve my ability to get stories across in the concise and informative way journalists and broadcasters need. The OCHA New York media team I inherited were nice but lacked drive and dazzle, and as part of the office restructuring in 2018 and 2019 we were able to bring in people with more star quality. That infusion of fresh thinking quickly translated into better material for journalists and a step up in the volume and quality of our press coverage, which Guterres' press team also noted with enthusiasm. During the pandemic, as I will explain later, it proved invaluable.

OCHA was not short of management problems when I left. There was still not enough rotation of staff between the field and headquarters, with some people holding on to desirable headquarters jobs for years on end. We still needed to be more agile as priorities changed. Yet in important respects, we had created a better OCHA. I was able to bequeath a financial surplus to my successor. The annual survey in which OCHA's partners rated our performance showed higher scores year on year. The organisation was more collaborative; senior managers behaved in a more collegiate way and were taking responsibility for the organisation as a whole rather than only the things they supervised directly. Fewer people spent their days bad-mouthing their colleagues. We had shifted resources from headquarters, cutting staffing in New York and Geneva from 600 to 520 posts and removing some duplication to free up more money for field operations. Processes under our control were more efficient. In particular, we were managing a lot more money through the central emergency response fund and the country funds with negligible increases in overheads. (We did though continue to labour under wasteful bureaucracy imposed by member states and other parts of the UN Secretariat.) And, importantly to me, when Guterres—who as head of the UN refugee agency for 10 years up to 2015 had had his own experience of OCHA—asked other people how we were doing, he got positive feedback. All these things helped a little as we struggled to cope with the scary increase in humanitarian need from one year to the next.

I faced a parallel set of challenges in trying to make the Inter-Agency Standing Committee more effective. I had private one-to-one conversations with all the chief executives who were members of the committee—essentially the heads of all the main humanitarian agencies, and NGO umbrella groups representing many more—before I took up the role. They were a diverse group, including many impressive individuals. Tony Lake, the head of UNICEF when I started, had been the US national security adviser under President Bill Clinton. (He was later succeeded at UNICEF by Henrietta Fore, previously the administrator of the US Agency for International Development.) Tedros Adhanom Ghebreyesus, recently elected as WHO director-general, had been Ethiopia's health minister and then foreign minister. David Beasley, head of the World Food Programme, a person of serious intent who nevertheless found something to laugh about every time he spoke, had previously been the governor of South Carolina. Natalia Kanem, a charismatic Panamanian doctor, ran the UN Population Fund. Michelle Bachelet, who had served two separate terms as president of Chile, was a fount of empathy and practical common sense as the UN High Commissioner for Human Rights for most of my tenure. As Sy, a giant Senegalese with decades of UN experience, deep insight, and a smile as big as his heart was warm, was now secretary-general of the federation of national Red Cross and Red Crescent societies. Peter Maurer, a grizzled former Swiss diplomat and now president of the International Committee of the Red Cross, was as shrewd, patient, and persistent as you would need to be if your job required constant negotiations with despots and warlords to persuade them to treat people in their prisons and torture chambers with more humanity. Filippo Grandi, born in Milan and educated at a Jesuit university in Rome, had had a distinguished 30-year career in the UN and now ran the UN refugee agency.

All 17 members of the Inter-Agency Standing Committee had demanding day jobs. In principle, they agreed that they should collaborate because no one agency could deal with any crisis anywhere without help from others, and the victims needed comprehensive, well-coordinated help. In practice, the agencies were all fighting for the same resources from the same donors. There was a lot of (mostly hidden) competitive tension. A recent review by the Overseas Development Institute had made clear that the members were frustrated with the meetings of the Inter-Agency Standing Committee—including, as several made clear to me in my first discussions with them, the way OCHA was managing them. Agendas were too full of bureaucratic paper-processing, involving signing off on or arguing over (while staff from each agency watched on) documents prepared by subgroups in which the chief executives had little interest. Some committee members told me frankly when I first spoke to them that they were not sure the meetings were a good use of their time.

I decided we needed a different approach. I convened a meeting three weeks after I took up my post, when all the members were in New York for the annual UN meeting of heads of government. The chief executives alone were invited, with their support staff remaining outside the room. I told them I thought OCHA's job was to help and support them, not try to control them. I suggested that in future we should make part of every meeting closed and private to facilitate frank discussion on the major crises and shared problems. I tried to speak as little as possible—not the normal UN approach for senior staff—and asked others to lead off discussions. I took personal responsibility for distilling the main points, anonymizing and diluting them to protect confidences, and sending a brief record round immediately after each meeting so members could pass them round their teams if they wished. These meetings proved valuable—to everyone, I think—for the information we all gleaned, but also in building rapport and a stronger esprit de corps. (In the true acid test, attendance by the chief executives remained very high.)

I also regularly convened subgroups to deal with specific issues where a common approach was needed. I made a point of frequently staying in touch with many of the chief executives individually to check whether they had concerns or wanted help, or just to resolve issues causing grief in one part of the humanitarian system or another. This was one of the aspects of my role as the ERC for which decades of attending and chairing meetings of departments across the British government, as well as earlier international responsibilities I had taken on, stood me in good stead. The reputation of the committee improved, which was reflected in requests from several additional UN bodies to be allowed to join. I headed those off because I thought the group was already too big and would be less effective if it grew further, but I found other ways to help some of the organisations who had wanted to join.

There were a parallel set of issues on coordination in each country in which humanitarian agencies were working. Coordination was organised by the UN's resident coordinator, who under the Guterres reforms reported through the deputy secretary-general to the secretary-general. Where there was a long-lasting humanitarian crisis or a large new emergency, they were also designated as humanitarian coordinator, in which guise they reported to me. This dual reporting system generally worked fine, but in places where most of the UN's work was as a practical matter humanitarian, it was essential to have the right coordinator. In some cases where new problems arose and we thought the resident coordinator needed bolstering—as, for example, in Venezuela in 2019 and Tigray in 2021—we appointed deputy humanitarian coordinators to take responsibility for emergency operations. Humanitarian coordination roles in places like Afghanistan, South Sudan, Syria, and Yemen are exceptionally demanding. They require not just expertise but reservoirs of patience, determination, resilience, and courage to stand up to frequently obstreperous people in powerful positions and persuade them that even their opponents should be treated with humanity and receive assistance when they needed it to survive. As in every walk of life, a few of the humanitarian coordinators I worked with were prima donnas or charlatans, but most were committed and capable, and they included some of the most impressive people I came across in the UN. Most days I spoke to some of them, and one of the main things I wanted the OCHA country offices to do was support and help them.

As humanitarian needs have grown over the past decade, the strain on this apparatus has increased. While the humanitarian sector has become a lot larger, with 25,000 jobs advertised for international staff in 2020, a commensurate investment is needed to build the management and leadership skills to enable it to perform as well as it needs to. Towards the end of my tenure, the US government offered to fund a humanitarian leadership programme organised through OCHA to build more capacity for the future. It took time to get it off the ground, and the pandemic slowed things down, but sustaining effort on this programme would be an investment with high returns. Humanitarian crises are not going away. Whether they are well managed makes a big difference.

EIGHT

Reforming Humanitarian Finance

IN MARCH 2021, LATE AT NIGHT from my small apartment in Manhattan, I spent several hours in a video call with villagers from Kurigram District in northern Bangladesh, not far from the border with Assam in India. Every year in recent memory, their homes had been flooded during the monsoon season, threatening their health, safety, and their few belongings. Najma, a 15-year-old student, told me how the floods made basic hygiene impossible for young women like her. Aklima, a 27-year-old with a small son, said her husband's income as an agricultural day labourer disappears in the flood season. Rupali described how her chronically sick daughter became even more vulnerable when their home was inundated and how difficult it was to elevate her bed above the water. For years, the government and aid agencies in Bangladesh have offered people like this help after disaster struck. Help in the aftermath is better than no help at all. But the floods are predictable. Why not take action in anticipation of them? One of the main things I tried to do at the UN was move the humanitarian system from a primarily reactive approach to one that acts faster, earlier, and in advance of predictable events. I was talking to the villagers of Kurigram at the beginning of their new day because for the past two years we had been piloting the provision of help before the floods for people whose homes we knew would be affected. They had a lot to say about the subject. But it boiled down to a simple, repeated message: Acting before the event is a whole lot better. "The best way to help is to give us cash. And do it fast."

Disasters and emergencies are predictable. We may not know exactly when and where the next one will be, but we know that droughts, earthquakes, floods, hurricanes, cyclones, and storms are a fact of life and, linked to climate change, are on the rise. The traditional approach to humanitarian crises has been to watch disaster and tragedy build—whether from famines, wars, storms, or disease—and then gradually decide, normally driven by public and political reaction to media coverage, that we need to respond, then to mobilise money and organisations to help, and then after that to start to get help to the people who need it.

That is a reactive approach. It saves many lives. But it is slower, and hence less humane and more expensive, than it needs to be. It would be better to take an anticipatory approach, where we plan in advance for the next crises. If a poor farmer knows that her seeds will not produce a harvest because of an imminent drought in her area, why would we not give her drought-resistant seeds, instead of waiting for her family to starve and her children to show up malnourished in a clinic? If we know that cholera is likely to break out in a particular location, would it not make sense to remind people to wash their hands, and make sure there are clean water sources and enough hydration medicine at the local clinic, instead of waiting until people are infected and fall ill?

I am talking here not about preventing crises in the sense of stopping them from happening at all, such as by diplomacy and mediation to resolve disputes before they dissolve into conflict, or investing in irrigation to reduce dependence on rain-fed agriculture in drought-prone places. Naturally, I am in favour of those things wherever possible. Anticipatory action in the humanitarian sphere, however, is about acting as soon as we know there will be a crisis, but before it actually strikes. It is about predicting disasters before they arrive and having a response plan with money available in advance to pay for it.

In developed countries, that is what happens. People take out insurance policies against emergencies. Governments do contingency planning and practice drills. Why are the same concepts not part of the routine approach to helping more vulnerable countries? For one thing, we have not previously had the data and tools that now allow us to predict many crises. (Weather models, for example, can now predict the path of storms days ahead of their arrival.) For another thing, it can be hard to mobilise the political will to act until we all see the suffering on our screens. Moreover, bureaucratic inertia and a misguided tendency to act only at the very last minute mitigate against anticipatory action.

My conviction that the humanitarian system would be much better if it behaved more consistently in anticipatory rather than reactive mode was informed partly by my training as an economist and an accountant. (There are, I found, surprisingly few financially literate people in senior positions in humanitarian agencies.) It was magnified by my experience of the world's worst-ever Ebola outbreak, in West Africa, which dominated my working life as the permanent secretary of DFID in late 2014 and 2015. The signs of trouble were evident in March and April 2014. Had there been a bit more money ($10 million probably would have done it), a few more medical organisations like Médecins Sans Frontières in place, and a better understanding in the countries concerned that addressing the problem early would have saved many lives and prevented much economic damage, the outbreak could have been brought under control quite quickly. But because it was allowed to get out of control, it developed into a global threat, with cases appearing in Europe and the United States as well as Africa in the autumn of 2014. It sent shivers through global stock markets. The ultimate cost of dealing with the outbreak ran into billions of dollars. It required the mobilization of thousands of international public servants, including from the US and British militaries, working alongside their West African counterparts. By the time the outbreak had been contained, more than 11,000 people had died, including over 800 West African health workers. Of course, as we were to learn in 2020, that was small beer compared to what could happen.

A first step towards a more anticipatory approach in crisis-prone poor countries is to make greater use of disaster risk insurance. In high-income countries, almost half of natural hazard costs are covered by insurance policies issued by private companies. That is not the case in poorer countries, which on average have just 5 percent coverage.

In December each year, OCHA publishes a major report, the *Global Humanitarian Overview*, setting out likely humanitarian problems across the globe for the following year, together with high-level response plans and details of the resources needed to implement them. The overview is followed up with detailed country plans, which for the major crises (Syria, Yemen, and others) are the subject of international fundraising meetings convened by the UN. The overview has in recent years developed a good track record in forecasting overall needs, though every year a number of new, unpredicted problems also arise. In 2019 the unexpected crises included the Ebola outbreak in the east of the Democratic Republic of Congo, in 2020 the coronavirus pandemic, and in 2021 the conflict and resulting famine in northern Ethiopia.

In 2018, my colleagues at OCHA estimated that 20 to 30 percent of the needs we identified in that year's overview could in principle be met through insurance. Interestingly, insurance companies like Swiss Re and Munich Re, asking the same question, reached roughly the same answer. The main kinds of disaster for which insurance can help are weather-related events—droughts, floods, and storms—but it also can cover some disease-related problems. Insurance providers are understandably wary of offering coverage for conflict-related problems, given that they arise from deliberate human decisions.

Climate change means weather-related natural disasters are becoming more frequent, intense, and destructive. In 2018, the total economic losses as a result of climatic disasters amounted to $165 billion. Insurance covered half of that. But because the poorest people and the most fragile countries are underinsured, expanding coverage for them could make a major difference in preventing shocks from becoming humanitarian crises. Insurance provides fast, predictable payouts. It also makes people more aware of risk. Whether the policyholder is a country, a business owner, or a family, buying insurance boils down to deciding that the cost of coverage is cheaper than footing the bill when disaster hits. Insurance markets only work when people trust that the policy they buy will be honoured. In many of the poorest countries, where institutions, contract enforcement, and property rights are weak and the rule of law patchy, insurance markets are correspondingly underdeveloped. But government action can address this problem. At the national level, governments can buy insurance. Sovereign risk pools, through which countries collaborate with each other to take out similar policies, can help reduce the cost of coverage.

For instance, the Caribbean Catastrophe Risk Insurance Facility set up in 2007 now offers policies to 21 Caribbean states for tropical cyclones, earthquakes, and excess rainfall. The government of the Bahamas received a payout of $13 million from its policy within days of Hurricane Dorian in 2019. The Pacific Catastrophe Risk Insurance Company, owned by five countries and supported by the World Bank, offers similar help to countries in that region. In 2018 the small Pacific island of Tonga received a payout after Cyclone Gita, the most intense storm ever recorded there.

Similar models have been developed for food crises. One important new initiative I tried to support is African Risk Capacity, an African Union–led financial entity supported by the African Development Bank and donor countries. It shares the risk of severe drought through a continental risk pool. Its policies pay out when satellite data says that not enough rain has fallen. It is also developing products for river flooding and tropical cyclones. An important feature of African Risk Capacity's approach is that it goes beyond the tenets of decent insurance policies, which provide automatic and rapid payouts once the covered event occurs. These policies are also conditional on the country using the funds to implement a preagreed contingency plan that targets the most vulnerable. In other words, countries do not get the coverage unless they have developed a response plan for the potential problem. Those arrangements help speed up the response when disaster strikes, because the plan is already in place. Up to 2019, African Risk Capacity made payouts for eight countries. One package, funding drought response in Senegal, Malawi, Mauritania, and Niger, totalled $34 million, helping two million people with food, water, and livelihoods.

Governments can do the same thing within their own countries. Since 2010, the government of Kenya has offered index-based livestock insurance for pastoralists. The policy pays out automatically once satellites detect that available forage is becoming too scarce for animals to survive. Pastoralists can therefore protect their animals before they starve or become sick. The insurance here, in other words, provides not just the resources to act but also the signal that action is necessary. A similar initiative, Global Parametrics, backed by the British and German governments, has been working on an insurance scheme potentially protecting four million people in Africa and Asia from climate-related threats to their livelihoods.

The great advantage of insurance is that it is predictable and fast. It also provides an opportunity to bring private sector resources and skills into disaster response. I spent quite a bit of time as ERC trying to encourage insurance companies to dip their toes a bit further into this water. Every January, three hours from Zurich in the Swiss ski resort of Davos, the World Economic Forum brings together thousands of executives from private sector companies, heads of government and their ministers, celebrities, and senior staff from international organisations like the UN, universities, NGOs, and the media for a week's conflab on the issues of the day. It is the ultimate talking shop. I had never been before I joined the UN, but the ERC had a standing invitation, so I took it up. My first conclusion was that Klaus Schwab, a business professor from Geneva, and his wife Hilda, who started the World Economic Forum, were geniuses. You would have to be geniuses to get the global elite to give up a week every year to slip and slide their way in their business attire around the treacherous frozen pathways of a ski resort several hours drive, from the nearest international airport. (Heads of government, billionaire tycoons, and important royals are allowed to arrive in Davos from Zurich by helicopter. Mere ministers and millionaires have to brave the roads.) Most of the meetings and events I went to at Davos added little, I thought, to the humanitarian endeavour. But some of the conversations with executives of the large global insurance companies, who are brought together in an insurance and development forum sponsored by the UN, seemed to have potential for something more consequential.

Generally, the initiatives trying to break new ground in this area are small scale. When Hurricane Maria hit Dominica in September 2017, the damage, mostly to housing and the electricity system, was estimated by the EU, UN, and World Bank at more than $900 million. The government's insurance policy from the Caribbean facility paid out $19 million. Much of the damage was to private property, but the payout was nevertheless tiny in relation to costs that would have to be met through the public purse.

The cost of enhanced coverage makes policies unaffordable for some people and some governments. Consequently, payout amounts are currently relatively small in relation to the damage done. A larger guaranteed payout would promote a faster and ultimately cheaper recovery from major disaster. Caribbean and Pacific storms appear to be getting more frequent and destructive. Numerous countries could find themselves in the path of one, but in any particular season most will not. Development banks like the World Bank and the Asian Development Bank would find good value for money in subsidising small countries' access to enlarged versions of the current insurance products, and, together with other donors, in being willing to subsidise the premium payments as well.

But beyond that, there were two other areas in relation to insurance where I was particularly keen to see progress. First, more insurance products that pay out earlier, ahead of a shock. Instead of compensating after the fact for a loss, would it not be better to pay out earlier to enable policyholders to mitigate the impact of a forthcoming shock?

Second, more insurance products that incentivise reducing and managing risk. To give an analogy, young people seeking car insurance in the United Kingdom can obtain cheaper premiums if they have speed restriction devices put in their vehicles. That arrangement works for insurers because it leads to fewer and smaller accidents and therefore payouts. More insurance policies for crisis-prone countries could be written to require advance planning for disaster response as a condition of any payout.

Even where pre-disaster payouts would be possible, policies currently still only cover actual or predicted loss after the event. (Life insurance policies in rich countries, by contrast, sometimes pay out before death, for example in the case of terminal illnesses.) A truly anticipatory insurance policy is yet to be developed at either individual or sovereign levels. I raised this issue with senior industry leaders in Davos in January 2020, and OCHA staff pursued discussions after that. Despite interest from the insurance and development forum sponsored by the UN to promote this kind of idea, insurance companies are currently hesitant to commit capital and staff time to bringing an anticipatory insurance policy to market in the absence of guaranteed market demand. The pandemic obviously has not helped.

A different way of bringing private capital into the same problem is through Catastrophe Bonds. They are another instrument that provides cash to governments immediately after a disaster—like an earthquake above 7.5 on the Richter scale. Institutional investors buying the bond are essentially betting that such a disaster will not occur. Typically, a third-party company is set up to issue the bond, make low-risk investments to grow the capital, and collect a premium from the government that is often less expensive than buying insurance. If things go the investors' way, they recover their capital in full, plus the interest generated, plus the government's premium. If a disaster happens, investors lose their capital, which goes as an instant payout to the government. Mexico, which has a history of earthquakes and hurricanes, is one of the market makers for this kind of product. UNICEF and some of the insurance companies OCHA worked with in Davos have recently developed a catastrophe bond dedicated to cyclones, with an expected total payout of $100 million over 3 years.

Another innovation with potential for greater use is the introduction of disaster clauses into states' general borrowing on the international capital markets. When it restructured its national debt in 2018–19, Barbados exchanged old debt it had issued for approximately $5 billion of new government bonds, which included clauses introducing payment holidays following major disasters. The concept is that when an independent organisation, like the WHO or a meteorological agency, declares that a natural disaster has occurred, debt service payments are instantly suspended for two years and are instead added to the end of the bond term. This reshuffling immediately frees up money to use in responding to the emergency. These instruments could be used for pandemics, potentially, as well as weather events or earthquakes. They are particularly useful for countries that have affordable access to the capital markets but are too rich to be eligible for the cheapest money from multilateral development banks. Interestingly, the cost to Barbados of the disaster clause—which one might think would make their debt less attractive to lenders—appears to have been low. One of the main attractions of instruments like this is that the financial benefit in time of disaster is automatic and instant. It is a better arrangement than time-consuming negotiations with creditors or handing round the cap for humanitarian aid grants.

Another idea that has attracted interest is humanitarian impact bonds. These are a variant of social impact bonds, which have generated much hype and excitement in some public policy fora over the past decade. The basic concept is that investors lend money on the basis that the return they receive is dependent on preidentified social outcomes being achieved. The idea is that private sector disciplines and capabilities can overcome what is sometimes perceived as public sector sloppiness. The only case study so far in the humanitarian world is an initiative launched by the International Committee of the Red Cross in 2017. They issued a five-year bond for $25 million, which was bought by a group of private investors. The investors will get their money back, with interest (which turns out to be around 7 percent a year) if the Red Cross successfully completes a physical rehabilitation programme for thousands of disabled people in Nigeria, Mali, and the Democratic Republic of Congo.

So the investors have lent the money and the Red Cross is spending it. Someone surely has to pay it back? Yes: the group of donors underwriting the project. They include the Belgian, British, and Swiss governments. The good news for them is that they don't have to pay up if the Red Cross fails to deliver what has been agreed. The bad news is that they are essentially borrowing money for the project at a much higher price than they pay for their general government borrowing.

This concept has turned out to be one of those ideas that looks too good to be true because it actually is. It is a good deal for the investors, who can be pretty sure of their return and enjoy the kudos of being associated with better lives for thousands of disabled people. The Red Cross has a strong incentive to deliver what it has promised because it faces a financial penalty and blow to its reputation if it does not. But the flip side is that the initiative is too expensive for the borrowers to want to replicate it on a significant scale. It was not wrong to try the experiment, but it is important to learn the lessons from it.

The potential role of the private sector has not yet been fully exploited in humanitarian financing. However, it is important not to overstate that role. For the private sector, there needs to be a financial return. In many of the places where humanitarian needs are most acute, and especially where the underlying cause is conflict, there is limited scope for combining financial return with humanitarian response. Most lifesaving work in these places will still need to be paid for by grants, or very cheap loans of the sort that can only be offered by publicly subsidized organisations like the World Bank.

Most governments organise contingency financing for themselves through their national budget process. But many poorer countries are unable, unwilling, or too fiscally constrained to do this to a sufficient degree.

Preagreed contingency financing from the multilateral system—especially the multilateral development banks led by the World Bank, in which all countries are shareholders—can give countries access to grants or loans at concessional rates to finance emergency response and reconstruction. There is a lot of scope for these multilateral lending institutions to help with crisis management. Historically, however, the development banks have not seen humanitarian crises as a priority area for their work. Help from them has been available at much too small a scale, and sometimes with too high an opportunity cost, to play the role it could in supporting responses to humanitarian disasters. As the ERC, I tried to help remedy that issue.

One of the earliest initiatives we supported was a famine action mechanism, the brainchild of Jim Kim in his latter years as the president of the World Bank. Drawing on similar proposals he made after the 2014–15 Ebola outbreak in West Africa, he took as the starting point the struggle humanitarian agencies had faced in raising resources to stave off famine in Nigeria, Somalia, South Sudan, and Yemen in 2017.

At the annual heads of government meeting at the UN in September 2018, Guterres and Kim, together with other participants including Google, Microsoft, and Amazon, hosted a meeting to launch the famine action mechanism. The concept was to use predictive data analytics to trigger financing for early action when the risk of famine first emerges. It was a classic example of the anticipatory approach, leveraging financing and swift action based on preagreed plans to avert famine and food insecurity, in contrast to the traditional approach of launching appeals only when the crisis was underway. The Bank in particular was interested in building analytical models to use to trigger responses, and attaching some of its own resources for instant release when the triggers were met. The financial and economic issues were clear cut. Studies show that investing earlier could save lives and money by allowing cheaper responses (such as cash or food aid) to protect people before they were so malnourished that only expensive therapeutic feeding programmes could save them. The long-term economic rationale was also compelling: famine raises child mortality, increases stunting, and impairs cognitive development, all of which have life-long ramifications. I was hopeful that the famine action mechanism could make a real difference. But the Bank's strong engagement in it unfortunately fell foul of the "not invented here" rule I have observed frequently in public organisations, in which good ideas pushed by one leader (irrespective of their utility) are dropped by their successors. When Jim Kim left the Bank, their enthusiasm waned.

We were, however, able to collaborate with them on other ideas in the same vein. One of the proposals was that the World Bank—because it is a bank—should have a comparative advantage in the provision of contingency finance. Just as private companies need credit lines to access money at short notice, and many households find it useful to agree overdraft facilities with their banks to cover unexpected short-term needs, so some countries (especially those with limited access to the international capital markets) have a similar need.

The development banks lend to their member countries. The World Bank, for example, sells bonds—in other words, borrows money—at commercial rates on the international capital markets, and then lends the money to its members. The members can borrow from the bank at a cheaper rate than the country can obtain itself from the capital markets. One form of that borrowing is a deferred drawdown option: negotiating the provision of the money and then using it at a time of the borrower's choosing. This concept has been extended in recent years to the bank's poorer countries, which receive cheaper loans and sometimes grants subsidized by donor contributions to the Bank's concessional lending arm, the International Development Association.

In May 2018, the government of Kenya used part of its entitlement to resources from the International Development Association for a new product, a Catastrophe Draw Down Option. It gave Kenya an entitlement to an instant $200 million in the event of a disaster. This was the first time International Development Association funds had been used in this way. There was an opportunity cost for the Kenyan government, because it reduced somewhat the other concessional resources it could get from the World Bank. But this arrangement means that Kenya now has an instant right to a payout when needed. Similar Catastrophe Draw Down Options provided $1.2 billion at the start of the COVID-19 crisis, and that money was some of the fastest-disbursed funds.

This is a form of contingency financing: the deal is that the money is available instantly at the request of the borrower, but that if it is not needed, it does not have to be drawn and therefore no repayment is required. This approach means that financing can arrive in days, rather than the months that it can take to mobilise funds from the donors or institutions at the moment. Because it is a large institution with a strong balance sheet, the World Bank could provide this kind of financing on a much larger scale. In some cases, it might never be used; but its availability would be worth a lot to disaster-prone countries.

The development banks can take a similar approach by earmarking resources for crisis response without preagreeing access to the money for specific countries, but simply holding it for release to any member struck by disaster. There are a number of new examples of this arrangement. Following the cyclones in the Pacific in early 2018, the Asian Development Bank provided a contingency financing payout, along with the abovementioned insurance payments, to affected countries. The Inter-American Development Bank has a similar contingent credit facility for natural disasters. In the wake of Hurricane Dorian, it gave the Bahamas a $100 million loan. In that case, the loan agreement explicitly encourages the government to use the funds for better future risk management and emergency preparedness and risk transfers.

The World Bank has in recent years recognised a need to improve its support for fragile and conflict-affected member countries that are particularly prone to humanitarian disasters. For the first time, in 2019 it developed a strategy for supporting those countries, calling on help from an advisory group it asked me to join. Some senior people in the World Bank have recognised that it should develop different policies and products for the most fragile countries, as well as hiring more staff with an aptitude and skills for working in tougher places, and adopting new processes that would allow it to act faster and more flexibly.

One of the most important developments in crisis financing in recent years has been the creation of the World Bank's crisis response window in the International Development Association. Between 2017 and 2020, it made $2 billion available. This facility was used to help people in Mozambique, Malawi, and Zimbabwe in the wake of the destruction wrought by Cyclone Idai in 2019. The money was intended to help re-establish water supply, rebuild damaged infrastructure, restore agricultural livelihoods, prevent disease, and scale up social protection. The current system for the crisis response window involves negotiating response packages as each crisis appears, which takes time. A natural next step for the most clearly vulnerable countries is to put the arrangements in place in advance. Obvious candidates would be Nepal for earthquake risk, and Somalia and Ethiopia for drought risk.

One of the things that came out of the work on the World Bank's 2019 strategy for fragile and conflict-affected countries was a further evolution of the crisis response window, in particular to provide faster assistance and change it from an instrument of last resort to an instrument of first resort. For the period 2021–23, it has set aside $500 million for early action through an early response facility as part of the crisis response window. In Somalia, the UN and the World Bank have developed an anticipatory action framework to respond to out-of-the-ordinary droughts. The idea is that this mechanism will release finance when a drought is predicted to lead to an intensification of humanitarian need, as was the case in 2010–11 and 2016–17. Funds will be released, for example, to distribute drought-tolerant seeds, provide supplementary fodder for livestock, and rehabilitate water points.

In a related World Bank initiative, the establishment of the Global Risk Financing Facility, with additional money from Germany and the United Kingdom, is also helping governments scale up risk financing and early action. In Malawi, for example, a country that has been experiencing increasing climate-change-related volatility in the maize harvest that feeds most of its population, this facility has provided a grant of $21 million to develop a safety net that can be scaled up and down according to the vagaries of the harvest.

All these initiatives are a step in the right direction, but they need to be expanded, because one of the reasons why the world's most vulnerable countries are falling further behind is that they are continuously knocked back by crises. The World Bank is stronger on analysing and developing new ideas than on carrying them out them successfully. Its contingency financing windows disburse slowly, and normally it must rely on the institutions of the country being supported to implement its programmes. In acute humanitarian crises, those institutions are often nonexistent or not supporting the most vulnerable people. The Bank needs to revisit its internal processes to recognise that fast money is worth more than slow money in dealing with crises, that announcements of willingness to assist are worth less than help actually reaching people, and that sometimes it needs other intermediaries—the Red Cross, NGOs, and even the UN—as partners. The Bank's shareholders should, on the basis of what has been learned in recent years, instruct it to play a much stronger role in crisis response in the most vulnerable countries. They have not done so. This was a source of great frustration during the COVID-19 crisis, as I will describe later.

———— ❖ ————

In addition, I thought, the main humanitarian agencies—the membership of the Inter-Agency Standing Committee in particular—needed to do more to promote anticipatory action from within the resources they controlled. This was not straightforward. Around 90 percent of the money we raised each year for UN-coordinated humanitarian responses came as earmarked contributions to specific appeals such as for Syria and Yemen. That money cannot be redirected into new problems—and nor should it be.

Much of the money that is available for first responses to new problems is held in the UN's central emergency response fund. Set up as a voluntary fund supported by member states after the 2004 Indian Ocean tsunami, it had been stuck at around $450 million a year for more than a decade, even as needs for it had grown dramatically. A year or so before I was appointed, the UN General Assembly adopted a target to increase the fund to $1 billion a year, still based on voluntary contributions. When I arrived, there was no game plan for how to raise the extra $500 million. It seemed to me that member states would need good reasons to contribute more. I thought we could make a compelling case for using the fund to help move the humanitarian system towards a more anticipatory approach.

There was some support for this goal, for example from pilots on forecast-based financing run by the Red Cross with money from Germany. There was also evidence inside the UN itself from the Food and Agriculture Organisation's forecast-based financing model. These funds were used to reduce the impact of severe drought on pastoralists in Ethiopia, Kenya, and Somalia in late 2016. Response triggers were based on the analysis of socioeconomic, health, and climate indicators, as well as data on factors like milk production, stunting rates in children, pasture coverage, and soil moisture levels. An impact study of the intervention showed that for every $1 the Food and Agriculture Organisation invested in the project to keep livestock healthy, pastoralist households received a cash benefit of $3.50. And there was experience from the central emergency response fund's own activities to draw on. A review of the added value of the fund's response to the 2016 El Niño–induced drought problems in parts of Africa found that its grants were some of the first international funding available, and that they catalysed increased donor support. However, the review also found that the fund would have had a greater impact had it kickstarted action before the humanitarian needs became glaring.

There was, as often with new ideas, some internal and external resistance to using the fund to scale up anticipatory financing. But this reluctance was overcome as it became clear that this was something that appealed to the fund's largest donors, especially Germany and the United Kingdom. The new team we had hired in OCHA's humanitarian financing division had strong backgrounds in economic and financial analysis, and they helped develop analytical models to allow us reliably to predict new humanitarian problems before they crystallised. For 2020 and 2021, I carved out a dedicated allocation of $140 million from the central emergency response fund for a suite of possible anticipatory projects covering a variety of shocks across different regions. This allocation guaranteed that money would be released instantly and automatically as soon as data revealed that warning thresholds had been crossed.

One of these pilots addressed food security risks caused by drought in Somalia. When the data revealed in June 2020 that the problem was imminent, we implemented the preagreed response plan. The central emergency response fund automatically released $15 million to provide 1.3 million people across Somalia with assistance in the sectors of health, nutrition, water, and sanitation with the aim of mitigating loss of livelihoods, deterioration of nutrition, and disease outbreaks. Part of the aim was to generate evidence to corroborate the value of anticipatory action. One finding in Somalia was that the preparatory work reduced the time needed for funding to be released by a factor of two to three.

Another pilot tackled the annual floods mentioned by the Bangladeshi villagers I had talked to in early 2021. In early July 2020, it had become clear who would be badly affected by that year's floods. The trigger to initiate a response from the fund was reached on 4 July 2020. Money was then allocated within four hours, allowing agencies to start delivering assistance to 220,000 people straight away, even though the waters had not yet reached the victims' homes. The London-based Centre for Disaster Protection independently reviewed this pilot, and confirmed that "through effective coordination and encouragement, even with a very short turnaround, partners took a major step in scaling up anticipatory action . . . demonstrating what it takes and the potential human impact." The review also confirmed that the pilot demonstrated "the feasibility of scaling up anticipatory action."

More than 10,000 beneficiaries and a control group were interviewed as part of an independent evaluation, again confirming the value of the approach. (There are surprisingly few high-quality independent evaluations of humanitarian responses: funding more of them would probably encourage faster uptake of validated ideas.)

A similar story involves the response to recurrent outbreaks of bubonic plague in Madagascar. In 2017, the Pasteur Institute predicted that the following year would see more than 2,700 cases of plague, one of the largest outbreaks in decades. We provided $1 million from the central emergency response fund to preempt it. Only 250 cases were finally reported and there was no spread to other countries—unlike the previous year.

On the basis of evidence collected on pilots so far, the rationale for anticipatory action has been corroborated: the approach does indeed lead to faster and cheaper responses. And there are additional benefits. Because they received help before the peak flooding began, beneficiaries in Bangladesh were empowered to prepare themselves and face the crisis on their own terms. Women and girls who received dignity or hygiene kits were more likely to access healthcare and continue their education. Beneficiaries reported high satisfaction rates, not least on the quality and timing of the help they got, which they said translated into significant quality-of-life improvements, better mental health, and reduced financial stress. None of this is very surprising, but it ought to motivate a much larger shift towards anticipatory action in humanitarian response.

Obviously, in order to act ahead of problems, you need to be able to predict them accurately. In general terms, it is well understood that droughts can lead to food crises, but it is harder to say exactly when and precisely where droughts will happen and exactly who will be most vulnerable. Good, reliable models can help answer these questions. We tried to develop new analytical models to help with this problem, going beyond the pilot projects for the central emergency response fund and collaborating with scientists and technology companies.

Predictive analytics can be drawn from expected but also unexpected places. For years, livestock sales have been used in assessing risk: people sell their animals if they think they will not survive water and pasture shortages, in an effort to get some value from them before it is too late. Some reporting from Somalia suggests that when a community is on the brink of food insecurity, mobile phone data usage is one of the first things to decline. This strong correlation means that it should be possible to use data from mobile phone companies to predict when we need to scale up social safety nets for vulnerable communities.

Work done by US scientists supported by the United Kingdom's DFID (before its abolition in 2020) identified new ways of predicting cholera outbreaks. It may now be possible to predict a first person becoming infected up to four weeks ahead of time, within a geographic area smaller than 250 meters by 250 meters anywhere in the world. OCHA developed a partnership with the Universities of Maryland and Florida to validate the global cholera risk model they developed with NASA funding. The model predicts the onset of cholera one month in advance by looking at data on environmental conditions, infrastructure, and human behaviour. Combining evidence from the model with rainfall forecasts might make it possible to predict significant disease outbreaks more reliably. Such predictions could help prevent the recurrence of the kind of cholera outbreak that infected more than a million people in Yemen in 2018. The next stage is to link the risk signals of the model to the release of money from the central emergency response fund (or elsewhere) to agencies like the WHO and UNICEF, which can put in place public communications campaigns and water, sanitation, and health interventions that can prevent an outbreak.

In December 2017, António Guterres and I opened a new OCHA Centre for Humanitarian Data, partly funded by the Dutch government, in The Hague. One of the aims was to support the development of new models and to run independent and impartial peer reviews to assess them against ethical, technical, and humanitarian standards. In 2020, we obtained a grant from the Rockefeller Foundation to accelerate this work. Using the capabilities that had been built, we were then able, in collaboration with leading universities, to model how the COVID-19 pandemic might play out in countries with large humanitarian problems, including by producing the first rigorous predictive model for the spread of the coronavirus in Afghanistan. Initiatives of this sort, which are relatively cheap but still hard to fund, have a lot of potential that remains mostly unexploited.

Pilots of the sort I have described are improving our understanding of how best to implement an anticipatory approach. For one thing, a lot of scientific models promise to predict humanitarian needs, but most of them are not independently reviewed or assessed against their usefulness for humanitarian action. A lot of data is used for advocacy. We need to be more rigorous in using data for better decision-making. Another point is that some people would like a scientifically perfect method to trigger the release of finance, whereas a mindset focusing on the balance of probabilities and risk mitigation might be a better approach. Otherwise, you risk waiting too long in the search for perfection and find you have missed the best opportunity to curtail the problem. A different consideration arises from how we respond to the fact that models can be incorrect. We can be paralyzed by the fear of getting it wrong, yet research finds that actions based on false alarms could be taken up to 60 percent of the time before the total costs would outweigh those of a single late response.

Anticipating problems is one thing; recognising their likely duration is another. Most humanitarian crises I dealt with had their origins in conflict. We know that in today's world, crises caused by conflict typically last a long time, and require sustained responses. The average conflict now lasts twice as long as in 1990. In six countries, we have had annual UN humanitarian appeals for 13 years in a row. Yet responses to crises which we know will be long lasting are still financed as though they are short-term problems.

An annualized response involves short-term procurement, short-term grants, and constant turnover of staff because their employment contracts cannot exceed the period for which funding is available. This all makes for a more expensive, more fragile, and less effective response for people affected by crises. Senior staff spend a huge proportion of their time chasing the next funding grant and negotiating with donors, and need large support teams to help with that work. Ultimately, of course, the donors end up paying for all this. The upshot is that overhead costs are higher and therefore the proportion of the available money being used to help the intended beneficiaries is lower than it need be.

The obvious solution is for funders to provide longer-term grants. Some donors say this is difficult, given the rules that legislatures set for spending on humanitarian aid. However, my experience talking to legislators in many countries was that when the issue was raised, they generally were open to reviewing the approach they took. Governments, after all, are well acquainted with long-term commitments in their domestic spending.

At a global summit on humanitarian issues in 2016, the participants agreed that donors would try to provide longer-term funding. We made a degree of progress. Between 2016 and 2018, the 11 countries providing more than 80 percent of humanitarian assistance through UN-coordinated response plans increased their multiyear funding from $2.7 billion to $4.8 billion. Nevertheless, a more significant shift is needed.

When asked what help they need, people caught up in humanitarian crises always say two things. First, they want protection from violence, which is what causes most displacement in the first case. Second, they want material support to get back on their own feet—and they would always prefer to have that support in cash, so they have maximum control and choice over their own lives.

Until recently, however, almost all the help people have received in humanitarian crises has been in kind rather than cash: if they are lucky, they might be given food, water, shelter, and medical services. All the decisions are made by the provider. The provision of assistance in kind has historically been the norm because some donors have preferred to contribute to humanitarian crises by providing commodities rather than cash. The United States in particular has given huge volumes of wheat and maize as food aid, grown on highly productive farms in the country's Midwest region and frequently distributed through the World Food Programme. As time passed, this practice provoked increased controversy, owing to concerns over the distortionary effects on agriculture in developing countries (as free imported grain undermines the market for local producers). It is now generally accepted that in most circumstances, it is preferrable to have agencies resourced through financial contributions rather than the provision of commodities. The logical next step, when agencies receive their income in cash, is for them to pass it on in the same form to their beneficiaries. But it has been a bit more complicated than that.

One of the most interesting areas of innovation in the work of international development agencies over the past 20 years has been in helping poor countries establish social safety nets. These schemes have been inspired by the way in which developed countries, as they grew richer over the last century, have created social security systems to protect their most vulnerable citizens—the old, the infirm, the jobless—and guarantee people minimal entitlements to food or income. Up to the 1990s, the received wisdom in international development agencies was that poor countries could not afford such systems. The thought was that it was better to help developing countries build the infrastructure that would enable their economies to grow faster and create more jobs. In time, greater employment levels would increase the tax base, making public and welfare services more affordable. At the turn of the 2000s, the combination of economic development in poorer countries and democratisation (which meant that politicians had to care more about their poorest voters), as well as the creation of social protection systems in Brazil and Mexico (which other countries started to emulate), began to change this way of thinking. Often set up with international support, good social protection schemes can be scaled up and down as needed when disaster strikes, whether the crisis is a flood, a drought, or another problem. Countries like Bangladesh, Ethiopia, and Kenya have created productive safety net programmes, which help saves lives and contribute to development goals. These schemes often receive support from development agencies in their early stages, with the goal of moving them over to governments' national budgets as time passes and economic conditions permit. New technology, especially digital money transfer systems that make it possible to give people money by text message, has made such schemes cheaper and easier to operate.

Just as in developed countries, sceptics have been hard to persuade of the merits of these schemes. Won't feckless people simply drink or gamble away state handouts? The controversy has meant that, for the past 10 years, these schemes have been among the most scrutinized and evaluated of any activities supported by international development agencies. Globally, the evidence is now voluminous and clear. Beneficiaries overwhelmingly use money they are given for three things: buying food, sending their children to school, and investing in some income-earning opportunity (e.g., goods for petty trading). These uses are particularly common when money is given to women rather than men.

The same debate, with a twist, has taken place in the humanitarian sector as well. Modern technology used for identification, like biometric data, combined with new secure means of recording transactions and transferring cash, are creating new ways of getting help to people even in the most insecure environments. Cash also has a big advantage in acute crisis situations in that it can give people a bit more control over their own lives. People fleeing disasters, as well as losing their homes and their livelihoods, are stripped of their dignity and agency, often to the point where they can decide almost nothing in their daily lives. They risk becoming helpless and permanently dependent. The people I met in the secondary school in Addis Ababa in early 2018, mentioned in the earlier chapter on the Horn of Africa, had fled ethnic fighting in southeast Ethiopia but had previously had jobs, homes and assets. They feared being reduced into a state of permanent dependency just as much as they feared hunger and poverty. One of the responsibilities of humanitarian agencies ought to be helping people regain and retain more control over their own lives. Providing help in the form of cash does that.

With all this in mind, accelerating the switch to the use of cash in crises was one of the things I tried to promote as ERC. On the face of it, we made some progress. Cash and voucher use increased by 60 percent between 2016 and 2018, and grew further in subsequent years. In December 2018, following months of discussion, the heads of the World Food Programme, UNICEF, the UN refugee agency, and I issued a joint statement setting out our vision for greater use of cash and joining up the systems agencies use to administer it. Typically, when cash was used in crises, each agency had been setting up its own system to administer it, with their own beneficiary list, information technology platform, and stand-alone monitoring and evaluation processes. This created lots of inefficiencies, and by collaborating we hoped to reduce potential problems.

Studies continue to show that cash was up to 50 percent better value for money than in-kind aid, and helped support local markets and empower recipients. There ought to have been a faster switch to cash. In practice, progress is still slow. Much of the so-called cash is in fact vouchers redeemable only for identified commodities, mainly for food. There are powerful vested interests inside humanitarian agencies for whom the provision of assistance in kind is part of the business model, and the move to cash threatens this model. Some donors—notably the EU and the United Kingdom—have tried to address those issues, not least to get better value for their money. But I increasingly felt, the longer I served as the ERC, that the bigger problem was that aid agencies are not accountable to the people they are supposed to be helping. There was too little focus on the two most important questions: what do people affected in crises say they want, and how do we give it to them? I will return to this issue later.

When I started as ERC in 2017, I thought humanitarian agencies spent too much effort easing symptoms in a palliative mode, rather than operating in a way that contributes to solutions as well as relieving suffering. To oversimplify the issue a bit, the Horn of Africa may provide a case in point: rather than expensively trucking water around drought-prone parts of the region, it would be much better to support longer-term efforts to improve water resource management systems including boreholes, irrigation systems, and drought-resistant seeds. And rather than simply providing food and shelter to displaced people in camps year after year, it would be better to invest in solutions, including through the provision of land and help with housing, as well as jobs and schools, all to give people a chance to rebuild their lives more quickly.

Wherever possible, it is best to support long-term solutions to the causes of crises rather than simply mitigate their symptoms. For example, it is estimated that in Ethiopia the cost of six to nine months of water trucking to camps for displaced people is equivalent to the cost of a semipermanent water supply system. Too often, we end up financing trucking for two years or more when it would be cheaper to establish a more permanent solution from the outset. Similarly, in the past, the Lake Tana Plains in Ethiopia flooded every year. Humanitarian organisations were spending more than $1 million a year to keep waterborne disease in check and replace the seeds that washed away. It turned out that the flooding was caused by the build-up of river sedimentation and weak riverbanks. One of the funds I managed allocated a small amount of money to desilt and rehabilitate the river banks. Thereafter, the farmers of Lake Tana no longer experienced excessive flooding every year.

These solutions require the right mix and sequencing of humanitarian and longer-term recovery and development financing. However, financial silos militate against that. Many of the leading donors have separated their support for longer-term development from their contributions to handling humanitarian crises. Sometimes these issues are handled by different ministries; even where that is not the case, the budgets and teams for development work are generally separate from those for humanitarian assistance. It is difficult to take advantage of potential opportunities for collaboration when silos keep funding and personnel from working together more easily.

The same issue exists in response agencies. There has always been something of a cultural chasm between those who work on humanitarian response and those, often from the same organisations, focused on longer-term development. The humanitarian mindset too often comes across as evangelical, holier-than-thou, and riven with the hero complex. We are here to save lives and the need is urgent, the philosophy goes, and any questions about the causes of the problem and the lasting effects of crisis response work would only get in the way. The development agency perspective, by contrast, militates towards longer periods of analysis and consultation, lengthier implementation timetables than are permissible in crisis situations, and an aversion to quick but often temporary fixes. *Your rapid rescue effort won't work in the long run*, say the development specialists. *In your long run*, the humanitarian workers reply, *these people will be dead.*

These attitudinal problems reduce the effectiveness of both sides. Humanitarian challenges are focused overwhelmingly in countries with the highest poverty and lowest levels of development. Reducing them requires faster and more comprehensive development. Equally, the observable fact is that the wider world is no longer willing to tolerate avoidable mass loss of life in humanitarian disasters, and is willing to spend ever-increasing amounts of money to prevent it. Without the work of humanitarian agencies, poverty and suffering would be even deeper and harder to escape. There is an overwhelming argument for making development finance and humanitarian finance complement each other to reduce suffering and address the root causes of the problem—but that is easier said than done. During my tenure as ERC, significant progress proved impossible because the ballooning of humanitarian crises overwhelmed the response agencies, leaving them unable to do much more than stave off the immediate catastrophe and keep people alive for the next few weeks and months. There is no alternative to that approach. Buying time and delaying the worst is better than tolerating large-scale avoidable loss of life. But it must be admitted that this approach does little to solve the problem. The key point is this: crisis settings are not the exclusive domain of humanitarian organisations. Conversely, we need to find ways for every humanitarian dollar to contribute to development outcomes.

Even more important than joining up the humanitarian and development sectors, though, is the need to recognise that, from both national actors and the international community, the intrinsic fragilities and vulnerability of crisis-afflicted countries need better-resourced responses. More of the international development system's effort and resources should be redirected to support countries that have not enjoyed the development progress most have over the past 50 years. The 30 or 40 countries, mostly in Africa and parts of the Middle East, that account for the bulk of humanitarian suffering are being left further and further behind. The COVID-19 pandemic, as discussed in a later chapter, has made that problem worse, but the basic problem predates the coronavirus. The 2017 *World Development Report* found that many countries are richer not because they have grown faster than poorer ones, but because they have had fewer episodes in which crisis or conflict shrank their economies.

Some efforts have been made in recent years to address that. The World Bank's recognition of a need for a strategic focus on fragile countries and regions is welcome, though it needs to go further. The proof of the pudding will be in the action taken to implement the strategy. More of the world's aid resources need to go to these places. Many places that suffer humanitarian need barely receive any development support. As a result, humanitarian organisations have been drawn into doing longer-term work with short-term funding. That is never going to work. The issues here go well beyond the scope of this book, but the humanitarian agencies will be increasingly overwhelmed and ultimately will no longer be able to save lives and reduce suffering as successfully as they have in recent decades unless we can find better ways to deal with the causes of the problems that have required their response. Fundamentally, that means the countries in which humanitarian suffering is long-lasting and most concentrated will need to receive much more attention. The fact that during the course of my own lifetime, the proportion of people on the planet living in the most extreme poverty has fallen from more than 50 percent to (before the pandemic) less than 10 percent demonstrates what is possible.

Between 2017 and 2020, we were able to increase funding for UN-coordinated humanitarian appeals by more than 50 percent. We also secured more money for the central emergency response fund, with contributions growing from $426 million in 2016 to $831 million in 2019. Contributions fell back to $624 million in 2020—and barely $500 million in 2021—as a result of the British government's aid cuts. Problem is that needs grew much more than the money available to meet them. Trying to get a better impact from the available money, in the ways I have described in this chapter, is part of the solution. What would be better, though, is to address the underlying causes of the growing needs. The chapters that follow will focus on the most complicated dimensions of these causes.

NINE

Wars Have Laws

WARLORDS ARE INVARIABLY TOUGH, shrewd, determined, and expert in the raw end of power. About 10 years ago, in Kismayo in Somalia, I met Ahmed Mohamed Islam. Better known as Madobe, he was then leader of the dominant paramilitary group in southern Somalia. He has spent decades flexibly re-aligning as political power ebbed and flowed around him—in one phase, he was aligned with al-Shabaab, the al-Qaeda franchise of Somalia, but latterly has taken up government positions including as president of Jubaland, Somalia's southern zone. He chose to convey his authority by keeping us waiting in the hot midday sun for an extended period beyond the agreed meeting time, before letting us in to his shaded open-air seating area.

I also recall meeting one of the senior Houthi leaders in Sana'a in 2018. I came in suit and tie; he in military fatigues, jiggling his loaded Kalashnikov against his knee as we spoke. At one point, I inadvertently sent an anxious frisson through the UN team accompanying me and our interpreters by complaining about the Houthis' recruitment of child soldiers—a topic, I later learned, that he knew more about than me because he had been one from the age of seven. In Khartoum in 2019, I met Mohamed Hamdan Dagalo, generally known as Hemetti, then deputy chairman of the Transitional Military Council, the armed forces counterparts to the new civilian-led government. He was assessed to be the leading power in Sudan through his control of the Rapid Support Forces, the most capable armed grouping, which, according to Human Rights Watch, had been responsible for crimes against humanity in Darfur in 2014 and 2015. He used his position in 2017 to take control of Sudan's gold mines, becoming among the richest people in the country. He had spent less than three years at school, something he diverted attention from by doodling pictures in a notepad as we talked, but he exuded intelligence from every pore. He was then in a phase of trying to do what is always hardest for warlords— gaining legitimacy and international acceptance as a statesman—and went out of his way to appear as reasonable as possible in our discussion. In Equatoria in South Sudan in 2018, I was shepherded by UN blue-helmeted peacekeepers around discussions with local people, who complained about the banditry and pillage of a local contingent of opposition forces. Rag-tag elements of these forces, dressed in rough uniforms and concealing their weapons, watched on warily from less than a hundred meters away as we spoke.

I have also had plenty of encounters with the fighting men of state armed forces, with whom it is fair to say that humanitarian agencies do not always see eye to eye, though there is often more professional respect in both directions than you might think. To my best knowledge, I have never met the leaders of any of the extremist jihadi groups who have contributed much in recent times to humanitarian suffering, though at one point I was unknowingly just a few kilometres from ISIS leader Abu Bakar al-Baghdadi. Our near-miss became clear only a few weeks later when American special forces killed him in his Syrian lair. People like this—warlords, soldiers, and terrorist leaders— keep humanitarian agencies unhappily busy, and what we are dealing with here is how to make that less so.

Most humanitarian need is caused by conflict. Needs are higher than they ought to be, and harder to respond to, because of widespread violations of the laws of war. It was ever thus. Throughout the whole of the 150,000 years of human history, our species is unsurpassed by any other organism in its violence against itself. Warring parties have forever deliberately or carelessly disregarded the distinction between combatants and civilians. We should not delude ourselves that there was ever a golden age in which war was conducted nicely. Nevertheless, the world did see a dramatic decline in violence and a reduction in the recorded number of direct victims of armed conflict over recent generations.

Wars between countries became rarer in the aftermath of World War II. Since the beginning of the nuclear age, the most powerful countries in particular have shown a strong disinclination to go to war directly with each other. That does not mean they have vacated the field; the United States in Vietnam and Iraq, and Russia in Afghanistan and Syria, are among the counter examples. In recent decades, military spending by the major powers has also increased, reaching $2 trillion a year. The reduction in conflict among the major powers does not, I think, mostly reflect a change in human values. Though the norms militating against war, and social support for these norms, are quite powerful in many countries—especially democracies—the decline in open conflict says more about the effectiveness of alliances and deterrents in preventing large-scale hostilities.

All that said, in the past 30 years the world has seen an average of 20 internal conflicts a year. Some arise from secessionist movements, many of which fail but some (like South Sudan) succeed. Others arise from terrorist insurrections, drug cartels, or ethnic tensions. The years immediately after the end of the Cold War saw a spike in the loss of life arising from conflict, with the biggest contributions coming in the mid-1990s from the Rwanda genocide and the civil war which consumed the eastern parts of the Democratic Republic of Congo. But after that spike, the numbers of conflicts, the deaths of soldiers on the battlefield, and the total casualties fell for nearly 20 years. Data gathered by Uppsala University in Sweden and others shows that the number of armed conflicts decreased by 40 percent between 1993 and 2005. Maybe even more remarkably, high-intensity civil wars—those with more than a thousand battle deaths a year—fell by 78 percent between 1988 and 2008. Total conflict deaths declined accordingly.

The geopolitical environment between 1990 and 2010 was conducive to these trends. The conclusion of the Cold War briefly ended superpower support for warring proxies, and enabled agreement on UN initiatives to end civil wars through mediation, peacekeeping, and human rights monitoring. Namibia, Cambodia, Guatemala, Sierra Leone, Liberia, Timor Leste, and Nepal are just some of the places where UN interventions helped countries stay the course in the difficult transition from war to peace. Many countries that once seemed hopelessly war-torn are no longer in the headlines. While they all face challenges they are now at peace, and largely prospering (at least before the pandemic).

The problem is that in the past 10 years, the situation in many places has deteriorated again. All the problems I described in Part One—in particular in Syria, Yemen, the Horn of Africa, the Sahel, and the Lake Chad Basin—are evidence of that. The clearest manifestation is in the change in numbers of displaced people. Conflict forces people to flee. They either become refugees in other, mostly neighbouring countries, or are internally displaced. In 1990, there were 40 million displaced people across the world, half refugees and half internally displaced, of a total population of 5.3 billion, or significantly less than one in a hundred. By 2000, it had fallen to 37 million—of a global total of 6.1 billion, nearer to one person in two hundred. But over the last decade it has risen, doubling to around 80 million—much more than one in a hundred. Early in António Guterres' tenure as High Commissioner for Refugees from 2005 to 2015, there was a serious discussion inside the agency about what they would do if the refugee problem disappeared. No-one is talking about that now.

One of the lasting consequences of World War II was the creation of a body of international laws and norms, trying to ensure that future conflicts would be conducted more in the spirit of the St. Petersburg Declaration, which in 1868 had laid out a philosophy for setting limits in war: "The progress of civilisation should have the effect of alleviating, as much as possible, the calamities of war, and the only legitimate object which States should endeavour to accomplish during war is to weaken the military forces of the enemy." It should not, in other words, impose arbitrary suffering on innocent and non-participating civilians.

International humanitarian law and the related norms are among the best-established areas of international law. They are enshrined in the Geneva Conventions of 1949, their Additional Protocols of 1977, and a number of other international treaties. All states around the world are party to the Geneva Conventions. International humanitarian law applies in situations of armed conflict—whether between states, between armed groups, or between one or more states and one or more armed groups—and it equally binds all parties. Consistent with the St. Petersburg Declaration, it aims to protect people who are not fighting, including civilians as well as wounded, sick, or detained fighters. It prohibits torture, rape, and other forms of sexual violence. It requires that the wounded and sick be collected and cared for, and it allows impartial humanitarian bodies to offer their services to parties to a conflict. The legal framework and associated norms also limit the methods and means of warfare to which the parties may resort. For instance, they prohibit genocide, ethnic cleansing, religious persecution, systematic massacres, starvation as a weapon of war, and the use of chemical and biological weapons. They also set out the fundamental rules of distinction, proportionality, and precaution in the conduct of hostilities, and prohibit tactics and weapons that cause indiscriminate injury or unnecessary suffering. Unfortunately, the changing nature of conflict over the past 20 years has eroded respect for these norms. The growth in humanitarian need in conflict arises not just from the increase in the numbers of people affected. It also arises from a decline in compliance with the legal framework and associated norms of conflict is conducted, for which the St. Petersburg Declaration provided inspiration.

What has caused this reversal? There are a number of interlinked factors. First, Western countries have shown decreasing willingness and ability to act as the world's policemen, in the wake of the experiences over the past two decades in Afghanistan and Iraq. Vladimir Putin's Russia has taken the opportunity to fill the resulting vacuum, which has opened space for disagreements and grievances to turn into fighting. The Arab Spring and severe governance deficits in significant numbers of African countries have exacerbated these issues. The number of conflicts has risen again over the past decade, increasing by close to 60 percent since 2009. Along the way, battle-related deaths of both soldiers and civilians have increased as well. A small number of high-intensity conflicts—Syria, Afghanistan, and Yemen—accounted for most of that rise.

Outside powers are also interfering militarily in civil wars on different sides of conflict, with planes in the air and boots on the ground. By 2019, UN reports suggested that over 40 percent of all intra-state conflicts involved other countries, compared to 4 percent in 1991. This trend manifests itself most tragically in Syria and Libya, blighted by a return of proxy war dynamics reminiscent of the Cold War. There are more internationalized civil wars today than at any point in the Cold War. Turkey and the Gulf States in particular have entered the club of those increasingly willing to interfere in others' affairs.

Then there are changes related to globalization, in particular the rise in illicit flows and organised crime and the spread of new communications technologies, including social media. These developments have lowered entry barriers to the market for organized violence. The means to engage in armed conflict have become more readily accessible through illicit flows of arms and money and new communications technologies like Facebook and Twitter. This shift has also driven a progressive fragmentation of nonstate armed groups. The average number of rebel groups fighting in civil wars has increased from 8 in 1950 to 14 in 2010. Syria provides a particularly stark example: at one point, OCHA counted more than 1,500 separate armed groups in the region, all with constantly shifting agendas, alliances, and sources of support. The result in many conflict zones is a complex web of groups, often with loose chains of command, fluid alliances, and little grasp of the laws of war. The motivation of many groups is purely profit: they thrive off the illicit economy, which requires instability and sometimes conflict to keep the rule of law out.

A related development is the rise and spread of terrorism and, crucially, governments' response to it. Some commentators are raising concern over what they see as the counterterrorism imperative trumping states' obligations under international humanitarian law. They have a point. But the origin of the problem is the behaviour of jihadi groups, whose nihilistic ideologies reject the laws of war and are often used to justify unspeakable violence against civilians. Terrorism as a tactic is, by intention, often indiscriminate and disproportionate. Its purpose is what it says on the tin: to spread terror to as many people as possible. The overwhelming majority of its victims are innocent civilians in poor countries.

Though the demise of the caliphate in Syria and Iraq has weakened the Islamic State in the Middle East, the group has expanded in Africa in recent years. Today, more than half the civil wars around the world involve ISIS, al-Qaeda, or an affiliated group. Close to three-quarters of today's battle-related deaths happen in fighting involving one of these groups, and they are responsible for the lion's share of civilian fatalities caused by nonstate armed groups. More than 70 percent of civilian deaths caused by nonstate groups in 2019 were the work of ISIS, al-Qaeda, and their affiliates. And, as noted, the emergence of jihadi groups has itself attracted a reaction from many states across the political and ideological spectrum to counter the terrorism they exhibit and promote. Countering terrorism itself is frequently violent, often with deleterious consequences for civilians and the humanitarian agencies helping them.

As the wider world has become more urban, so has conflict. In 1960, a third of the world's population lived in urban areas. Today, that share has risen to 55 percent. As a result, many of today's armed conflicts are fought in cities and other urban areas, affecting an estimated 50 million people worldwide. Civilians and civilian infrastructure like water, health, and electricity systems have been increasingly exposed to the impact of war.

A further important trend is the emerging preference among the leading military powers for the use of remote warfare and, especially, aerial bombing with so-called precision-guided smart weapons. (There is a similar issue with nonstate armed groups too, with widespread use of improvised explosive devices often set off remotely, and the forced use of civilians, including children, as involuntary human bombs.) Over the past 20 to 30 years, in countries with advanced militaries, citizens' tolerance for casualties in what they see as discretionary military interventions overseas has declined. The consequence of this is an increasing reliance on remote warfare and airpower to pursue military objectives, regardless of the collateral impact. This trend has played out particularly clearly in Libya, Syria, and Iraq, where Western countries limited their exposure largely to air campaigns often in support of allied proxy forces on the ground. The ground forces, experience has shown, often lack the capabilities, willingness, or training to adequately protect civilians. And in any case, the much-touted "surgical strikes," where citizens are genuinely protected, are all but impossible against nonstate armed groups that consciously embed themselves among the civilian population. The Counter-ISIL Coalition's campaign to eliminate ISIS from its Raqqa headquarters in Syria, for example, left 80 percent of the city destroyed.

A related consequence of the declining willingness of many advanced countries to risk their own military personnel in distant conflict is the growing prominence of private security companies and contractors. As a study for the UN by the Atlantic Council put it, "Mercenaries are no longer Kalashnikov-toting soldiers of fortune who show up in wars of decolonisation." Increasingly, they fly attack helicopters, drive tanks, and pilot armed patrol boats. They are distant from the scrutiny, visibility, and accountability that may apply to states. The Wagner Group, for example, a private military company widely believed to be closely tied to the Kremlin, has deployed hundreds of soldiers in Sudan, the Democratic Republic of Congo, Libya, and the Central African Republic. They are alleged to have committed various atrocities but their legal status in Russia is murky and it has been difficult to hold them to account. In what may prove an interesting test case, human rights NGOs have started filing legal cases against the group in Moscow for war crimes committed in Syria.

A particularly disturbing feature of 21st century conflict has been the breaching of recently established—if fragile—taboos. Again, Syria has been the most prominent theatre for this, with the repeated use of chemical weapons, widespread use of starvation and siege as weapons of war, and industrial-scale sexual abuse and torture of both men and women. These behaviours are bleeding into other places. Sexual atrocities are a frequent tactic of extremists in the Sahel, especially the enslavement and exploitation of young women and girls. Yet there is clear recent evidence that states also have been engaging in the systematic and organized use of such tactics—as in the cases of the Rohingya forced out of Myanmar, and violations committed by Eritrean soldiers and other men in uniform against women and girls in Tigray.

As a result of these factors, the duration of civil wars has been trending upwards over the past three decades. Armed conflicts ending in 1991 had lasted an average of 12 years. Those ending in 2015 had been going on for nearly 27 years. And in contrast to the early 2000s when, for the first time in history, most civil wars ended in negotiation, today they are increasingly likely to be pursued beyond previous limits in the search for a one-sided victory.

The role of humanitarian agencies in conflict has evolved as well in recent years. During the Cold War, the provision of humanitarian aid to the victims of conflict was largely limited to refugees who managed to escape violence by fleeing to neighbouring countries. Only the International Committee of the Red Cross consistently operated inside those parts of countries affected by civil wars. That limited outreach was one of the reasons why loss of life was so high among civilians in many conflicts in the 40 years after World War II—including in Ethiopia in the mid-1980s, where a million people lost their lives in a conflict-induced famine. At that time, humanitarian agencies were much less present to save lives and reduce suffering. However, following the Ethiopia experience, the Russian invasion of Afghanistan in the late 1980s, and the turmoil that followed the American-led war against Iraq in the early 1990s, international humanitarian agencies, including those of the UN, began to operate on a larger scale inside conflict-affected countries. In some cases, that work involved cross-border assistance, as in Afghanistan. Conflict in the Balkans in the early 1990s helped draw increasing attention to the needs of internally displaced people. Their plight previously had not been considered an issue of real international concern. Largely as a result, and as discussed earlier, UN-coordinated humanitarian assistance efforts increased from roughly $2 billion per year in 1990 to $5 billion by 2000 and $10 billion in 2010. This expansion in humanitarian assistance helped significantly drive down mortality rates in war-torn countries.

The current prevailing mindset among humanitarian agencies is that it is essential to try to meet the needs of all people caught up in crises, regardless of who they are, where they are, and who exercises control over them and their environment. This thinking runs into some controversial territory, given the UN's founding principles around state sovereignty and noninterference. It also runs into the realities of state power, as reflected for example in the negligible access humanitarian agencies have to the Uighurs in China or vulnerable communities in North Korea. (In early 2021, most of the few remaining international humanitarian staff were withdrawn from North Korea, together with the final remnants of the diplomatic community.) But other elements impose limits as well. Some of the most challenging humanitarian situations are those facing the 60 to 80 million people, roughly 1 percent of the global population, who are living somewhere not controlled by a state. They include people in areas dominated by drugs cartels, as in parts of Latin America, or by other criminal gangs like those pillaging the timber and mineral resources of eastern Congo. For such groups, lawlessness, chaos, and state absence is an essential requirement of the business model. Growing populations also are stuck in places under the sway of jihadi and other extremist groups that oppose national and local governments but also refute the legitimacy and impartiality of humanitarian organisations. Increasingly, the modus operandi of such extremist groups has included the kidnap and murder of people working for independent relief organisations.

Humanitarian agencies therefore find themselves in a wicked dilemma: they are driven by an imperative to help people in need, but are practically limited in doing so by the requirement to manage the risk to their own staff and operations. The conflict management toolkit, which was designed in the post–World War II era primarily with conflict *between states* in mind, was extended over time to try to respond to the reality of conflict *within states*. Efforts to strengthen and expand peacekeeping, peacebuilding, mediation, extended uses of sanctions, and acquired experience in running complex emergency relief operations in conflict settings are reflections of that trend. (The UN's most extensive peacekeeping operations are now all dealing with intra-state conflict.) In truth, however, humanitarian agencies are struggling and overstretched in many conflict situations, and lately the problems they face have become much worse.

What can be done to try to recover some of the ground lost in recent years in protecting civilian populations against the effects of conflict and to enable humanitarian agencies to support people better? The question is important, because conflict is the main driver of humanitarian need. There are no easy answers, especially in a geopolitical context where the leading powers find it difficult to collaborate. Nevertheless, there are opportunities. I see four main themes for stronger action.

First, it would help to add further energy to the public debate on the causes of the recent erosion in compliance with the laws of war. States all signed up to the Geneva Conventions and the associated arrangements for a reason. Compliance has benefits. There is a debate over how far morality, values, and a sense of horror, as opposed to judgements based on narrower interests, drove changes in thinking about warfare after World War II. Certainly, the evolution of national and international public policy has had a moral and humane core. But going back to the mid-19th century origins of the first Geneva Convention, naked and enlightened self-interest were also important considerations. Those creating the rules wanted to ensure that their wounded soldiers, war prisoners, and civilians would be cared for and protected when in the hands of the enemy. To achieve that, they realised they would have to do the same, simply to solve the tit-for-tat problem. The entire international rules-based system was created because states thought it served their interest, and that has not changed. In 2018, the International Committee of the Red Cross published an important study on the roots of restraint in conflict. That year, the UN held a series of events to discuss this question, but the issues failed to gain enough senior and sustained attention. A resumed effort would be desirable, particularly if it focuses on the benefits of compliance. More trained and experienced negotiators—a rare commodity—would help.

Numerous studies, not least by military intellectuals, have produced compelling evidence that few factors have done more to fill the ranks of jihadi groups in places like Afghanistan, Syria, and Iraq than the widespread violations of international humanitarian law and other abuses committed by state security forces in the name of counterterrorism. Research by the UN Development Programme, based on hundreds of interviews with former members of jihadi groups, confirms that unrestrained military counterterrorism has accelerated jihadi recruitment. Likewise, the International Crisis Group has found that excessive and disproportionate military action against extremists has fuelled recruitment by ISIS and al-Qaeda by allowing them to present themselves as protectors of the population against predatory regimes. It is evidently in the interests of states combatting violent extremists to work harder and be more careful to win the hearts and minds of civilian populations, including their local leaders.

In a similar vein, choices of weapons and tactics to try to minimise civilian harm, which are required under the international humanitarian law provision for proportionality, also support local counterinsurgency goals. At the same time, too many states still exercise disproportionate or excessive force, despite the evidence suggesting that doing so undermines the objective being pursued. One potentially valuable initiative in this area is Ireland's promotion of a political declaration in the UN on the avoidance of explosive weapons with wide-area effects in urban areas. More than 80 countries have subscribed so far. The choice of weapons is of course partly determined by what belligerents can get their hands on. Weapons exporters could contribute to increased compliance with the laws of war if they exercised more self-discipline in what items they sold to who.

A commitment by state military forces to institute professional systems to track and tabulate data on civilian harm in military operations has also been shown to help. The process of gathering the information and analysing it led to changes in tactics to the benefit of civilians in Afghanistan, and attempts are being made to replicate the approach in the Sahel.

There is also scope for more collaboration between humanitarian agencies and states' military forces to protect civilians. This does, however, require genuine commitment by the military side, which is sometimes claimed even when it is absent. The recent history of notification and deconfliction systems designed to protect humanitarian agencies working in conflict zones illustrates that. The deconfliction system set up by OCHA in Syria in 2014 notified the United States, Russia, and Turkey of humanitarian premises, movements, and convoys to facilitate their compliance with the legal obligations to protect humanitarian operations from harm from military operations. As mentioned earlier, the notification system was broadly successful until 2018. Few incidents damaged aid operations until the Russians and Syrians decided to target them instead of protecting them. The notification and deconfliction system in Yemen, by contrast, has been remarkably effective in helping the Saudi-led coalition avoid damage to aid operations despite a nationwide bombing campaign. That was an imperative for the coalition, because those who supplied their weapons (primarily the Americans and the British) were hyper-sensitive to breaches, in part to avoid falling foul of their own obligations under international humanitarian law. (Unfortunately, in the early years of the bombing campaign that sensitivity did not extend sufficiently to collateral damage to civilians and facilities that were not part of the aid infrastructure.) The UN and state military forces could make greater use of such deconfliction and notification systems, but a high degree of vigilance is needed to make sure the deals are respected.

Compliance with humanitarian norms can also be advanced by training and awareness raising for military entities on the norms and laws. The International Committee of the Red Cross has a leading role here. Its work has demonstrated that training increases battlefield restraint. It ought to be more fully funded by donors: the current level of effort verges on the tokenistic. Interestingly, these approaches have been shown to work not just with state forces but also with opposition and informal groups. OCHA staff have over the years regularly been asked about international humanitarian law by commanders of armed groups, who appear interested in what they must do to avoid being sent to the international courts in The Hague.

The second area of work to contain the erosion of compliance relates to calling out violations when they occur. Some of my former UN colleagues think such advocacy deters repetition of the worst violations. What I can say is that it is often a thankless, tiring, and unrewarding task, one that too rarely leads to any visible remedial action, as I found through more than a hundred Security Council meetings at which I gave presentations between 2017 and 2021. It is nevertheless important to do it. Perpetrators commit violations when they think they will not be seen, caught, or punished. The more doubt that can be created in their minds over their impunity, the better, and the starting point is advocacy and the reporting of abuses. This is a core role of the UN's human rights machinery, and many NGOs do excellent work in this area. The UN secretary-general has appointed special representatives on genocide and sexual violence in conflict, and their work adds to the drumbeat of condemnation. The Security Council has also, through the adoption of a set of new resolutions in recent years, created a stronger platform for advocacy. Resolutions in 2016 calling for accountability for attacks on medical personnel, in 2018 on the use of starvation as a weapon of war, and in 2019 on sexual violence in conflict require the UN Secretariat to draw the attention of Security Council members to violations. The effect is to increase the public profile of atrocities. All this machinery needs to be used to the fullest extent. One of the cheapest worthwhile investments for countries and organisations concerned about these issues is to finance investigations, research, and media products exposing them.

Third, new and clearer-eyed thinking is needed on dealing with non-state armed groups, particularly jihadi extremists. It bears restating that those who suffer most at the hands of terrorists are the people who live in the areas they control. The experience of local people under the tyranny of ISIS is ample testimony to that. ISIS fighters became expert in rape and sexual enslavement, public executions, abductions, torture, and starvation, and publicized their acts both to draw international attention to themselves and to terrify local populations into submission. A state-led military response is required in such cases, and is justified to protect local populations. Humanitarian agencies have struggled to work out how to react to this. As a practical matter, they have had very little access to people in places controlled by terrorist groups that regard the humanitarian system itself as a legitimate target. Traditionally, humanitarian agencies have operated on the basis of negotiated consent: that is, persuading parties to let them operate.

But what if that consent is deliberately and as a matter of strategy withheld? That has been the experience with many extremist organisations in recent times. Efforts through secret dialogue to find some common ground have had only limited results. (One positive example was the continuation of the anti-polio campaign in ISIS-controlled northern Syria, in which we gave ISIS operatives doses of the vaccine to distribute.) But large populations in places including the Lake Chad Basin, other parts of the Sahel, northern Mozambique, and parts of Yemen are often out of reach because the extremist groups controlling them will not permit humanitarian agencies safe access.

The dilemma faced by humanitarian agencies is well illustrated by the events of the past 10 years in northeast Nigeria. A decade of conflict and violence perpetrated by the Islamic State affiliate Boko Haram and other nonstate armed groups has devastated communities, as I heard from many local people in visits in 2017, 2018, and 2019. Between 2016 and 2018, the Nigerian military took back large parts of the region previously ravaged by the insurgents, but renewed violence and displacement left seven million people in need of assistance by late 2019. It was clear to me—as I said publicly—that military measures were a necessary and legitimate part of the Nigerian government's response. But the military was also responsible for atrocities and human rights abuses, and the government failed to put in place the necessary accompanying measures—services, development activities, and cash—to win over local people.

NGOs and others were loud in their criticism of this, to the point where some allowed themselves to be perceived as believing that there was a moral equivalence between the terrorists and the legitimate state institutions combatting them. That mindset was particularly ironic given that nearly 40 staff members of NGOs had been killed in the decade after 2011, mostly by Boko Haram, and sometimes in executions that were recorded and then widely circulated. The Nigerian military, who lost many more servicemen to the insurgents, persuaded themselves that legitimate international NGOs may have been colluding with the extremists. In 2019, they suspended the activities of leading NGOs, including Mercy Corps and Action Against Hunger, thereby cutting off 400,000 people from food support and other assistance from these NGOs. Following discussions with the federal government in Abuja, the state governor, and military commanders in Borno during a visit in October 2019, I was able to get the suspension lifted and help establish new fora in which the Nigerian authorities and the humanitarian agencies could discuss how they could work together effectively in future. But there has been little real progress, and by mid-2021 the insurgents were still wreaking havoc across large areas.

The handling of these issues has been made more complicated by the growing tendency of states facing opposition groups to brand them as terrorists, often for political reasons, in circumstances where the label does not appear to be justified. Recent examples in Myanmar and Ethiopia illustrate that particular trend.

For humanitarian agencies, the best approach for navigating this minefield is to seek dialogue with opposition groups in order to test the scope for access in which agency staff can safely assess and provide for the needs of local people. That dialogue needs to be on the basis of the humanitarian principles: that whoever needs assistance should receive it through agencies that act in independent, neutral, and impartial ways. Where such access is achievable—as, for example, it was for 20 years in Taliban-controlled parts of Afghanistan before it regained nationwide control in 2021, as well as in Colombia, the Occupied Palestinian Territories, and elsewhere—states need to be persuaded to tolerate it. Doing so will generally be in their own long-term interests; the opposite approach will further alienate local people.

Where extremist groups refuse access or persist in attacks on aid agency staff, humanitarian agencies need to be more open about the challenges, including condemning atrocities, not least in discharge of their responsibility to speak out for the people affected. This tactic will require judgement and dialogue, and a good understanding of the perspective of local influencers, including chiefs, clan heads, and religious leaders. In a significant number of cases, opposition groups motivated by local, legitimate, and reversible grievances may through dialogue be incentivized to comply with humanitarian norms. At present, distinguishing between those cases and others where there is no realistic prospect of compliance with humanitarian norms is a key challenge that too often is not being met.

Counterterrorism legislation has complicated the process of humanitarian agencies entering into dialogue to seek access to areas controlled by proscribed terrorist groups, because that contact itself may be found to be unlawful. States need to take steps to amend their counterterrorism legislation, guidance, and practice to assure legitimate humanitarian agencies, if necessary on a case-by-case basis, that they will not be egregiously pursued through the vehicle of such legislation. Again, such situations need to be handled sensitively and carefully, reflecting the legitimate intent of and requirement for measures to deal with violent extremists.

In many conflict situations, there is also a need for better understanding of the inner workings of nonstate armed groups. Such understanding requires research and analysis of their sociological, political, ideological, and economic motivations. Given the fluid structures of many of these groups, which appear, merge, split, and disappear faster than our understanding of them, this analysis will need to be updated constantly. There is no one-size-fits-all route to improving their compliance with humanitarian norms and laws.

The fourth area in which enhanced action is needed to improve respect for humanitarian norms is the most important and most difficult to achieve: meaningful accountability for perpetrators of crimes and atrocities. In the halcyon period of the immediate post–Cold War era, progress looked possible. One development was the establishment of the International Criminal Court in The Hague in 1998, intended to ensure that the most serious crimes do not go unpunished in cases where national authorities are unable or unwilling to take action. International criminal tribunals on Rwanda and former Yugoslavia—which led to the prosecution, conviction, and incarceration of Serb leaders, including Slobodan Milošević, Ratko Mladić, and Radovan Karadžić, for crimes against Muslims in former Yugoslavia—ensured a degree of justice after those conflicts. But in the harsher realties of the previous decade, international collaboration towards justice has withered. China, Russia, and the United States—three members of the P5—are hostile towards the International Criminal Court, reducing the likelihood of referrals there.

At the national level, however, the situation is less bleak. Under the principle of universal jurisdiction, investigations and prosecutions on genocide, crimes against humanity, and war crimes have become more common in the EU, with nearly 3,000 cases by 2019. In early 2021, more than 140 suspects were arrested, detained, or on trial in 18 countries. Significantly, they include defendants against allegations of atrocities committed in Syria, on which the German courts are particularly active.

There is also scope for greater use of other penalties for violators. Sanctions against named individuals are now commonly used by individual countries and the EU as a group, and sometimes by the Security Council. They constrain the freedom of movement and finances of those accused of violations, and tarnish their reputations. President Assad, for instance, has barely left Syria in a decade. President Bashir in Sudan was effectively prevented from travelling even within Africa in the latter years of his regime for fear of arrest. The judicious instigation—and removal—of sanctions can create helpful incentives, albeit only marginally in some cases.

Finally, there is a need to scan the horizon for future challenges to humanitarian norms. Conflict is not going away, yet it will continue to change. Analysing the potential impact of cyber operations, for example in disrupting critical civilian infrastructure like water and health systems, is one issue that would benefit from further study. One obvious challenge is the difficulty of identifying those responsible for such attacks. Humanitarian organisations also need to pay attention to the evolution of autonomous weapons. Their use appears antithetical to the principle of precaution, which is part of the bedrock of humanitarian law and norms. If a weapon can decide on its own who, what, and when to attack, how can distinctions between civilian and military targets be ensured?

These will be among the most difficult challenges for humanitarian agencies in the years ahead. The old shibboleth that prevailed when I started my career, that no warring parties would target aid agencies, has broken down, and aid workers now constantly come under attack. In 2017, 139 aid workers were killed in the line of duty. Agencies have to take risks to reach people who need their help, but they also owe a duty of care to their own staff. Some agencies need more staff with military experience in order to coordinate effectively with belligerents in conflict situations. The best civil-military coordination staff in aid agencies tend to have a military background themselves, but most former military personnel are not cut out for this work. Building capability to assess needs and provide assistance remotely, such as by using digital technology to transfer money to people in need, will also be important, especially in the growing number of crises that involve extremist groups.

TEN

Women and Girls

THE YOUNG WOMAN, DRESSED IN THE LIGHT-BLUE tunic many UN staff in field operations wear, took me to the side and directed me down the short corridor. She opened the door and pointed to the empty wooden chair in which I was to sit. She followed me in, closed the door, and sat behind me. In front of me, seated in another chair facing my own, was the woman I had come to meet. She held her hands in her lap, twiddling her fingers, and glanced briefly at me, a little uncomfortable, before averting her gaze.

"My name is Mark, and I work for the United Nations in New York," I said. "Thank you for talking to me. Could you tell me what happened?"

It was March 2019, and I was visiting the Democratic Republic of Congo with UNICEF head Henrietta Fore and International Federation of the Red Cross Secretary-General As Sy. Today, we were in Goma, a sprawling city in the far east of the country which has been an epicentre of humanitarian crises for nearly 30 years. We had come to Heal Africa, a hospital that provided medical, surgical, and psychosocial care to survivors of sexual violence and aimed to help them to rebuild their lives. We had had the normal series of introductions and briefing meetings, and had now split up to meet some of the people Heal Africa were supporting.

The woman, who looked to be in her fifties, had been gang-raped, beaten, and cast aside by a group of armed men dressed in military fatigues who had rampaged through her village. Her physical injuries were severe but, as UN Population Fund head Natalia Kanem has frequently noted, "The greatest wound is the one the doctor cannot see." She had been mentally paralysed by what had happened to her, and supporting her psychological recovery was as important as dealing with her physical injuries. She had done nothing wrong, but after the attack the people of her village had stigmatized her and it was impossible for her to return home. The staff of Heal Africa were helping her establish a new livelihood elsewhere. She knew she had been wronged, and she wanted justice and to see the perpetrators punished.

These four things—medical care, psychological support, help to rebuild their lives, and justice—are almost invariably what women who survive such attacks say they want. I listened to similar stories from women I met in many countries. I always felt uncomfortable and inadequate in these conversations, but I was aware that the encounters were a lot harder for the people I was listening to, being asked to respond to painful questions from a powerful, elite, greying white man from the other side of the world. The courage and resilience women displayed as they told their stories was a constant source of amazement.

In a visit to the Democratic Republic of Congo the previous year, I met Monga Albertine and her children in a camp near the shores of Lake Tanganyika in the east of the country. Her husband had been killed in tribal fighting, and she fled to try to save her children. She was living under a plastic sheet on a wet, slippery hillside, with not enough to eat, no school for the children, and no way of making a living. Two months after that, I met a woman called Fatima in a camp in South Kordofan in Sudan. She described the risks she took every day, gathering firewood in an area where women are frequently assaulted and raped. Most people facing humanitarian crises round the world are just like this. The majority are women and girls, and most of them are caught up in conflict. And the problem that makes it hardest to help them is how the men with guns and bombs behave towards them in those conflicts.

In my dozens of visits to countries in crisis, the stories of women and girls stuck with me more than any others. Stories of escape from violence and terror. Stories of barbaric acts committed against them. Stories of fear for their children and loved ones. But stories also of resilience and hope. Women and girls remaining defiant. Mothers determined to ensure that their children were safe and had the chance to go to school. Young girls with ambitions to be doctors, engineers, and leaders. Women heading households, who had resolved to take control of their lives, start businesses, and provide for their families. Brave survivors, not just helpless victims.

Even though it is well known that humanitarian crises in the 21st century disproportionately affect women and girls, humanitarian agencies and the donors who pay for their work have historically not adequately recognised or responded to that fact. They do a good job in saving lives, but not nearly a good enough job providing the particular help that women and girls need and men do not.

———————◆———————

The subjugation of women by men has been a dirty feature of humanity for tens of thousands of years. When in 2019 I was researching and writing a book on the lives and times of 120 of my own and my wife Julia's ancestors between the 1650s and 1950s, I was reminded that efforts to address that subjugation are still very new, even in a country that by global standards is relatively advanced (for all that it has a lot still to do) in gender equality. My female ancestors in the 17th and 18th centuries were largely treated as the property of their fathers and husbands, with very few rights of their own. It is barely a hundred years since British women first received the right to vote and were allowed to enter universities, the professions, and Parliament. It took the Sex Disqualification Removal Act of 1918 to allow them to serve on juries. In the 1950s, married women needed their husband's signature on hire-purchase agreements to buy consumer durables like washing machines. In the early 1960s, when I was born, it was not a crime for a man to rape his wife. Domestic violence was then regarded as a private matter. But social attitudes in the United Kingdom and other developed countries have changed, and with them laws and how people behave.

Violence against women remains frighteningly common everywhere, especially violence perpetrated by the men they sleep with. WHO data show that more than one woman in four will be beaten or sexually abused by a partner over her lifetime. This violence has lifelong consequences, including reduced earnings, emotional stress, depression, and suicide attempts. Children who see their fathers beat their mothers are more likely themselves to become victims or abusers. Most Western countries have now criminalised domestic sexual violence, and it is less prevalent than it was in previous eras. But in poorer places and conflict situations—in other words, the places where humanitarian crises are found—the problem of violence against women is much worse. In conflict situations, men consistently behave atrociously towards women. This phenomenon is not new and does not seem to be declining. There is a robust statistical correlation between physical security of women and the levels of conflict in a country. When asked, something like one in five displaced women say they have recently experienced sexual violence. In Afghanistan, 80 percent of women say that husbands are justified in beating wives in some circumstances. Women and girls are at greater risk of violence at food distribution points or if they have to travel long distances to get water. There is clear evidence that as food insecurity increases, levels of domestic violence also go up.

Customs that make women dependent on their husbands, like restrictions on women's property rights, exacerbate the situation. It takes time to change these customs. Education—especially of boys, and especially by role models like male sports coaches—helps. But abusers must also face a credible threat of redress, which means changing the laws on violence against women and the behaviour and attitudes of those who enforce them. Similarly, reducing women's economic vulnerability, for example through work or cash transfer programmes, helps by improving women's standing and bargaining power.

Some of the worst atrocities committed against women and girls are those systematically adopted as weapons of war by states and non-state armed groups. These violent acts have the explicit objective of terrorising, brutalizing, and shocking civilian populations, both men and women, in order to control them or expel them. The rape and other horrific sexual abuses of Rohingya, Tigrayan, and Syrian women, mentioned in earlier chapters, are in that category. So is the tactic, used by Boko Haram and others in northeast Nigeria, of strapping explosives to the bodies of young girls and forcing them to walk into crowds of civilians before detonating the bomb. Adolescent girls and young women continue to be traded, sold, and trafficked as sex slaves in the brothels of war.

Then there is the suffering of women and girls in humanitarian crises arising from the lack of services they need but men and boys do not. The paucity of reproductive health services means that more than 500 women and girls die from pregnancy and childbirth complications in crisis-affected countries every day. Inadequate help with menstrual hygiene limits girls' mobility, keeping them in tents and shelters and preventing them from accessing services. Lack of basic hygiene supplies is one of the reasons why girls in conflict zones are more than twice as likely as boys to be out of school.

The central role that women often play in caring for their families can also contribute to their added vulnerability. In the 2018–19 Ebola outbreak in the Democratic Republic of Congo, twice as many women were infected as men. It was the women, many of them heads of households, who were in charge of caring for the sick, bringing them to hospital, and preparing bodies for burial. Because Ebola spreads by contact with infected bodily fluids, these women were exposing themselves to the disease with little in the way of protection or sanitary measures to prevent its transmission.

Violence against women is preventable. It is not an inevitable by-product of war. What needs to change is the behaviour and attitudes of men and boys. Examples show that the right kind of action can make a difference. A project funded by the UK's former DFID in the Democratic Republic of Congo supported faith leaders to work in their communities to address violence against women. This programme successfully reduced domestic violence from 69 percent to 29 percent, and sexual violence from 21 percent to 4 percent. In Bangladesh, I spoke to religious and community leaders in Cox's Bazar in 2019 who were working on similar ideas with men in the Rohingya community. This kind of activity, however, is conspicuous by its rarity.

In February 2018, Oxfam, one of the world's most admired and respected international development charities, hit the headlines over a sexual abuse scandal. The leadership of the organisation were accused of covering up the sexual exploitation of women and girls by Oxfam staff who had been involved in the relief operation after the 2010 Haiti earthquake. Sexual abuse by aid workers of people they were supposed to be helping sickened and appalled people across the humanitarian sector, as well as politicians, celebrities, volunteers, and many others who supported their work and expected better of them. People rightly found it particularly repugnant for abuses to be committed by men working for organisations whose mission was to protect the most vulnerable from exactly this sort of problem. Oxfam's leadership had in fact previously investigated and addressed what had happened in Haiti in 2010, but the enquiries lacked rigor, adequate follow-up, and transparency. Oxfam had left itself open to criticism, and in fact the scandal burst into life because of concerns expressed through the agency's own whistleblowing systems that leadership had not properly dealt with the Haiti case. In the ensuing furore, most of the agency's senior staff either resigned straightaway or moved on in the subsequent months, including several who had done nothing much wrong but rightly accepted responsibility. My take—as someone whose family had been providing monthly contributions to Oxfam for decades—was that the organisation still did a great deal of good in the world and, as often, this crisis provided an important opportunity. We doubled our monthly contributions, and I started to think about what I could do to reduce the risks of a recurrence of similar violations in other humanitarian agencies.

Many organisations—across politics, the Catholic Church and other religious institutions, business, the media, sport, and Hollywood—have suffered similar scandals in recent years. The UN has had its own share of problems, especially in conflict settings and humanitarian crises that create the kind of circumstances where atrocious behaviour by men has been all too common. The Inter-Agency Steering Committee readily agreed that we needed to use the Oxfam crisis as the trigger for an energetic strategy and programme of work to deter sexually abusive behaviour in aid agencies by men who in the past might have thought they could get away with it. We recognised that we needed a determined, long-term commitment to get to the roots of the problem. We agreed that we would henceforth put this issue on the agenda for every meeting to ensure sustained attention. Agency heads took turns for a year at a time to champion the cause: first Filippo Grandi from the UN refugee agency; then Henrietta Fore at UNICEF; and then, starting in the months before I left my post, Natalia Kanem from the UN Population Fund.

We adopted new mechanisms to report abuse, investigate complaints, enforce disciplinary proceedings, and provide assistance to victims. All staff were required to take mandatory training, so no-one had the excuse of not knowing what was expected. I tracked the data on OCHA staff completion of the training, and told everyone I was doing so—which had the desired effect, because participation rates increased substantially. We tightened the guidelines governing sexual relationships between staff members and beneficiaries, so that staff would be subject to disciplinary action if there were even a perception (much less an actual element) of coercion. I was in a minority of agency heads who wanted to go further and ban all sexual contact between staff and beneficiaries, but the majority view was that this would be both an infringement of rights and in practice unachievable. From OCHA's own budget, I created a fund to which any agency linked to the Inter-Agency Standing Committee could apply for money to pay to investigate allegations they did not have the capacity to look into themselves. We strengthened information sharing through employment vetting and referencing systems to make it harder for perpetrators to move from one organisation to another. We also set about strengthening investigatory capacity, including through meetings between the heads of investigating bodies and managers from organisations in the Inter-Agency Standing Committee. All this was done in concert with similar initiatives across the whole of the UN. (The UN humanitarian agencies were already party to these efforts, but at that time other agencies were not.) The idea was to replicate and give genuine effect to the UN policy of zero tolerance for sexual exploitation, abuse, and harassment.

Tackling sexual exploitation and abuse is not straightforward, and it is easy inadvertently to make things worse. I thought that the British government's decision to cut funding to Oxfam (and subsequently also to Save the Children), as it did in the wake of the Haiti scandal, may have been counterproductive. The effect was to hamper much good work the agencies were doing. Moreover, their internal systems were more likely than some others, which the British government continued to fund, to identify and punish miscreants. I also saw a spate of what turned out to be fabricated, mendacious, and normally anonymous abuse allegations against aid workers. People with a grievance, including local administrative officials, saw that aid agencies were trying to clean things up and thought they might be able to get rid of aid staff they did not like by concocting malicious allegations against them. (Often, the targeted staff were the ones doing their jobs with energy and integrity, which meant that they had made local enemies.) That was the flip side of a more common problem, when suspicions against staff could not be substantiated to justify action even where they seemed likely to be true. That often happens when victims think it is too risky to provide evidence.

I have no doubt that the measures we took in the Inter-Agency Standing Committee made a difference. Yet they did not, and on their own cannot, solve the problem entirely. Until the places in which international humanitarian agencies work are less riven by huge gender inequalities, and the rights of women and girls in those areas are better protected through legal, societal, and behavioural changes, violence and subjugation will continue and aid agencies will have to be constantly vigilant in upholding higher standards in their own operations. That sad truth was brought home to me in 2020 by the revelation, following a commendable and exhaustive investigation by *The New Humanitarian*—one of the leading media websites tracking humanitarian issues—of widespread sexual misconduct by employees of the WHO and other aid agencies involved in the response to the Ebola outbreak in 2018 and 2019 in the east of the Democratic Republic of Congo.

A starting point for providing better help for women and girls in crises is gathering better data. In the past, aid agencies tended not to collect enough information detailing the specific needs of women and girls as opposed to men and boys in humanitarian crises. Inadequate data are a key barrier to designing, implementing, and monitoring humanitarian action that can benefit women and girls. In preparing OCHA's annual *Global Humanitarian Overview* from 2017 to 2021, we tried to improve the coverage on women and girls and to disaggregate data more consistently according to the gender of intended beneficiaries. We also tried, with more limited success, to persuade donors to invest more in data gathering. Alongside those efforts, working with the Norwegian Refugee Council, we sought additional funding to deploy gender and protection experts from the beginning of any crisis response to shape the overall approach. The Norwegian Refugee Council is headed by Jan Egeland, one of my ERC predecessors, and it is one of the leading NGOs on gender issues in humanitarian crises. We reinforced the guidance material provided to frontline staff in the early stages of crises so that, for example, they would pay more attention to making sure that camps were well-lit, toilets and showers had locks, and women and girls had safe spaces. The idea was to try to make sure the camp manager, the local mayor, the food distribution contractor, and everyone else involved in a relief operation all thought more about how their activities could better protect women.

One of the most important initiatives was to try to increase the number of women in senior positions in humanitarian agencies, both at headquarters and in frontline operations. António Guterres had made gender parity at the senior level of the UN a central plank of his pitch when campaigning for election as secretary-general. He achieved that within his first three years for the appointments within his personal control at the most senior levels, which provided a strong incentive to do the same at the middle levels.

As a senior UN official, there are not many things over which you have a high degree of control. (In my experience, you spend most of your time suggesting, encouraging, pleading, begging, and cajoling.) Who gets appointed to what job in your organisation, however, is one thing you can normally decide. When I became the ERC, 30 percent of the most senior posts in OCHA (i.e., the top 110 posts in the headquarters and field offices) were held by women. At the end of 2018, it was 42 percent. According to the figures I received just before I left in June 2021, it was then exactly 50 percent. Getting to that point required constant nagging and focus, as well as a more intrusive approach to the selection of people for posts several rungs down the ladder than it would be normal for someone in my position to adopt. I suspect this kind of obsessive focus will need to be sustained if the progress made so far on gender parity is not to be lost.

In October 2017, I visited Pulkha, the small town in Borno in northeast Nigeria that had been captured briefly and declared a "capital" by Boko Haram insurgents. There, I met a young woman working for the IOM. Having grown up in Borno, she had previously been a teacher, but when conflict broke out, she wanted to do more to relieve the suffering of her people, so she became an aid worker. She was committed and knowledgeable, and had clear leadership skills, and she had been promoted into a management position. But certain barriers make it harder for other women to achieve the same thing. Many jobs in the front line of humanitarian operations require people to be away from their homes and families most of the time. Too often, that requirement has prevented women from progressing into senior positions. More enlightened personnel policies that address maternity leave, health, and well-being, and that aggressively fight all forms of harassment in the workplace, are still needed.

For whatever reason, more women leaders in relief operations translates into a greater focus on the needs of female beneficiaries. Women convene assistance networks. They provide psychosocial support. They raise funding, spread awareness, and mobilize for peace.

———————

One of the most significant requirements in improving humanitarian responses for women and girls is to devote more of the funds raised for their benefit, so they can receive a proportionate share of the things (like food) that everyone needs but also obtain the things they need but men do not, like reproductive health care. This remains challenging. The donors all decide for themselves what programmes to fund. Under the Trump administration, the United States, which is by a huge margin the biggest source of finance for humanitarian agencies, cut funding for women's reproductive health. Other donors stepped up to some degree, but resource gaps remained large. Some donors were sceptical that UN Women and the UN Population Fund, the agencies expected to play a leading role in providing assistance to women, had the frontline capacity to deliver programmes effectively, and limited their funding for that reason. There was something in that line of thinking, I thought, but the donors missed the Catch-22: without more funding, the agencies could not build capacity. The leading agencies had designed a minimum services package to try to ensure basic health support was always available, but often there was not enough money even for that. This is a sad missed opportunity: evidence suggests that every dollar spent on contraceptive services saves $1.70 to $4.00 in maternal and newborn care in humanitarian crises.

Only 3 to 4 percent of all humanitarian spending goes to protection activities. Even less—around half of one percent—is spent on reducing gender-based violence. From resources under OCHA's own control, both the 19 country funds we ran in the places with the most protracted humanitarian need like Syria and Yemen, and the central emergency response fund, we took steps to try to ensure women were better supported. I instituted a system in which no-one could apply for money from the central emergency response fund without explaining how women would benefit. Applicants had to provide data on the intended numbers of male and female beneficiaries. I asked the humanitarian coordinators, the senior UN field staff who were responsible for the allocation of money from the country funds, to prioritise programmes benefitting women.

But none of these steps could overcome the central challenge, that as each year in my tenure passed, overall humanitarian needs around the world grew. Although we raised more money year after year, the gap between the needs and the available funds kept increasing. The agencies charged with focusing on women and girls were especially squeezed. We needed to do something new to deal with that.

One of OCHA's roles is to coordinate advocacy and fundraising for humanitarian agencies to seek support for relief operations for the biggest humanitarian crises. I spent a lot of time organizing funding conferences, pledging events, and similar meetings. In an attempt to bring greater structure and predictability to that work, from 2017 we published future plans for the largest and most important events in the annual *Global Humanitarian Overview*. Most of these events focus on a particular crisis—Syria, Yemen, the Sahel, and so on—

but I thought it would be worth trying drawing attention to broader themes. When I met Ine Eriksen Soreide, the charismatic and energetic Norwegian foreign minister, at the UN heads of government meeting in September 2018 I asked whether Norway would be interested in co-hosting with OCHA an event the following year on gender-based violence in humanitarian crises. As a result of some exploratory discussions between my Swedish deputy chief of staff, Sofie Karlsson, and Norwegian diplomats, I knew Ine was interested in the topic. I was sure Norway, which has a long track record of generous support for humanitarian agencies, would be able to attract high-level attendance from lots of countries and serious commitments to do more to tackle the problem.

Largely thanks to Ine's efforts, we were able to persuade the governments of Iraq, Somalia, and the United Arab Emirates to co-host a conference in Oslo over two days in May 2019. Nearly 50 governments, UN agencies, and other organisations announced financial contributions totalling nearly $370 million, as well as hundreds of policy commitments, including for new national legislation, regulations, or good-practice guidance to protect women and girls better in crisis situations. There was also a commitment to monitor and report on whether what was promised was actually completed. Encouragingly, a year later, when progress was reviewed at a follow-up video conference meeting, more than 90 percent of the promised money had indeed been provided. It turned out, however, that this was a temporary improvement in funding. As described in the next chapter, it proved exceptionally difficult to raise money to tackle violence against women and girls during the COVID-19 pandemic, even while other humanitarian financing increased.

No major organisation or society can say they have achieved gender equality. Humanitarian agencies have made a start, but not more than that. Crisis zones are typically characterised by even deeper, more embedded, and more severe discrimination and abuse against women and girls than the rest of the world. It is not difficult to see what needs to happen, but it looks like it might take generations to achieve it. And progress is easily eroded in times of stress. The coronavirus unleashed not just a pandemic of disease but also a pandemic of domestic and sexual violence, with a dramatic deterioration in the behaviour of men in many countries around the world as societies struggled to cope.

ELEVEN

Pandemic

ON 6 JANUARY 2020, JUST AFTER THE HOLIDAYS, António Guterres called a few senior UN staff, including WHO Director-General Tedros Adhanom Ghebreyesus and me, to a meeting on pandemics. A new report had just sounded the alarm that the world was vulnerable to a deadly new airborne disease (or, in the technical jargon, a respiratory pathogen), with the potential not just for large scale loss of life but also huge damage to the world economy. Like previous reports, this one said the world was not very well prepared. In the discussion, we agreed on a series of measures to take, including advancing readiness across the UN itself by conducting a major simulation exercise in which Guterres would be a key participant. At the end of the meeting, Mike Ryan, the experienced, energetic, ebullient Irish doctor who is the head of emergencies at the WHO and with whom I had worked closely in recent years, including on the 2018–19 Ebola outbreak in the Democratic Republic of Congo, said his team were currently gathering information about a new virus in China. They did not yet know much about it, but they thought it could be significant. That was my introduction to the coronavirus.

The COVID-19 pandemic has been the biggest new problem the world has faced for more than 50 years. A deadly disease caused by a highly infectious new virus is an intrinsically difficult challenge. When it starts, the most important information is unknowable: how the virus is transmitted, what symptoms it causes, how long it takes for those symptoms to appear and disappear, whether it is transmitted even if the carrier shows no symptoms, what sort of people are most vulnerable, who will recover and who will not—and, above all, how it can be stopped. The virus therefore has a huge headstart, and responders inevitably risk mistakes while playing catch-up. In some ways, the most surprising thing about the COVID-19 experience is not how bad the response has been, but how good it has been, especially in the speed of the development of vaccines. Yet the global response could have been so much better, and the damage in the most vulnerable countries so much less. Leading the UN's humanitarian response was immensely frustrating: we knew some of the things that needed to be done, but we were unable to persuade those with the wherewithal to take the necessary action.

Much of the discussion so far on how the world can improve its response to future pandemics—and a number of international review exercises have already reported on this question, even though the COVID-19 crisis is far from over—have focused on addressing failures in preparation and readiness. The difficulty with this is that problems like COVID-19 cannot realistically be forestalled by preparation alone. What matters most is how people respond when the problem appears. It is crucial to understand why some of the obvious things that could have been done to help the poorest countries cope better, which would have benefitted everyone else as well, were not pursued. Otherwise, no-one should expect a better response next time.

———————

The human species has had previous encounters with pandemics. There have been plenty of them, going back more than 5,000 years to the dawn of agriculture, when greater human contact with animals facilitated the transmission of new diseases. The bubonic plague still holds the prize for the largest contribution to human death. Fifteen hundred years ago, as wars raged across the Roman Empire and harvests failed,

Constantinople was forced to import large quantities of grain from Egypt. Unfortunately, the city unwittingly imported plague-carrying rats in the process.

Once introduced to Europe, the bubonic plague reverberated periodically around the continent for centuries. Seven hundred years ago, the worst episode, the Black Death, spread rapidly across the continent through trade routes and killed between one-third and two-thirds of the entire population. This experience generated one important insight that is relevant even today: that the disease was contagious and could be mitigated by quarantine. A further important insight arose from the spread of cholera epidemics in the middle of the 19th century: that countries could reduce the impact by working together. The first International Sanitary Conference took place in Paris in 1851.

The Spanish flu pandemic of 1918–19 reinforced international cooperation. It infected and killed a much higher proportion of the global population than COVID-19 has done. Because of its scale, and because people could see how easily and quickly it had become a global not just local problem, it catalysed the creation of the Health Organisation of the League of Nations. The Spanish flu also prompted countries to see that governments had to take more responsibility for public health, rather than relying on private or voluntary efforts. It also introduced something else with which we are all now familiar—the wearing of face masks, a practice that originated in China and Japan.

Although pandemics have always been part of the human experience, the risk appears to have grown recently. In the past 40 years, we have seen SARS, H1N1, MERS, Zika, and Ebola. Why is that? The global population is bigger—there are nearly five times as many people now as there were a hundred years ago. It is older, more urban, and more mobile: ports and border crossings counted 1.5 billion international arrivals in 2019. (A disturbing number of them were me.) Human encroachment into animal habitats is leading to more transmission of infections from animals to people. Once that happens, the nature of today's globalized societies makes it very difficult to prevent spread. That is especially true for those infectious viruses whose carriers sometimes develop symptoms either slowly or not at all.

———◆◆◆———

There was no shortage of experts and reports warning of the risks of a new airborne disease. Many governments, like the United Kingdom, had pandemics at the top of the list of risks to national life that required more preparation. The World Bank, the G-20, and the World Economic Forum all conducted simulations. The UN meeting mentioned at the beginning of the chapter, held on 6 January 2020, took place in the wake of the new Global Preparedness Monitoring Board report which warned that "there is a very real threat of a rapidly moving, highly lethal pandemic of a respiratory pathogen killing 50–80 million people and wiping out nearly 5 percent of the world's economy. The world is not prepared." This statement turned out to be all too true.

The few preparedness initiatives that existed at the time failed partly because they did not reflect the reality of how different societies actually work and how people behave. The standard mix of measures for dealing with diseases spread through human contact all aim to reduce damaging interactions: they focus on handwashing, practising physical distancing, wearing face masks, reducing socializing (including at work and especially where large groups of people gather), using testing and tracing to identify who might be carrying the virus, and introducing quarantines and isolation. There are daunting practical, legal, political, institutional, and social constraints to implementing all these measures, even before considering the huge economic costs they imply. Their feasibility varies considerably between countries. Levels of preparation and past experience help determine what is realistic in different societies. By the end of March 2020, the virus had reached essentially every place on the planet. Everyone was having to deal with it. But there were many different sorts of response, reflecting the differences between countries.

A first category, those countries with recent experience of SARS, H1N1, and MERS, were mostly in Asia. They were alert to the danger, had invested in public health systems, and had governments that enjoyed levels of trust facilitating broad voluntary compliance with severe restrictions (or, in some cases, had authoritarian systems capable of enforcing compliance on the population). These countries tended to act early and, as it appeared for much of 2020, relatively effectively.

A second group of countries, including many in Europe and North America, had relatively large and effective medical systems (as distinct from public health systems) but less recent relevant exposure. In some cases, like the United Kingdom, they had cut back on investments in public health institutions as part of the austerity measures following the 2008–09 global financial crisis. Some countries, including the United States, tended to overestimate their capacity, underestimate the risk, and had leaders high in confidence but limited in relevant experience or temperamentally and ideologically unwilling to take measures that would slow the spread of the virus but limit people's freedoms. Typically, these countries acted slower, later, and more weakly. They suffered high death tolls.

A third group of countries, including a number of African countries, had been at the forefront of the Ebola and HIV crises. They knew their capacity to act was weak but at least had relevant recent experience. They acted early and decisively, taking the limited measures feasible for them—and they may also have benefitted from having younger populations less threatened by the virus and, being less urbanised, living conditions less conducive to its spread.

A fourth category includes those with limited relevant capabilities and no relevant recent experience. They included some middle-income countries, for example in Latin America. But this group also included most of the world's poorest, conflict-affected, and fragile countries, often with significant refugee and displaced populations. In the early weeks and months of the pandemic, many people thought these countries, which are where humanitarian agencies mostly work, would be hit worst of all. That has turned out to be true. Not primarily, as was expected, through the direct impact of the virus itself on human health and mortality, but rather as a result of the economic carnage it has wrought. The tragedy is that some of that economic damage could and should have been avoided.

Overall, countries that placed a large premium on individual freedoms, had limited relevant recent experience of widespread infectious diseases, had less strong public health systems than their level of development might have implied, had been experiencing a decline in trust in government, and had leaders less well personally equipped for such a crisis, underperformed. (This group of countries includes both the United States and United Kingdom.) Nonetheless, some of these countries had two huge compensating advantages: they could cope better with the economic contraction, and they had the scientific and industrial capabilities to develop vaccines and treatments faster than anyone else. They could, had they wished, also have done a lot to help the most vulnerable countries. Doing so would not just have been generous, it would have served their own interests as well.

In the second quarter of 2020, governments, businesses, and many families and individuals in the developed world took decisions that had the effect of temporarily closing down substantial parts of the world economy, with the goal of slowing the spread and impact of the virus and buying time to find solutions—especially vaccines and treatments. This remarkable approach to handling the problem, never previously adopted, was feasible only because the better-off countries were able to protect their citizens from the worst effects of the economic lockdown. They threw out the fiscal and monetary policy rulebooks and introduced a vast array of furlough schemes, business loans, social payments, tax holidays, asset purchases through central banks, wage subsidies, and other extraordinary innovations. The measures were not formally coordinated across the major economies, but they all did the same sorts of things in a synchronized way, which reinforced the impact. The cost, running into tens of trillions of dollars, is dizzying and will ultimately need to be addressed. Nevertheless, this was the right thing to do. But the better-off countries signally failed to offer an adequate helping hand to the poorest countries, which faced the same economic crunch but lacked the resources, institutions, or access to markets to take similar measures. The poorest countries have faced a collapse in their commodity earnings, tourism revenues, and remittances from citizens working abroad, as well as the economic costs of global and in some cases nationally imposed lockdown measures. While the better-off countries threw more than 20 percent of their national incomes at the protection of their own citizens, the poorest countries could access only 2 percent of their (much smaller) incomes.

Writing in the *Guardian* in early May 2020, I set out what I saw was happening and proposed an agenda for limiting the global damage. I said that the biggest economic slowdown in living memory would have a devastating and destabilizing effect in the world's poorest countries:

> We should be ready for a rise in conflict, hunger and poverty. The spectre of multiple famines looms. . . . As countries with weak health systems attempt to fight the virus, we can expect an increase in measles, malaria, cholera and other disease as vaccinations are put on hold, health systems buckle under the strain and medical supply chains are disrupted. . . . Recent history shows us that what happens in the world's most fragile places has knock-on effects, whether it's through uncontrolled migration, terrorism or global instability. Leaving the virus to spread unchecked in the world's most fragile countries and free to circle back round the world is in no one's interest. Nor is economic collapse and instability in the poorest nations.

The cost of protecting the most vulnerable 10 percent of people in the poorest countries, I estimated, would be approximately $90 billion. This, I said, was a lot of money, but—

> [I]t is an affordable sum, equivalent to just 1 percent of the global stimulus package the world's richest countries have put in place to

save the global economy. About two-thirds of it could come from organisations such as the World Bank and the International Monetary Fund. They will need support to change the terms on which they help the most vulnerable countries: front-loading money, reduced interest rates and further debt relief. The remainder will need to come from official development assistance—the money wealthy countries spend on foreign aid. That currently stands at about $150 billion each year. A one-off 20 percent increase over the next twelve months would generate the $30 billion needed.

I repeated similar arguments through the first year of the pandemic in a string of opinion articles published in the *Washington Post*, the *Financial Times*, *Le Monde*, and many other papers, as well as in countless interviews for the broadcast and print media. Many other people offered comparable analysis and made similar proposals.

———— ✦ ————

Meanwhile, we set about doing the things humanitarian agencies could do, with the resources available to us. In February, before there were any recorded cases in any of the countries where OCHA was working, we took our first practical action: to provide a grant to the WHO and UNICEF from the central emergency response fund to help them start public information campaigns and get testing kits and protective equipment to as many countries as possible. The last major international trip I took before the global lockdown was at the end of February into early March. I went to Fiji, New Zealand, Australia, through Dubai to Saudi Arabia, then to Turkey down to the border with Syria and then back to New York. Everywhere I went, people were talking about the virus and how to cope with it—though in most places there were still few, if any, cases.

We thought the public information issue was crucial. One of the main problems in the world today is that too many people believe things that are not true, and do not believe things that are true. That is exacerbated by one of the world's biggest growth industries: fake news and misinformation. This is all potentially catastrophic in the highly charged atmosphere of the early stages of a pandemic, where fear, anxiety, and myths abound, and correct information struggles to be heard.

We recognised in the UN that there was an important role for us to play here. The Edelman Trust Barometer, a respected annual survey, had been reporting that trust in the UN had been growing around the world over recent years. Many people in much of the world trusted what we said more than they trusted governments or parts of the media. As a result, one of the things we tried to do was ensure that every person on the planet knew a few basic facts about the virus and what they could do to protect themselves. The UN's "Verified" campaigns in the first months of the pandemic, delivered with the help of more than 110,000 volunteers in 100 countries who spotted and reported dodgy claims that needed correcting, reached more than a billion people in multiple languages. They were greatly facilitated by collaboration from responsible media organisations around the world. I had consistently found that the leading global broadcasters with serious professional standards—CNN, the BBC, Al Jazeera, and others—wanted to cover the major humanitarian stories and did so in an informative, even-handed way. The high-quality professional media, as well as the scientists and the pharmaceutical companies, are among the institutions that have acquitted themselves well during the COVID-19 crisis.

The WHO's declaration of a pandemic on 11 March led to a frantic fortnight in OCHA, during which we prepared and then on 25 March launched what became our largest ever response plan: the Global Humanitarian Response Plan for COVID-19. In order to help put it together and organise the follow-up, I convened the chief executives of the Inter-Agency Standing Committee—who normally meet twice a year—on a weekly basis in the early months of the crisis. We set clear objectives. First, and most difficult, to contain the spread of the virus and decrease mortality and morbidity. Second, to stem the deterioration in human rights, social cohesion, food security, and livelihoods, which we could already observe. Finally, to protect the people who we feared might be the most vulnerable of all—including refugees, people displaced inside their own country (normally because of conflict), migrants, and the host communities for all these groups. The COVID-19 response plan was successful up to a point. We raised a billion dollars in the first few weeks, and $3.8 billion by December.

Some of the uses agencies found for the money were what humanitarian agencies always do. During the course of 2020, we provided cash transfers worth $1.7 billion to vulnerable people across more than 60 countries who had lost their incomes. We assisted 33 million refugees, displaced people, and vulnerable migrants, many of whom were stuck in prison-like conditions as lockdowns closed the borders. We improved water, sanitation, and hygiene facilities for more than 70 million people; delivered essential health services to 75 million; and provided community-based mental health and psychosocial support to 75 million.

But the unique circumstances also required innovations. In March and April, commercial airline flights mostly disappeared or were banned, especially in the places where humanitarian agencies work. The UN had 50,000 staff working on the front lines in humanitarian crises. The NGOs had even larger numbers. The vast majority were nationals of the countries in which they served, but there also were thousands of international staff, who in war zones normally work on rotations of six weeks on and two weeks off to allow some respite from the extreme circumstances they face. If we wanted relief operations to continue—and pre-existing humanitarian crises only grew worse during the pandemic—we needed to be able to get staff and supplies in and out. So the World Food Programme, with a pump-priming grant we provided from the central emergency response fund, swiftly created a new air service to replace the vanishing commercial airlines we had previously relied on. Between May and August, it transported 25,000 humanitarian workers from nearly 400 organisations to and from the humanitarian front lines, and carried vaccines, medicines, and other supplies. These flights allowed the staff to stay and deliver services, albeit often at personal risk and under extremely tough conditions.

We had also to arrange for medical help for staff who got serious cases of COVID-19. Given the paucity of medical facilities in places where humanitarian operations are needed, particularly intensive care facilities, the only immediate option was to try to negotiate access to hospitals in better-off countries to which specialist air services could medically evacuate sick staff. Alongside that, working with the UN operational services department that supports peacekeeping operations, we set up dedicated new facilities in countries willing to receive sick UN staff. That system, which we subsidised through another grant from the central emergency response fund, also covered international staff working for humanitarian NGOs. These arrangements provided just enough confidence for many staff to be willing to stay in post despite the risks.

These elements of the humanitarian response in the poorest countries were all very well. They helped in a modest way and it was important to pursue them. But the cold truth is that they did little more than take the edge off the worst of the problem.

In December 2020, we launched the *Global Humanitarian Overview* for 2021. It is the most comprehensive, authoritative, and evidence-based assessment of humanitarian need available. We forecast that 235 million people would need assistance to survive the next year—40 percent more than the previous record number the year before. The increase was almost entirely due to the pandemic. We developed UN and NGO plans to meet the needs of 160 million of those people. They were costed at $35 billion, another record. If implemented, those programmes would prevent large-scale loss of life. But a dramatic increase in other support was necessary to give the most fragile countries a chance to recover from the pandemic in parallel with the larger economies of the G-20 and the Organisation for Economic Co-operation and Development (OECD).

Once it became clear by the autumn of 2020 that scientists were anticipating success in developing vaccines against the coronavirus, an energetic public policy debate began about the most rational way to roll them out. In the UN, everyone from Guterres down repeated ad nauseam in every public meeting the mantra that, because no-one would be safe from the virus until everyone was safe, the world should take a collective approach to vaccine roll-out. For understandable reasons, it was clear that the new vaccines would be used first in the countries whose scientists, pharmaceutical companies, and taxpayers had done most to develop them. The question, then, was how and how fast would they be made available to the rest of the world. A new initiative, known as COVAX—co-led by the WHO, Gavi (the Vaccine Alliance, previously called the Global Alliance on Vaccines and Immunisation), and the Coalition for Epidemic Preparedness Innovations—was established to coordinate funding and access for poorer countries.

In January 2021, with Jeremy Farrar, the head of the Wellcome Trust—one of the world's most highly regarded medical research institutions—I published an opinion article in the *Daily Telegraph* arguing that Britain's national interest would be best served by starting to give some of the vaccine supplies it had ordered for domestic use to poorer countries. We made similar arguments with the United States and the EU. A global pandemic left very little option but to have broad horizons. Keeping the United Kingdom's citizens safe, we felt, depended on not leaving other countries behind:

> If a variant arises somewhere in the world, it will come back to the UK. Each new infection is an opportunity for mutation—as we are now seeing with the new, highly infectious variants first identified in Britain, South Africa and Brazil. If the virus is left unchecked in large parts of the world, more variants will arise. The more that develop, the higher the risk of the disease evolving to an extent where current vaccines, diagnostics and treatments no longer work. To reduce the chances of new variants arising, we need to reduce the

amount of virus circulating and lower transmission. In an inter-connected world, that means speeding up the rate of vaccination not just at home, but everywhere. Britain has a unique opportunity—and the capability—to lead the way in tackling this pandemic, en-suring fair global access to all COVID vaccines, treatments and tests. . . . If Britain shared a small percentage of doses each quarter, instead of waiting to donate doses after all adults are vaccinated, it would galvanize other countries to do the same. Our best chance of getting ahead of this virus now is if all wealthy nations, especially those with multiple deals with vaccine manufacturers, contribute a portion of the doses they receive each quarter.

We also emphasised the economic case for sharing vaccines sooner rather than later:

New analysis this week highlights the economic case, suggesting wealthy countries vaccinating themselves by the middle of the year, leaving poor countries largely shut, could knock $9 trillion off the global economy—nearly half the costs accruing to wealthy coun-tries themselves. As a trading nation, the UK can't start rebuilding its economy unless all countries can start rebuilding theirs. If we fail to fast-track vaccine rollout on a global scale, and ignore the sci-entific and moral certainties, we will fail to establish any kind of lasting control of this endemic disease. It will reverberate for years to come, continuing to devastate our communities, taking more lives and crippling our health systems and economies. We are fac-ing the biggest, most challenging vaccination campaign in history. We need to speed things up across the world. Covid-19 is not wait-ing; neither can we.

I was also concerned about two other challenges in relation to vaccine roll-out in poorer countries. The first was ensuring that the fi-nancing for COVID-19 vaccines for the very poorest countries did not come at the expense of other activities that could save more lives in those countries. As I said at a public event on the pandemic hosted by the Brookings Institution in December 2020, "it would be perverse, and probably in fact increase loss of life, to pay for the COVID vaccine by cutting funding for things like food security and routine immunization against diseases like measles." The second challenge related to the limitations of the vaccine delivery system in fragile and conflict-affected countries. I recalled unhappy previous experiences with donors chopping and changing priorities as a result of delivery difficulties. For example, I was involved over a 10-year period in northern Nigeria with successive bursts of enthusiasm for polio eradication and malaria control, only to discover that these initiatives were being pursued at the expense of routine immunisation. It would be a real challenge to add delivery of the COVID-19 vaccines to the to-do list of weak health systems without causing unintended damage to other important objectives. This issue was not receiving nearly enough attention.

Richer European and North American countries made good progress with vaccine roll-out in the first six months of 2021. But the situation in most of the world improved little if at all. New and seemingly more infectious variants of the virus coursed through many countries, with India particularly badly affected in the second quarter of the year. Very few doses of the vaccine reached low-income countries, and in some cases the doses supplied could not be used because the recipients did not have the required health workers and public information campaigns in place. Some countries even returned vaccine supplies they had received from COVAX.

It was clear that much more urgency and ambition would be needed for a larger, faster, and more comprehensive plan to vaccinate the world. In May, the IMF unveiled a $50 billion proposal to end the pandemic by vaccinating 40 percent of the global population by the end of 2021 and 60 percent by mid-2022. "That," I told journalists who asked me about it, "is the deal of the century." The cost would pale into insignificance compared with the value of the global economic recovery it would make possible. All eyes swivelled to the G-7 summit of heads of government, to be hosted in June by the British government in the southwest tourist centre of Cornwall.

For the first time since the beginning of the pandemic, the leaders were able to meet face to face. Importantly, they committed themselves to multilateral collaboration of the sort that had characterized the response to the 2007–08 financial crisis but had been absent in the years of the Trump administration. But the broad principles were not converted into practical action, and the detail of what was agreed in Cornwall flattered to deceive—it was weaker than it was made to sound. The communiques at the end of the summit said that the leaders had agreed to provide a billion doses of vaccine to poorer countries. They sought, and got, friendly publicity. But what was needed was a plan to vaccinate the whole world, and this amounted to a plan to vaccinate 10 percent of the population of middle- and low-income countries, mostly in a year's time. It also transpired that some of the vaccine offered would be from the stocks that governments held that were nearing their expiry date, for which there was no useful alternative but to give them away.

I was doing a series of end-of-tenure interviews in the days after the summit, and was asked by Reuters about the outcome. I was blunt: "These sporadic, small-scale charitable handouts from rich countries to poor countries are not a serious plan and will not bring the pandemic to an end." The White House complained when I spoke to them on a prearranged call the day after the story was published. What did you expect us to do, they asked. I thought the G-7 should have agreed a plan to take to the G-20 meeting later in the year. I referred to the IMF proposal; emphasized the need for an urgent large-scale global vaccination plan backed by all the leading economies (i.e., the G-20); and said that the most fragile countries also needed help with oxygen, testing, and protective equipment while they waited for vaccines, as well as more fulsome economic support. If the vaccine manufacturers saw a market for 10 billion doses backed by funding guarantees from the largest economies in the G-20 and coordination through COVAX, they might make more serious efforts to address the constraints to scaling up production. By the middle of 2021, most G-20 members were making meaningful progress with vaccinations, but progress in Africa and other places with major humanitarian crises was negligible. Remedying that would have been an act of self-interest by the bigger economies, because they would all be threatened by new variants emerging in places where the virus continued to run out of control. Some scientists believed that the risks of dangerous new mutations were particularly high in places with large populations infected with HIV, like many African countries. Twenty years ago, the G-7 had the weight to push such an agenda through. It transparently no longer does, and unfortunately the state of geopolitical relations among those who now could—the G-20 countries, which between them account for 80 percent of global income—seemingly puts this kind of rapid collective action challenge beyond their reach.

It is dispiriting, as I write this the best part of two years since the pandemic began, to see that many of our direst projections have been realised, and that the remedial measures agreed internationally remain pathetically paltry. The failure of international solidarity is surprising, because the experience of the 2008–09 financial crisis made it evident what needed to be done. That crisis, of course, had a lesser impact: global gross domestic product fell by 0.1 percent then, compared to the much bigger reduction of 4 to 5 percent in 2020. The obvious measures that were taken to support the most vulnerable countries during the 2008–09 financial crisis, including the issuing of Special Drawing Rights (supplementary foreign exchange reserves) to all IMF members, the recapitalisation of the multilateral development banks, and generous replenishments of their funds for the poorest countries, have either not happened at all or been too timid and too slow during the pandemic. (An issuance of Special Drawing Rights to all IMF members was finally agreed in August 2021, but there was no agreement on how to maximise the benefits to the poorest countries.) There was also a failure to address the growing debt burden of the poorest countries; many were being dragged ever deeper into the mire.

The cost to the richer G-20 and OECD countries of more generous measures would have been minimal, especially in the short term. The fact that they were not taken represented a governance failure in leading countries, which had in the past acted collaboratively for the global benefit and in their own self-interest. As a result, the economic and social consequences of the pandemic in countries where humanitarian agencies work are much worse than they would have been had international action been better.

For the first time since the 1990s, extreme poverty has increased. When the final numbers are crunched, they will probably show that by the end of 2021, up to 150 million people fell back into extreme poverty (on the World Bank's $1.90 a day measure), bringing the number to nearly 750 million. That amounts to 9.5 percent of the world's population, compared to 586 million, or 7.5 percent, without the COVID-19 crisis. Predictably, the burden fell particularly heavily on women and girls.

Health services in the poorest countries have been heavily compromised. Life expectancy is falling. The annual death toll from HIV, tuberculosis, and malaria is set to double. In mid-2021, the WHO and UNICEF reported that in 2020 at least 25 million children had not received routine immunisation for measles and other preventable diseases. Vaccination rates, improvements in which have been one of the global success stories of the past generation, fell almost everywhere. In India, the number of unvaccinated babies and toddlers doubled, with 3 million missing out. The number of people facing starvation also doubled, though as of mid-2021 the strenuous efforts made by the UN and others to avoid large-scale famine appeared to be working.

There has been a lot of press coverage and policy discussion in better-off countries about the pandemic-related toll on mental well-being and psychosocial stress in their populations. Lord Gus O'Donnell, the former head of the British civil service, and Larry Summers, the former chief economist of the World Bank, have noted that putting a value on this suffering and its associated impact on productivity dramatically increases the overall cost of the pandemic. That impact is evident in the most fragile countries as well. The plague of violence against women and girls particularly demands attention. The pandemic has caused fear, and heightened tension and anxiety. Many people have been cooped up in cramped conditions for long periods of lockdown. That unfortunately took its toll on the behaviour of men, too many of whom violently took out their frustration, stress, and anger on their intimate partners. In some countries, calls to dedicated helplines increased by over 700 percent. Support services were overwhelmed.

While all countries suffered, and there were daunting problems in both middle-income and better-off countries, the human carnage was concentrated in the poorest, most vulnerable parts of the world. As the Bill and Melinda Gates Foundation's Goalkeepers report put it in September 2020, the first six months of the pandemic threatened to unravel 25 years of progress in some key development activities, like immunisation. It is worth remembering what many poor countries were like 25 years ago. I was working in a country then where a quarter of children never saw their fifth birthday, most never went to school, and 1 woman in 18 died in childbirth. There were many other places like that then.

The problems now brewing have the potential to come back to bite everyone. All the poverty, hunger, sickness, and suffering will fuel grievances, hopelessness, and despair. In their wake will come conflict, instability, migration, and refugee flows, all giving succour to extremist groups and terrorists. The consequences may reach far and last long. There is, in other words, a serious risk of a significant reversal of the substantial global progress over the past 50 years in reducing poverty, increasing life expectancy, improving literacy and access to education, and reducing hunger. The biggest economic and social effect of the pandemic, when measured over the long term, may turn out to be that arising from the disruption to the education of hundreds of millions of children. Children everywhere have had their education disrupted by the pandemic, but again the impact is greatest in the poorest countries. Up to 25 million children, pushed into work and early marriage, may never return to the classroom. The World Bank has estimated that the cost in lost lifetime earnings could be more than $10 trillion. The effects may not all be visible, but they will be there just the same.

It would not surprise me if the recovery in better-off countries is brisk. By mid-2021, we could already see the signs of that in countries that had vaccinated a high proportion of their citizens. In the poorest countries, however, I think the COVID-19 hangover is likely to be long and harsh, especially if there is no improvement in international collaboration. Real incomes fell by more than 5 percent in fragile and conflict-affected states in 2020. The IMF has projected that their per capita incomes will not recover to their 2019 levels before 2024. By that time, nearly 40 percent of the people in the world living in extreme poverty will be in those countries, and they are at significant risk of falling even further behind. That is bad news for them, but also dangerous for the rest of the world.

TWELVE

A Better Humanitarian System

MY 12 PREDECESSORS AS THE ERC between 1991 and 2017 served for an average of a little more than two years each. In the middle of 2019, Guterres asked me to extend my two-year contract for another two years. I found the job stimulating, thought I was making a worthwhile contribution, and also thought OCHA would benefit from some further continuity to bed down the changes I had been overseeing. But I also missed my family, who were mostly in London, and some of them needed more support than I could offer when spending so little time at home. So even though I signed on for two more years, I privately thought the best thing might be to serve just one more year. Talking it over at home during the 2019 Christmas holidays, we decided I would aim to leave the UN by the end of 2020, making clear my plan by the middle of the year in order to leave plenty of time for a successor to be selected. But when the pandemic broke, it was obvious that it would not be responsible to announce that summer that I would be leaving. By the autumn of 2020, though, when it was clear that vaccines were about to arrive and could bring the pandemic to an end, things looked different. Late in the year, I asked Guterres to agree to release me; he said he would have preferred me to stay a few more years, but was gracious in understanding why I wished to leave. I sent in my resignation letter in December, effective from the end of March 2021, but made clear I was ready to stay until he had chosen a replacement. It was not until February that my departure was announced, and in the end it was not until late June that I signed off and handed over to the UN's Yemen envoy, Martin Griffiths. (Martin had been the head of the OCHA Geneva office decades previously.) In all, I ended up staying for almost four years.

Everyone who has been the ERC has thought they were doing the job in demanding times. That is the nature of the role. Objectively, however, the 2017 to 2021 period was, in terms of the quantity, scale, and complexity of humanitarian crises, unusually challenging. These were genuinely dire times for many. The number of people in need grew dramatically to never-before-seen peaks. The size and costs of operations to help them reached new records, too. In addition to the large-scale crises I have covered in the course of this book, culminating in the pandemic, there were plenty of others. I have visited Afghanistan frequently since 2003 and have seen the ebb and flow of humanitarian need there, with spikes caused both by natural events like droughts and by the human factor during upsurges in fighting or political instability. In early 2021, the pandemic, drought, and renewed conflict together took a terrible new toll, and by then almost half the country needed help from humanitarian agencies. (While I was writing this book in the late summer of 2021, we saw the return to power of the Taliban, with all the additional threat that posed, especially to women and girls.)

When in 2019 I visited Venezuela, a country whose large natural oil reserves ought to give it significant wealth, politicians had squandered their national assets and created a crisis requiring the mobilization of the humanitarian system and appeals totalling more than $2 billion both for people inside the country and those forced to flee to neighbouring countries. Drought in Southern Africa—exacerbated in places like Madagascar and Zimbabwe by abject governance and economic folly—when I travelled there in 2019 also necessitated help from humanitarian agencies to stave off acute hunger. A few months later, I saw during a short visit how Haiti, the poorest country in the Western Hemisphere, is perpetually at risk of earthquakes and one bad hurricane away from total disaster. But there, too, the biggest risk is human; that is evident from the fact that the Dominican Republic, the other half of the island of Hispaniola, with the same geography and climate as neighbouring Haiti, is relatively prosperous.

That distinction between two countries on the same landmass and with much of the same history, where one is developed and the other disastrous, is even starker on the Korean Peninsula. Seoul, the capital of South Korea, is prosperous, welcoming, comprehensible, and an easy and nice place to visit. Pyongyang and the surrounding provinces in North Korea, where I went in 2018 and over which three generations of the Kim dynasty have sustained an impressive indoctrination and subjugation of 25 million people, gave me the creeps. The UN's offers of help with food security and combatting drug-resistant tuberculosis and other health problems there have been rebuffed.

As I have described, humanitarian crises have been getting worse in recent years because their causes are not being tackled. Problems get bigger and last longer. In late 2020, my office analysed the humanitarian problems the UN had been dealing with over the previous 25 years. The findings are sobering. Between 1995 and 2020, the average duration of crises requiring a UN-coordinated response increased from less than two years to nearly seven years. The number of responses also more than doubled, with more countries—like Syria, Libya, several in the Sahel, and Venezuela—being added to the list of those where humanitarian assistance was needed. And the size of response plans grew even more dramatically, from just over $2 billion in 1995 to nearly $40 billion in 2020. Some of that was the effect of the pandemic, but most was not. The 2019 figure, before the pandemic, was already $30 billion. Funding for responses has grown enormously, too. In 2016, the year before I started as the ERC, $12 billion was raised for UN-coordinated humanitarian responses. In my first year in the role, 2017, we received $14 billion. In 2018, it was $15 billion; in 2019, more than $17 billion; and in 2020, $20 billion—a 65 percent increase in four years. But the requirements had grown even more, so unfinanced needs were larger than ever, averaging nearly 40 percent in recent years.

Funding has become ever more reliant on a small group of Western donors. The United States on its own accounts for 30 to 40 percent of the resources raised by the World Food Programme, UNICEF, and the UN refugee agency, which are the largest humanitarian agencies. The four largest donors—the United States, Germany, the European Commission, and the United Kingdom—have between them in recent years accounted for 70 percent of the money raised for UN appeals. The drastic British aid cuts in 2020 and 2021 concentrate the burden even more on the top three. Funding for the UN's humanitarian activities is voluntary, unlike contributions to peacekeeping or the general subscription countries pay for UN membership, which are assessed on an agreed formula related to member states' economic weight. Some large countries chose to pay very little towards UN humanitarian appeals—China, Russia, and France among them. So the sharing of the burden is skewed in a way that looks increasingly unfair. As time passes, it is unlikely to be sustainable.

Humanitarian agencies, especially the larger, most professional, and best managed UN agencies, Red Cross organisations, and international NGOs do a good job with the money they can raise. More than a hundred million people in countries affected by crises have benefitted from UN-coordinated responses in each of the last few years, receiving food, shelter, health services, education for their children and other assistance. Millions of lives are saved every year. The situation worldwide would be a lot worse without that work, not just in terms of a larger death toll but also larger refugee flows and other spillovers, creating problems in the neighbourhood of countries in crisis as well as more widely. The humanitarian aid sector has grown as the number of crises has mushroomed. Local organisations—and individuals and families helping their friends and neighbours—are consistently the fastest and most generous responders when a new disaster strikes or conflict displaces more people. However, international agencies across the world that employ hundreds of thousands of people play a prominent role in these efforts.

Despite all its good work, the humanitarian sector is overwhelmed. Needs are growing faster than the capacity to handle them. This imbalance will continue, to rub the point in, for as long as the underlying causes of humanitarian crises remain inadequately addressed. It is unrealistic to expect funding to meet all the needs. How will the agencies cope with the growing strain? How do they stretch the available resources further? Although the current arrangements have been effective in saving lives, no-one can pretend that they are the most efficient way to help people. Kofi Annan found 20 years ago that there was no appetite for major reform in the basic architecture in which multiple agencies compete for resources and are encouraged to collaborate in using them. There is still no appetite for a redesign of the humanitarian system. Meaningful reform would, however, be possible—and looks to me to be essential.

What can be done on the most important issue, to address the causes of humanitarian crises? Some of the issues are acutely intractable. One example is the impact of climate change, much of which is already baked in for the poorest countries. Likewise, geopolitical arrangements to prevent, resolve, and contain conflict appear to be a tall order at a time when the leading powers see many issues through the prism of "what's bad for my adversary must be good for me." Even the skimpiest analysis quickly reveals the flaws in that mindset, given the tendency for conflict to generate negative spillover effects ranging from migration to organised crime, narcotics, people trafficking, the spread of infectious diseases, and other problems that ultimately affect everyone. Such thinking, however, is prevalent.

Despite these constraints, there is broad scope for improving the situation in many countries beset by long-lasting humanitarian crises—and for preventing others that have been made more vulnerable by the pandemic falling into the same morass—by increasing the volume and improving the quality of the support they receive to sustain their economies and provide basic services to take the edge off the frustration and misery many people suffer. Humanitarian problems are concentrated in fragile and conflict-affected countries that are falling further behind the rest of the world, and the pandemic has been widening that gap. One of the most obvious ways of addressing these discrepancies would be to redirect the energies and resources of the international financial institutions, in particular the IMF and the World Bank, to focus more seriously on these countries. Others—not least former British Prime Minister Gordon Brown in his 2021 book *Seven Ways to Change the World*—have made similar proposals. Moving the international financial institutions in this direction would require not just the harnessing of their financial firepower, but also retooling their products and processes and bringing in new personnel with the skills, experience, and aptitude for such demanding work. There is scope for stronger collaboration with UN agencies, many of which are highly focused on the most challenging environments but lack the financial resources and analytical rigour the international financial institutions can bring to bear. Both the IMF and the World Bank have begun to move in this direction, but so far only with baby steps. More serious efforts are required.

In the meantime, humanitarian agencies must continue to battle away. Most of what they need to do is more of the same. Doing it faster and in anticipation of predictable problems would have huge benefits, as described in the earlier chapter on reforming humanitarian finance. But further progress is also necessary in ensuring the relief agencies are meeting the essential needs of the most vulnerable and previously overlooked groups, in particular women and girls and people with disabilities. Similarly, there is much to do to provide more comprehensive assistance, particularly in the areas of mental health and psycho-social support and, in long-lasting crises, education.

A specific reform that would make a difference would be to finance the UN's central emergency response fund through the kind of assessed contributions that member states make for peacekeeping and their regular contributions to the UN budget, rather than relying on voluntary contributions. This could enact the proposal endorsed several years ago by the UN General Assembly that the fund should reach $1 billion a year. Such change would have a number of benefits. It would make it easier for the UN to act faster and in anticipation of new crises, and lead to a cheaper and more humane response with a smaller risk of spillover effects into other countries. It would be a step towards addressing what I think is the increasingly unsustainable reliance on a small number of mostly Western countries to finance humanitarian action. The cost for most countries would be modest, particularly if those countries that already contribute generously to the fund were to agree to sustain their contributions at recent levels for a period while the new funding system was phased in.

———————

One of the things that worried me increasingly about the humanitarian sector as my UN experience grew was how little weight all the agencies, even the most well-meaning among them, gave to the wishes and preferences of the people they were trying to help. It is hard to address the "we know best what you need" mindset. Agencies have their own mandates and areas of specialism. Everything looks like a nail to someone whose only tool is a hammer, and relief agencies tend to be attentive to the needs they specialise in meeting and deaf to other requirements. The fact that they have to comply with the demands of their donors if they want to stay in business amplifies the problem. I addressed these concerns in a speech at the Center for Global Development in Washington in April 2021:

The humanitarian system is set up to give people in need what international agencies and donors think is best, and what we have to offer, rather than giving people what they themselves say they most need. . . . Ultimately, organisations or decision makers can choose to listen to people and be responsive or they can choose not to. There are no real consequences for the choice they make. There are weak incentives to push them in the right direction. . . . People in dire need are frequently selling aid they have been given, to buy something else they want more—a clear indication that what is being provided does not meet people's needs and preferences.

The failure consistently to ask people what help they need and then track whether it is being provided has two deleterious consequences. It introduces unnecessary costs and inefficiencies: why go to the trouble of procuring and distributing goods that people then turn around and sell? When there are so many unmet needs, this is particularly regrettable. But beyond that, and to my mind potentially more corrosive, is the fact that it strips people in need even further of the ability to make choices for themselves, adding to the humiliation and disempowerment the victims of humanitarian crises suffer. Some of these concerns have echoes in the debate about "decolonising development," which has gathered steam in academic circles in recent years and which points in the direction of reducing the sway of intermediaries, including international agencies, in favour of empowering local people.

To address these issues, I suggested the creation of an independent commission for voices in crisis, to be tasked with listening to people and then grading the aid agencies on the extent to which the help they were offering was what people were saying they wanted. These assessments would not solve the problem, but they would subtly tilt the playing field back in the direction of the people the agencies say they are trying to help. My proposals initially attracted two sorts of critical response (as well as a fair degree of support). One critique, in parts of the right-wing press, claimed that I was saying that aid agencies should not be supported because they do not actually help people.

That critique was predictable, but bogus and dishonest. I had gone out of my way to say that the humanitarian system does a great deal of good, and pointed out things would be much worse without it; the question, as I saw it, was how to make it even more effective. In a way, the second objection troubled me more. It came from some quarters inside the humanitarian system, from people who said that the concerns I was raising had already been addressed and solved. For that view to be expressed in the face of the evidence seemed to me to prove my point. Saving lives in dire times means putting people first.

ACKNOWLEDGEMENTS

THOUGH I AM RESPONSIBLE for all the errors, many people contributed, knowingly or otherwise, to the writing of *Relief Chief*. My friend Andrew Wilson was first off the mark, suggesting before I even started the job that I should think about writing a book about it. He conducted a series of lengthy private interviews with me from 2017 to 2019 in which, stream-of-consciousness style, I recorded my thoughts. The transcripts of these interviews were the main source for many of the contemporaneous personal judgments peppered through the text. He and Claire Bolderson also wielded the casting votes on the title.

Most of the book was written in the three months after I left the UN in June 2021, but some chapters draw significantly on lectures and speeches I gave before that. The chapter on Yemen is an expanded version of a talk I gave at the Blavatnik School of Government at Oxford University in the spring of 2021, which John Ratcliffe, Asmaa Chalabi, and George Khoury helped me prepare. The Syria chapter builds on a presentation given at the Geneva Graduate Institute in the spring of 2021, for which I benefitted from conversations with Ali Al Za'atari, Imran Riza, Kevin Kennedy, and Yacoub El Hillo, as well as the work of Sebastian von Ensiedel. (Sebastian von Ensiedel was also heavily involved in preparing a lecture I gave at the London School of Economics in June 2021, which became the foundation for the "Wars Have Laws" chapter.) For the chapter on reforming humanitarian finance, I drew on talks at the Ministry of Foreign Affairs in Dublin and the London School of Economics in 2018 and 2019, and discussions with Stefan Dercon, Dirk-Jan Omtzigt, and Juan Chavez were invaluable in developing these talks. In December 2020, I spoke at the Brookings Institution in Washington about the impact of the COVID-19 pandemic in conflict-affected countries, drawing on analysis Kate Yarlett helped assemble. This talk forms part of the raw material for the chapter on the pandemic. Zoe Paxton made important contributions to many of the statements I made and opinion pieces I wrote for newspapers around the world in 2020 and 2021, several of which I also have drawn on.

Masood Ahmed, Charles Kenny, Sarah Rose, and Jeff Feltman provided invaluable advice on the text before it was finalised, correcting many errors, misjudgements, and omissions.

I am extremely grateful to Emily Schabacker, who masterminded the editing and production process, and to those who helped her, notably Sean Bartlett, Stephanie Donohoe, Eva Taylor Grant, Holly Shulman, Shannon Granville, Marissa Eigenbrood, and Joanna Bennett.

I owe an enormous debt to António Guterres, not merely for appointing me but even more for his support, encouragement, friendship, and advice as I struggled to deal with the challenges we faced. I also want to record my gratitude to the late Jeremy Heywood for his support in the complex process through which the British government decided it wanted to nominate me for the post.

The principals on the Inter-Agency Standing Committee between them do a lot to make the whole humanitarian system work, notwithstanding the idiosyncrasies of its design arrangements. I felt lucky to have the colleagues I did on the Committee between 2017 and 2021, and would like to pay tribute to them, in particular David Beasley, Tedros Adhanom Ghebreyesus, Qu Dongyu, Natalia Kanem, Michelle Bachelet, Zeid Ra'ad Al Hussein, the late Bill Swing, Antonio Vitorino, Sam Worthington, Abby Maxman, Achim Steiner, Sean Callahan, Dominic MacSorley, Henrietta Fore, Tony Lake, Filippo Grandi, As

Sy, Peter Maurer, Jagan Chapagain, Cecilia Jimenez-Damary, Maimunah Mohd Sharif, Gareth Price-Jones, and Ignacio Packer. I must also acknowledge the (sometimes inadvertent) contributions they made to forming my views.

The staff of my personal office as the ERC were great colleagues and lasting friends, and particular gratitude is due to Yasser Baki, Sofie Karlsson, Rania Abdulrahman, Daniel Pfister, Natasha Geber, and Daniel Alcaide. I learned a great deal from many other people in OCHA, too numerous to list, but I would like to thank Ursula Mueller, John Ging, Gwi Yeop-Son, Lisa Carty, Reena Ghelani, Ramesh Rajasingham, Rein Paulsen, Abdul Haq Amiri, Aidan O'Leary, Alf Blikberg, Alice Sequi, Amy Martin, Andrea Noyes, Andrew Alspach, Andy Wylie, Annette Hearns, Aurelien Buffler, Belinda Holdsworth, Cathy Howard, Cindy Issac, Crispen Rukasha, David Carden, Dieudonne Bamouni, Edem Wosornu, Elin Asgeirsdottir, Frida Hoxholli-Menendez, Gintare Eidimtaite, Greg Puley, Heli Uusikyla, Ian Ridley, Ignacio Leon, Jean Verheyden, Joseph Inganji, Julie Belanger, Justin Brady, Jutta Hinkkanen, Khalid Almulad, Malene Kamp Jensen, Marcy Vigoda, Maria Rosaria Bruno, Markus Werne, Marina Skuric-Prodanovic, Menada Wind-Andersen, Modibo Traore, Molly Little, Nathalie Weizmann, Paula Emerson, Paul Handley, Peter Ekayu, Ruth Mukwana, Sajjad Sajid, Samantha Newport, Samir Elhawary, Sanjana Quazi, Sarah Hilding, Sebastian Rhodes Stampa, Sebastien Trieves, Severine Roy, Shelley Cheatham, Sheri Ritsema-Anderson, Sofie Garde Thomle, Steve O'Malley, Suzanne Connolly, Tareq Talahma, Trond Jensen, Victoria Saiz-Omenaca, Vincent Hubin, Wafaa Saeed, Wendy Cue, and Zola Dowell.

Other UN colleagues also contributed to my understanding and navigation of the organisation and the wider world, notably David Gressly, Bintou Keita, Jean-Pierre Lacroix, Phumzile Mlambo-Ngcuka, Pramila Patten, Kelly Clements, Jamie McGoldrick, Denise Brown, Najat Rochdi, Martin Griffiths, Amina Mohammed, Rosemary di Carlo, Geir Pedersen, Staffan de Mistura, Melissa Fleming, David

Shearer, Maria Luiza Ribeiro Viotti, Volker Turk, Catherine Pollard, and Martha Helena Lopez.

My family were relieved to be spared much of the time-consuming work imposed on them by my last book, but they still made countless tangible and intangible contributions this time as well. Anyone intrigued by the nameplate in the photo of me briefing the Security Council might like to know that my daughter Helena gave me the enhanced role.

NOTE ON SOURCES

I OFTEN ENJOY FOOTNOTES and references in books, but decided that *Relief Chief* would work best as a continuous narrative interrupted as little as possible by citations and explanatory material diverting the eye to the bottom of the page or the end of the volume. The quid pro quo is that I felt I should explain here a little about the sources of my information.

Many of the facts and figures cited come from UN sources. OCHA has numerous excellent websites, and much of its material is posted on reliefweb.int, one of the world's leading internet sites for humanitarian issues. All the material in the annual *Global Humanitarian Overviews*, for example, is on there. Other UN documents, notably from the UN Development Programme, were the source of other data on countries referred to in the text.

Most of the more than one hundred briefings I gave to the UN Security Council covered the regions referred to in Part One, and I have drawn on that material. The statements I made in open sessions (most of them), which the UN staff prepare with care, attention to detail, and a desire not to exaggerate or overstate, are freely available to all in the records of the Security Council.

The @UNReliefChief Twitter account contains the public statements I issued as the ERC, as well as articles and opinion pieces I published. I have on occasion used material contained in my email correspondence.

Where I have drawn information from other places, including books and articles, I have generally made it clear in the text. I have also tried to make clear where something I have written is a personal judgment or conclusion.

PHOTO CREDITS

Briefing the Security Council. *Credit: Sofie Karlsson.*

Woman in the orange head scarf, Cox's Bazar, Bangladesh, November 2017. *Credit: OCHA/Anthony Burke.*

With Mia Seppo, the UN Resident Coordinator; Antonio Vitorino, head of the International Organisation for Migration; and Filippo Grandi, UN High Commissioner for Refugees, Cox's Bazar, April 2019. *Credit: OCHA/Anthony Burke.*

Cox's Bazar, April 2019. *Credit: OCHA/Anthony Burke.*

"This child cannot survive": Aden, Yemen, November 2017. *Credit: OCHA.*

Displaced people in a makeshift settlement north of Sana'a, Yemen, November 2018. *Credit: Suliman Al Moalemi.*

Complaining live on Saudi television about bombs being dropped near the OCHA headquarters in Yemen, November 2017. *Credit: Sofie Karlsson.*

The Saudis hand over a cheque for $500 million, September 2019. *Credit: Sofie Karlsson.*

A Syrian boy protects his baby sister from the war planes. *Credit: OCHA.*

Khaled had fled with his family from Palmyra to escape Islamic State: Homs, January 2018. *Credit: OCHA.*

Getting briefed by the Jordanian military commander on northern border with Syria, January 2020. *Credit: OCHA.*

Listening to the stories of women who had fled Boko Haram: Diffa, Niger, September 2017. *Credit: OCHA/Ivo Brandau.*

Visiting people who had fled ethnic conflict in southeast Ethiopia with UN Development Programme head Achim Steiner, January 2018. *Credit: UNOCHA Ethiopia.*

People in crises want the same things as everyone else: makeshift school in camp for displaced people, Juba, South Sudan, May 2018. *Credit: UNMISS/Eric Kanalstein.*

UN peacekeepers provide the protection in Equatoria, South Sudan, May 2018. *Credit: UNMISS/Eric Kanalstein.*

The earthquake and tsunami turned everything upside down: Palu, Sulawesi, Indonesia, October 2018. *Credit: OCHA.*

With Guterres in Davos, January 2019. World Food Programme chief David Beasley is in the background. *Credit: OCHA.*

With Guterres in Palu. *Credit: OCHA/Anthony Burke.*

With the staff of Heal Africa, Goma, Democratic Republic of Congo, April 2019. *Credit: OCHA/Tommaso Ripani.*

Listening to women in Kassala, eastern Sudan, November 2019. *Credit: OCHA/Saviano Abreu.*

With Filippo Grandi visiting displaced people near Kabul, Afghanistan, September 2018. *Credit: OCHA/Philippe Kropf.*

Cover photo © cloverphoto / istockphoto.com.

Cover design by Steve Kress.

INDEX

Barbados, 158
Barbuda, 122
Bashir, Omar al-, 10, 36, 110–111, 196
BBC, 220
Beasley, David, 51–52, 109, 146
Belgium, 84, 159
belligerents. *See* conflicts and belligerents
Benin, 98
Biden, Joseph and administration, 53, 114
Bill and Melina Gates Foundation, 142, 229
Blair, Tony, 5
Blinken, Tony, 53
Boko Haram, 89, 91, 93, 96–97, 193, 202, 207
BRAC (formerly Bangladesh Rural Advancement Committee), 22
Brahimi, Lakhdar, 64
Brazil, 172
Brookings Institute, 225
Brown, Gordon, 236
bubonic plague, 167, 213–214
bureaucracy, avoiding, 131–132
Burkina Faso, 90, 93–94. *See also* Sahel humanitarian crises

Caesar Civilian Protection Act (2019), 68
Cambodia, 2, 181
Cameron, David and government, 59
Cameroon, 90, 95. *See also* Sahel humanitarian crises
Canada, 58, 84
Caribbean, 11, 122–123, 126–127, 128, 154, 156, 162. *See also specific countries*

Caribbean Catastrophe Risk Insurance Facility, 154
Carty, Lisa, 142
Catastrophe Bonds, 157–158
Catastrophe Draw Down Options, 161–162
Catholic Church, 204
The Cave (movie), 73
Center for Global Development, 237
Central African Republic, 186
Central Bank of Syria, 58
Central Bank of Yemen, 48–50
central emergency response fund: coordination of use of, 144, 145; for COVID-19 pandemic relief, 219, 221–222; finance reform and, 164–168, 177, 237; for natural disaster relief, 120–121, 125, 127; for women's and girls' crises relief, 209
Centre for Disaster Protection, 166–167
Centre for Humanitarian Data, 168–169
Chad, 90, 95, 96–97. *See also* Sahel humanitarian crises
chemical weapons, 59, 62–63, 65, 79, 186
children and youth: child soldiers, 32–33, 36, 79, 97–98, 178; domestic violence effects on, 201; education of (*see* educational systems); famine and food crisis effects on, 161; immunisation statistics, 228, 229; natural disaster effects on, 120, 126; Rohingya experiences, 18, 19, 26; Sahel crisis effects on, 89, 93, 97–98; Syria war effects on, 60, 68, 70–71, 79;